THE THEOLOGY OF
REINHOLD NIEBUHR

The Edward Carnell Library

*An Introduction to Christian Apologetics,** 1948

Television: Servant or Master, 1950

The Theology of Reinhold Niebuhr, 1951

A Philosophy of the Christian Religion, 1952

*A Christian Commitment,** 1957

*The Case for Orthodox Theology,** 1959

The Kingdom of Love and the Pride of Life, 1960

The Burden of Søren Kierkegaard, 1965

*The Case for Biblical Christianity,** 1969

*These reprint editions also include Edward Carnell's Presidential Inaugural Address, "The Glory of a Theological Seminary," presented at Fuller Seminary in 1955. This appears at the end of these books.

The Theology of
Reinhold Niebuhr

by

Edward John Carnell

Professor of Apologetics
Fuller Theological Seminary

WIPF & STOCK · Eugene, Oregon

Wipf and Stock Publishers
199 W 8th Ave, Suite 3
Eugene, OR 97401

The Theology of Reinhold Niebuhr
By Carnell, Edward J.
Copyright©1960 Becker, Jean Carnell and Carnell, John
ISBN 13: 978-1-55635-265-2
ISBN 10: 1-55635-265-4
Publication date 2/6/2007
Previously published by Wm. B. Eerdmans, 1960

Foreword

Edward J. Carnell (1919–1967) is one of the most fascinating figures in twentieth-century American evangelicalism. By age forty he had produced a corpus of major writings more impressive than many scholars produce in a far longer lifetime. Nor was he, like some, writing essentially the same book in differing forms. His writing was marked both by creativity and by remarkable development during his relatively short productive career. He was also, by all accounts, the most popular teacher at Fuller Theological Seminary, where he taught from 1948 until 1967 and served as president from 1954 to 1959. For a few years, at the peak of his brief career, he was regarded as the leading intellectual representative of evangelicalism in the larger American theological community. Although his writings are today not as well-known as they were in the past—a regrettable situation that we can hope this volume will begin to remedy—he played a major role in setting the tone for much of future evangelicalism, especially the kind of approach represented these days at Fuller Theological Seminary.

The son of a Baptist pastor, Carnell received his BA from Wheaton College, where he was influenced by the philosopher Gordon H. Clark (1902–1986). Graduating from Wheaton in 1941, Carnell went on to Westminster Theological Seminary where he studied with apologist Cornelius Van Til (1895–1987). In 1944, the same year that Carnell completed his BD at Westminster, Clark and Van Til became engaged in a sharp controversy concerning Clark's more rationalistic apologetic and Van Til's presuppositional approach. Carnell, who sided with Clark, was searching for his own resolution of these differences. He also sought to engage the Protestant intellectual mainstream of the day, going on to Harvard Divinity School for a ThD, where he wrote on Reinhold Niebuhr. While in the Boston area he enrolled in a second doctoral program in philosophy at Boston University. He wrote his doctoral dissertation there on Søren Kierkegaard and received his PhD in 1949. Eventually he turned these works into books on these prominent figures.

More remarkably, while he was engaged in these two doctoral programs, he produced his first major book, *An Introduction to Christian Apologetics*, published in 1948. This volume, which addressed issues that Carnell had been wrestling with in his studies with Clark and Van Til, received the "Evangelical Book Award" of $5,000 (a comfortable year's salary) from William B. Eerdmans Publishing Company.

When in 1948 Carnell took a position at Fuller Theological Seminary in Pasadena, California, he was already established as a prodigy of the "new evangelical" movement that was emerging out of fundamentalism. Fuller Seminary had been founded just the previous year to be the intellectual flagship of this movement. Harold J. Ockenga (1905–1985), pastor of Park Street Church in Boston, was the leader of this movement and served as Fuller Seminary's president *in absentia*. Fundamentalist radio evangelist Charles E. Fuller (1887–1968) provided solid funding. The seminary was to be made up of theological "stars" of the movement and Carnell joined Carl F. H. Henry (1913–2003) as one of the brightest younger lights.

Having accomplished so much before the age of thirty, Carnell had the highest ambitions for the movement of which he was a part and for his role in it. In his efforts to revolutionize evangelical apologetics, he frankly aspired to be the evangelical equivalent of Paul Tillich or Reinhold Niebuhr, the best-known Protestant theologians of the era; he looked to have, as these theologians did, a major national audience. His hopes to be a popular commentator soon met with disillusion when his small book, *Television: Servant or Master?* (1950), despite its balanced approach, proved to be a commercial failure. Nonetheless, his determination to change the face of the theological world remained intact.

In 1952 he published a second major work on apologetics, *A Philosophy of the Christian Religion.* In this he departed from his earlier emphasis on the law of non-contradiction and "systematic consistency" and emphasized more that Christianity best satisfied the heart's desire for meaningful values. Five years later, in 1957, he published a third apologetic work, *Christian Commitment: An Apologetic*, this time with a major commercial publisher, Macmillan in New York. Addressing Christianity's "cultured despisers," this highly original volume emphasized the existential appeal of Christianity. Particularly Carnell emphasized the commonalities between the experiences of believers and non-believers and how Christianity best accounts for universal moral sentiments, such as moral outrage or a sense of injustice. The book, although creative, did not have the impact that Carnell hoped. Part of the problem was that Carnell, despite his immense intelligence, was less and less working within a tradition. Béla Vassady, a distinguished Reformed theologian from Hungary who was briefly a colleague of Carnell, later commented that he was amazed at the degree Carnell believed he could reconstruct Christian thought on his own. Theologian John G. Stackhouse Jr. has suggested that Carnell was a sort of "intellectual Thoreau," depending on insights into his own experience and then generalizing to all humanity. These perceived traits may help to explain why Carnell did not gain a larger public constituency.

In the meantime Carnell had been elevated to the presidency of Fuller Theological Seminary where he encountered some other problems. In May 1955 he delivered his inaugural address, "The Glory of a Theological Seminary." In it he emphasized the need for mutual tolerance and for emphasizing Christian love over fine points of theological difference. Fuller Seminary in 1955 was too close to its partly fundamentalist origins for these sentiments to pass unchallenged. Conservatives on the faculty suggested that Carnell's sentiments smacked of theological compromise and blocked the publication of his address. (Only after Carnell's death did his former student, President David Hubbard of Fuller Seminary, have it published.)

The controversy over Carnell's inaugural address at Fuller was part of the background for the most controversial part of his much-discussed book, *The Case for Orthodox Theology* (1959). By the later

1950s, even though Carnell had not had the national impact for which he had hoped, he did have the satisfaction that mainline Protestant leaders were recognizing him as one of the most thoughtful evangelical spokesmen. He was honored to play this role when he was chosen by Westminster Press to write a book on evangelicalism to complement books on Protestant liberalism and neo-orthodoxy in a three-part series. While Carnell defended broadly Reformed orthodoxy, the most notable part of his book was his polemic against fundamentalism. Not only did he attack dispensationalist theology and fundamentalist anti-intellectualism, but he also singled out conservative Protestantism's most renowned scholar, J. Gresham Machen (1881–1937), for some of his strongest criticism. Carnell characterized Machen, the founder of Westminster Theological Seminary and the Orthodox Presbyterian Church, as promoting a "cultic mentality" which Carnell saw as one of the worst features of fundamentalism. Even though Carnell had resigned from the Fuller presidency at just about the same time that *The Case for Orthodoxy* appeared, the book brought widespread criticism from conservatives and fundamentalists to Fuller Theological Seminary and to its sponsor, Charles E. Fuller.

Carnell resigned the presidency largely because of deteriorating mental health. His condition was doubtless exacerbated by the immense pressures of the presidency while also continuing with his scholarship. In the subsequent years he suffered from bouts of severe depression and during the worst period in 1961–62 he was hospitalized for five weeks and then continued an extensive series of shock treatments or electroconvulsive therapy. Nonetheless, he continued his teaching and some writing, although as a teacher he was only a shadow of himself. He also maintained his role as an evangelical spokesperson on the national scene, continuing to write for the *Christian Century* and other journals articles that would be collected posthumously in *The Case for Biblical Christianity*, edited by Ronald H. Nash. Most notably he accepted, despite his illness, the great honor of being one of the "young theologians" chosen to dialogue with theologian Karl Barth on his much-heralded visit to the United States in 1962.

Before the most severe onset of his illness, Carnell had completed yet another apologetic work, *The Kingdom of Love and the Pride of Life* (1960). Once again he shifted his emphasis and tone. In dealing with his psychological difficulties he had been reading Freud and he incorporated insights from modern psychology into his work. As in much of his writing, he generalized from personal insight into the human condition. In this case he emphasized the universal need for love that Christianity offered as a counter to destructive pride. His only major publication after his illness was *The Burden of Søren Kierkegaard*, which drew on work he had done for his Boston University doctoral dissertation.

In May of 1967 Carnell was to be one of three keynote speakers at a Roman Catholic ecumenical conference in Oakland, California. On the day of the conference he was found dead in his hotel room from an apparent accidental overdose of sleeping pills.

Carnell's spectacular successes, his even higher ambitions, his disappointments, and his profound inner struggles make him one of the most intriguing figures in this history of American evangelicalism. His writings often combine incisive logic with introspection. In them one can both find the products of one of the finest minds of the time and get glimpses of what might be characterized as "the burden of Edward J. Carnell."

—George M. Marsden
2007

Preface

In fairness the reader must be advised in advance of the limitations of this book. Reinhold Niebuhr is profoundly a many-sided thinker. He cannot fully be evaluated in the pages of one small volume. Mindful of this, I have restricted my labor to the delineation of one controlling concept — *the dialectical relation between time and eternity* — assuming that if the reader can clearly grasp this fundamental point, he will then be in a position to interpret the corpus of the literature for himself.

The exact plan I have elected to follow in this excursion is detailed in the table of contents. There is nothing to be gained in repeating it here.

No finite thinker is ever wholly in or out of the truth. Therefore, I have found it both natural and necessary to divide my estimate of Niebuhr's final worth. On the one hand, his fundamental psychological understanding of the inevitability of pride and egotistic self-assertiveness in all individual and collective expression (save for his interpretation of the first and second Adam), plus his excellent expression of *agape* love as the final definition of the law of life, are, as a whole, both profound and convincing. No serious individual can rest at ease in Zion after studying Niebuhr. I myself have been made uncomfortable no few times in the preparation of this manuscript. On the other hand, the epistemological and metaphysical piles which support these insights are hardly adequate. Niebuhr tends to draw implications from his initial observations which are far from compelling.

Since my own faith is most accurately expressed in classical Reformation theology, I naturally evaluate Niebuhr from the perspective of orthodoxy. One cannot shed his own presuppositions as he would a jacket. I trust, however, that I have been both fair and objective in my labor. If I have failed, it is from want of personal skill, not resolution.

e. j. c.

Acknowledgements

The author cheerfully expresses a feeling of great indebtedness to both Charles Scribner's Sons and Harper & Brothers for their unhesitating permission to quote from the basic works of Reinhold Niebuhr in the preparation of this work. To Charles Scribner's Sons for the use of Niebuhr's *Beyond Tragedy, Christianity and Power Politics, Discerning the Signs of the Times, Faith and History, Human Destiny, Human Nature, Moral Man and Immoral Society,* and *The Children of Light and the Children of Darkness.* To Harper & Brothers for the use of Niebuhr's *An Interpretation of Christian Ethics.*

Thanks go also to the following publishers for their permission to quote from other copyrighted material. Abingdon-Cokesbury Press: "The Ethic of Jesus and the Social Problem" by Reinhold Niebuhr. [Reprinted from *Religion in Life,* Spring, 1932. Quoted from Thomas S. Kepler (ed.), *Contemporary Thinking About Jesus.*] The Beacon Press: F. S. C. Auer, *Humanism States its Case* and Curtis W. Reese, *The Meaning of Humanism.* Harper & Brothers: E. Aubrey, *Present Theological Tendencies;* E. Burtt, *Types of Religious Philosophy;* W. Horton, *Realistic Theology* and *Contemporary Continental Theology.* Harvard University Press: Arthur O. Lovejoy,*The Great Chain of Being.* Houghton Mifflin Company: William McGovern, *From Luther to Hitler* and J. Randall Jr., *The Making of the Modern Mind.* King's Crown Press (Columbia University Press): J. Neal Hughley, *Trends in Protestant Social Idealism* and Mary Frances Thelen, *The Doctrine of Man as Sinner.* Meador Publishing Company: Walter Lowrie, *Our Concern with the Theology of Crisis,* Princeton University Press: Kierkegaard, *Concluding Unscientific Postscript, The Concept of Dread,* and *The Sickness Unto Death.* The Christian Century Foundation: for quotations from *The Christian Century*. The Macmillan Company: Walter Lippmann, *A Preface to Morals*, Reinhold Niebuhr, *Does Civilization Need Religion?*, and S. Matthews, *The Faith of Modernism*. Oxford University Press: Karl Barth, *The Epistle to the Romans* and Kierkegaard, *The Journals of Sören Kierkegaard*. The Westminster Press: E. Brunner, *Revelation and Reason*. Simon and Schuster: Charles F. Potter, *Humanism, A New Religion*. Watts & Company: Julian Huxley *et al.*, *Humanism*. The New American Library of World Literature: Wm. Scarlett (ed.), *Christianity Takes a Stand*. Zondervan Publishing House: Karl Barth, *The Word of God and the Word of Man*. Also to Dr. Cornelius Van Til for use of his volume, *The New Modernism*.

The New Testament quotations in this publication are from the Revised Standard Version of the New Testament, copyrighted 1946 by the International Council of Religious Education and are used by permission.

CONTENTS

PART ONE

Background for the Dialectical Theology

PART TWO

The Construction of Dialectical Theology

PART THREE

The Christian Dialectic

PART FOUR

Concluding Implications

Part I

BACKGROUND FOR THE DIALECTICAL THEOLOGY

I

Why Neo-Orthodoxy?

INASMUCH as dialectical theology is reformational in spirit, being informed by the plan to revitalize a defunct, liberal optimism, the mood of the movement can be understood and appreciated only after an introductory study of the rise and fall of liberal theology itself. Immanence is the backdrop against which neo-orthodoxy originally took its rise, and in contrast to which it presently continues its distinctiveness.

I. The Spirit of the Theology of Immanence

Modernism boasts of no *Summa,* no *Institutes of the Christian Religion.* Its coordinating genius lies in its method. Modernism is an attitude toward life. It is a mode of free thinking. "Modernists are unified by their approach to theology, not by their theological conclusions."[1] Modernism "is not a philosophy but a group of philosophies reflecting no single controlling principle, whether metaphysical, methodological, or ethical."[2]

The medieval mind turned to dialectic as the queen of sciences. Dialectic treats the conceptual, the universal, the eternal. With the rise of the scientific method, however, men began to abandon *a priori* logic in favor of empirical experiments. They turned from the concept to the percept, from the universal to the particular, from the deductive to the inductive. Instead of coming to the universe with an *a priori,* the new empiricists decided to let nature tell her own tale. "Nature to be commanded must be obeyed; not by the anticipation of Nature in some magic dream, but by the study and interpreta-

1. Edwin E. Aubrey, *Present Theological Tendencies,* (N. Y., Harper and Brother, 1936), p. 25.
2. Edwin A. Burtt, *Types of Religious Philosophy,* (N. Y., Harper and Brothers, 1939), p. 285.

tion of Nature will there rise the kingdom of man."[3] Modernists have cast their lot with this method. They disdain submission to authority, be it ecclesiastical or revelational. They follow the scientific method — come what may. "The Modernist movement is a phase of the scientific struggle for freedom in thought and belief."[4] Modernism, hence, courts the spirit of criticism. "The habits of medieval Catholicism and national churches, the appeal to some supernaturally authoritative church or Bible, arguments based neither upon a study of the nature and history of either Bible or church, but upon usage or ecclesiastical action, do not satisfy free minds. There is an indubitable struggle between ecclesiastical authority and free scientific method."[5] The medieval mind, in the main, compared authoritative texts. The modernist demands fresh, empirical evidence. "Modernists are Christians who accept the results of scientific research as data with which to think religiously."[6] If science shows that man evolved from higher primates, then neither pope, council, nor Bible can alter that fact. Conclusions must be subjected to the test of present experience. "One result of the new study of nature with 'the free mind' was a tremendous change in the views of the world handed down from the past. Systematic observation, instead of confirming, contradicted most of the things which had been believed for centuries. One after another traditional idea was shown to be erroneous, and gradually an entirely new picture took the place of the old."[7]

---

3. John Randall, *The Making of the Modern Mind,* (Boston, Houghton Mifflin Company, 1926), p. 224.
4. Shailer Mathews, *The Faith of Modernism,* (N. Y., The Macmillan Company, 1924), p. 23.
5. *Ibid.,* p. 28. "But whether helpful or injurious, the spirit of criticism and liberty is here, and we cannot, even if we would, escape its control. The vote of the church can no longer make us believe that the sun moves around the world, and the vote of a scientific association cannot make us believe that anything is true which denies the evidence of systematized experiment . . . The modern man yields only to that he finds to be real." Mathews, *The Gospel and the Modern Man,* (N. Y., The Macmillan Company, 1912), pp. 52-53.
6. Mathews, *The Faith of Modernism,* p. 29.
7. Arthur McGiffert, *The Rise of Modern Religious Ideas,* (N. Y., The Macmillan Company, 1921), p. 31. See A. D. White, *A History of the Warfare of Science and Theology,* (N. Y., Appleton, 1896), two volumes.

A natural corollary of this dependence on science was a faith in the complete rationality of the universe and the reign of natural law. "The boldness of the faith of modern science lies precisely in the fact that it insists on an ideal of intelligibility that spurns all limitations; for its implicit conviction there is absolutely nothing in nature, however capricious to ordinary observation, that is not at bottom reducible to universality of law. Every relation is regular if we but penetrate to its determining conditions."[8] While others contend that there is a fringe of the non-rational in reality, the modernist prefers smooth rationality. "The modern man cannot conceive of any break in the causal, genetic process. True, he is ready to admit that there may be events which are not yet located in any of its known formulas, but in such a conception there is no place for that which, before its recent apologetical manipulation, the word miracle stood, — an event out of a causal series."[9]

Modernists also follow the mood of the *Aufklärung,* the critical passage of the mind beyond voluntary immaturity. Reason is supreme. Any stratum beyond or above reason is chimerical.[10]

Destructive, higher criticism of the Scriptures was swiftly accepted. Whatever in Scripture was found to be a valid experience of the church was retained, and whatever was not was rejected. Orthodoxy believes the Bible to be God's coming to man; modernism believes the Bible to be man's coming to God. "The Bible is essentially a record of man's past religious

---

8. Edwin A. Burtt, *Religion in an Age of Science,* (N. Y., Frederick Stokes, 1929), pp. 45-46.

9. Mathews, *The Gospel and the Modern Man,* p. 46. The miracles are "now interpreted naturally as they were once interpreted supernaturally." McGiffert, *op. cit.,* p. 41.

10. "The movement had this curious feature, that though professing to prove everything by reason the Rationalists hardly appear to have raised the question what reason is. The common assumption was that everybody knew. In each human mind, so the theory went, there is to be found an ascertainable outfit of intellectual, moral, and religious convictions whose validity is a matter of universal agreement." H. R. Mackintosh, *Types of Modern Theology,* (N. Y., Charles Scribner's Sons, 1937), p. 16. Modernists, therefore, actually exchanged one authority for another.

experience, reflecting at each stage the fallibilities and limitations of his outlook as well as his dominant loyalties, ideals, and needs."[11]

Philosophy joined with science to undermine the theistic proofs. Kant demolished these Maginot and Siegfried lines of Thomistic dialectic. He showed, with Hume before him, that once one draws the content of his knowledge from *earthly* experience, it is impossible to demonstrate the existence of a *transcendent* God. "Thus, both by empiricism and by philosophical rationalism, in the persons of their greatest exponents, the possibility of demonstrating the existence of God was denied, and philosophy was at one with natural science in closing the traditional roads to God, whether from the world of nature or the world of ideas."[12]

Having become satisfied with the destruction of transcendentalism, modernism refurbished the ancient Greek concept that God, like the Logos of Heraclitus, is an immanent principle that runs through the changing process of history, but which itself somehow remains unchanged through time. This was believed scientific, inasmuch as science itself presupposed the unity and rationality of the universe. No special revelation was called for, and no authority outside of reason and experience need be appealed to.

Spinoza, who was greatly admired by the father of modernism, Schleiermacher, had already given philosophical credence to immanence. And Hegel followed by pumping some rich blood into the idea. Time became real in Hegel. Time had been an embarrassment in Spinoza's pantheism. Modernism is by no means Hegelianism, but the mood is clearly there. Hegel gave a religious motif to immanence. He supported the doctrine of human progress. He gave a rosy hue to progress in history. His philosophy of history was informed by rational and moral optimism. "He definitely rejected the doctrine of

11. Burtt, *Types of Religious Philosophy*, p. 324. "The Bible when properly arranged on the basis of satisfactory evidence is a trustworthy record of human experience of God." Mathews, *The Faith of Modernism*, p. 47. The modernist never fully explained why the *Christian* experience is normative for all men, however.

12. McGiffert, *op. cit.*, pp. 59-60.

the fall of man as taught by orthodox Christianity and the idea that man has slowly degenerated from a golden age in the distant past as taught by many of the classical philosophers."[13]

The greatest encouragement for immanence came, however, with Darwin's hypothesis of evolution. Natural selection was one of the final links in the faith of modernism. It was presupposed as an indubitable scientific truth that history was on the way to inevitable progress. Modernists quickly adopted a one-dimensional, linear theory of history. "Never in our outlook upon man's earthly future can we go back to the endless cosmic cycles of the Greeks or the apocalyptic expectations of the Hebrews. We are committed to the hope of making progress, and the central problem which Christianity faces in adjusting her thought and practice to the modern age is the problem of coming to intelligent terms with this dominant idea."[14] The die was cast.[15]

II. The Structure of the Theology of Immanence

A. *Metaphysics: Immanence.*

In his excellent study of contemporary realistic theology in America, George Hammar properly defines liberalism "as that theology which attempted to establish a synthesis between Christian dogmatic tradition and the philosophical idea of immanence, whereby the Christian concept of revelation was more or less dissolved."[16] The scientific earnestness of modern-

13. William McGovern, *From Luther to Hitler,* (Boston, Houghton Mifflin, 1941), p.292.

14. Harry Emerson Fosdick, *Christianity and Progress,* (N. Y., Fleming H. Revell, 1922), pp. 41-42.

15. "This, then, is the method of modernism. It is clear that modernism is an attitude rather than a creed. Accordingly, the modernist is not committed in advance to any formula of belief. He reserves the right to reformulate his position as new knowledge comes within his ken . . . It follows from this that the modernist is able to co-operate with any man who is honestly seeking light, be he arch-conservative or humanist, because they both have the same objective." Aubrey, *op. cit.,* pp. 28-29.

16. George Hammar, *Christian Realism in Contemporary American Theology,* (Uppsala, Sweden), p 160. "A second and closely akin characteristic of the modern world is its conception of God as immanent in this process rather than an extra-mundane monarch." Shailer Mathews, *The Gospel and the Modern Man,* p. 43.

ism betrayed it into a premature hope that all the clues to history are contained within the process of history itself. This is pure immanence. The world itself has all of the data required to explain itself. *Ab extra* revelation is superfluous. God is the soul of history. "With the old static idea of the universe a transcendent God, the maker of the world machine, himself entirely above and apart from it, was almost a necessity. But the new idea of the world as in process of evolution, through the play of forces resident within it, makes possible a different conception of God's relation to it . . . With the increasing prevalence of the idea of the world as an organism, ever growing and developing through the constant play of inherent forces, has steadily grown the idea of immanence at the expense of the old notion of transcendence."[17] Immanence should lead to sheer pantheism, but most modernists have recoiled from this implication. If all is an "expression of one all-pervading divine energy or of one all-embracing divine being,"[18] it would seem to follow that modernism ought to be a pantheism.

With God everywhere, the liberal detected no essential difference between the miraculous and the natural. A miracle was simply the natural seen through consecrated eyes. Schleiermacher called a miracle the religious name for any event. Consequently, since God always functions within the limit of natural law, Biblical miracles were quickly explained away. "The Resurrection, for example, was no more than recovery from apparent death; the feeding of the multitude is erroneously set down as if it implied a marvel, whereas the real facts were much more simple — the crowd, following the lead of Jesus and the disciples, took provisions out of their pockets and handed them around. At the Transfiguration, an unknown friend of Jesus, hidden in the morning mists, called out in the hearing of the apostolic three, 'This is my beloved Son.' "[19]

---

17. McGiffert, *op. cit.*, p. 180.
18. *Ibid.*, p. 201.
19. Mackintosh, *op. cit.*, p. 16.

B. *Epistemology: Feeling.*

Revelation, in the sense of an *ab extra* entrance into history of propositions inaccessible to experience was, obviously, a superfluity to the modernist. "Revelation is the awakening of human consciousness to the presence of the divine, or the eliciting of human devotion to a divine ideal; and to be religious is simply to have this consciousness or this devotion."[20] Schleiermacher defined religion as the feeling of absolute dependence. It is through feeling, not special revelation, that we find God. "The feeling of dependence is most complete in us when in our consciousness we identify ourselves with the entire world, and when we unite in a common thought all that appears to us as separated and isolated."[21] The attributes of God are not ontologically objective entities, existing *in rerum natura,* but rather the various ways in which our feeling of dependence is related to God. God's "eternity" is his absolute timeless causality. His "omnipresence" is the absolutely spaceless causality of God which conditions all space. "Sin" is the consciousness of an action as having arisen within ourselves. "The consciousness of sin is produced when we feel that the religious consciousness is arrested in its free development, and that it has not been able to permeate the other active elements of our consciousness."[22] Christ is the Lord of men in that He was more God-conscious than others. This was his sinlessness.[23]

C. *Anthropology: Inherent Goodness.*

Perhaps there is no point in liberalism against which Niebuhr recoils more markedly than the high estimation which the school of immanence has of man. Progress in history, together with a lofty estimation of man's nature, form the *prin-*

---

20. McGiffert, *op. cit.,* p. 302.
21. L. Lichtenberger, *History of German Theology in the Nineteenth Century,* (Edinburgh, T. & T. Clark, 1889), p. 147.
22. Lichtenberger, *ibid., p.* 149.
23. Niebuhr is still a liberal here. His concept of "myth" will correspond very closely to this liberal structure. For him, as for the liberals, Christ is sinless only provisionally.

cipium individuationis of the theology of immanence. "Liberalism may be defined as respect for the worth of the individual."[24] Liberals speak about a "defection" in man, but this is a mild term. It has only "an ethical idea, and not a forensic conception."[25] "Sin may be due simply to imperfect development, racial as well as individual."[26] Inherent goodness is one of the fundamental pillars of liberal anthropology, and against it the neo-orthodox theologian stands pitted. "The premise of liberalism is faith in man and his highest values as the clue to the nature of God. This faith in man makes possible confidence in human reason and insight as the basis of authority in religion. It makes possible the emphasis upon the immanence of God. It makes possible the identification of the divinity of Christ with his ideal humanity. It makes possible the optimistic faith in progress which is now under such a cloud . . . I think that the best short-cut to an understanding of the present theological situation is to realize that liberalism diverges from orthodoxy and neo-orthodoxy in its various forms in its doctrine of man, and that other differences follow from that."[27]

Because man was too intrinsically good to be subject to damnation, liberal theologians submerged the punitive side of God beneath the *agape*. God is defined in terms of man's ideal possibilities. Liberalism refuses the idea that an infinite *qualitative* difference separates the divine order from the human. "Divine and human ceased to be alien conceptions — the two terms of a disjunctive proposition — and were recognized as truly one. Christ, therefore, if human, must be divine as all men are . . . Where a thoroughgoing doctrine of divine immanence is accepted, the contradiction between divine and human, which alone justifies the denial of Christ's deity in the interest of his true humanity, is done away, and the two parties are at one in asserting that he is at once human and divine."[28]

24. Aubrey, *op. cit.*, p. 36.
25. Winfield Burggraaff, *The Rise and Development of Liberal Theology*, (New York, 1928), pp. 189-190.
26. McGiffert, *op. cit.*, p. 184.
27. John C. Bennett, "After Liberalism — What?" *The Christian Century*, Nov. 8, 1933, p. 1403.
28. McGiffert, *op. cit.*, p. 207.

"Small wonder that Man the Omnipotent, the Omnipresent, the Omniscient, should begin to fancy himself in the role of Supreme Deity, erecting skyscraping temples to himself, and dreaming stupendous, grandiose dreams of the splendor of his future achievements."[29]

D. *Philosophy of History: Optimism and Progress.*

Since history can bear its own meaning, and since evolution is the clue to the direction in which history is moving, it was easy to conclude that temporal process is moving upward to perfection. Progress is the key. Man is the locksmith.

This issue need not be labored, for it is one of the sorest points of contention between dialecticians and the liberals. In the subsequent study of the theology of Niebuhr, the meaning of the liberal view of history will be fully unfolded.

III. The Decline of the Theology of Immanence

Liberalism started to decay in the first quarter of the twentieth century. In the December 4, 1935 issue of *The Christian Century,* for example, Harry Emerson Fosdick published his famous article, "Beyond Modernism." The handwriting was on the wall. The uneasy conscience of the theologians of immanence was protruding. There was a general realization that the time for revitalization had come.

In the meantime, however, modernists discovered themselves caught between the crossfires of fundamentalism on the one hand, and humanism on the other. The former contended that the modernists had left Christianity, while the latter argued that they had not come far enough to be called scientific. Let us trace these attacks in this order.

A. *The Counteract of the Fundamentalists.*

Although a rather sizeable army of poorly trained minds enlisted on the conservative side against modernism, the honor of coming to grips with the opposition in effective strategy fell

29. Walter Horton, *Realistic Theology,* (N. Y., Harper and Brothers, 1934), pp. 57-58.

to J. Gresham Machen, a militant conservative and a master at argumentation. He set down his case against immanence in his classic volume, *Christianity and Liberalism*. The work remains today as one of the best defences of the conservative faith against modernism. His arguments apply, *mutatis mutandis,* to neo-orthodoxy likewise.

Machen's case rested on the conviction that there is really only *one* way to determine what Christianity is, and that is by studying the documents upon which the system rests. *What* Christianity is can be discovered only by a meticulous study of history as given in the New Testament. There is no other source. "The question can be settled only by an examination of the beginnings of Christianity . . . At the foundation of the life of every corporation is the incorporation paper, in which the objects of the corporation are set forth. Other objects may be vastly more desirable than those objects, but if the directors use the name and the resources of the corporation to pursue the other objects they are acting *ultra vires* of the corporation. So it is with Christianity. It is perfectly conceivable that the originators of the Christian movement had no right to legislate for subsequent generations; but at any rate they did have an inalienable right to legislate for all generations that should choose to bear the name of 'Christian.' It is conceivable that Christianity may now have to be abandoned, and another religion substituted for it; but at any rate the question what Christianity is can be determined only by an examination of the beginnings of Christianity."[30]

Machen then showed that the metaphysics of Scripture is theism, not immanence. "Jesus was a theist, and rational theism is at the basis of Christianity."[31] God is wholly above the process of history as well as being immanent within it. God is Sovereign over history. He is in history in the sense that time and space are completely dependent on Him. But His essence is independent of creation. The God that Jesus preached is a heavenly Father, quite distinct from the process of history.

30. Machen, *Christianity and Liberalism,* (Grand Rapids, Eerdmans, 1946), p. 20.
31. *Ibid.,* p. 57.

Machen contended thus, that while the liberal had a perfect right to construct a theology of immanence, he had no right to say his theology was *Christian.* The New Testament teaches that God's essence is transcendent over history as well as immanent within it; liberalism denies God's transcendence; therefore, liberalism is not Christianity.[32]

Machen perceived on the pages of the New Testament an epistemology quite foreign to the feeling theology of immanence. Christ followed the Rabbinic tradition that the Old Testament was God's *ab extra* revelation to man and that not a word of it would perish until all was fulfilled. The apostles joined in this view of special revelation. There is not a passage in the New Testament which encourages one to believe that the Trinity can be known in essence apart from propositional revelation.

The uniform witness of the Bible is that man is a sinner, not an inherently good creature. "According to the Bible, man is a sinner under the just condemnation of God; according to modern liberalism, there is really no such thing as sin."[33] The liberal has privately invented his view of man. It is not Christian. "None is righteous, no, not one. Their throat is an open grave, they use their tongues to deceive. The venom of asps is under their lips. Their mouth is full of curses and bitterness. Their feet are swift to shed blood, in their paths are ruin and misery, and the way of peace they do not know. There is no fear of God before their eyes . . . All have sinned and fall short of the glory of God" (Romans 3:10-23). The very intention in Christ's entrance into history was that of saving lost sinners. "For I came not to call the righteous, but sinners" (Matthew 9:13). Hence, Machen argues: "Modern liberalism has lost all sense of the gulf that separates the crea-

32. This argument is so clear that it is surprising others fail to appreciate it. "It is true that liberal theology is intellectually an immanentism, but when Machen pronounces the liberal theologians destitute of the right to be called Christians, he shows that he is blind to the fact that American liberal theology is Christian and evangelical in its devotional attitude." Hammar, *op. cit.*, p. 143.

33. Machen, *op. cit.*, p. 64.

ture from the Creator; its doctrine of man follows naturally from its doctrine of God."[34]

Machen saw lucidly that the Bible teaches a two-facet philosophy of history. On the one hand, history has meaning and the "kingdom of God is in the midst of you" (Luke 17:21). While on the other, the kingdom is something which the children of God will inherit at the *end* of history. " 'Come, O blessed of my Father, inherit the kingdom prepared for you from the foundation of the world' " (Matthew 25:34). The New Testament teaches an optimism within a pessimism. The kingdom must be striven for at all times, but the Christian is nowhere in the New Testament given any encouragement to believe that through his efforts the kingdom will be made actual.

Machen rested his case there. The liberals do not teach what the Bible says; the Bible is our only source of information of what Christianity is; therefore, liberalism is not Christianity. "The liberals have yet to answer Dr. Machen."[35]

B. *The Challenge of the Humanists.*

From the left there came the swift reprisal of humanism. Its attack was brilliantly executed. The humanist enjoyed an initial advantage over Machen, for whereas Machen was trying to call the modernists *back*, the humanists were urging them *on*. The latter, therefore, presupposed the advantage of momentum. The liberal was on the way to humanism. Logic demanded that he make a complete break with historic Christianity and go all the way with science. Humanism soon won the day. "When the more scholarly fundamentalists, such as Professor Machen, pointed out the real divergencies between the liberal Gospel and the New Testament Gospel, it was still possible to profess allegiance to the 'abiding experiences' which underlay the outmoded 'categories' of early Christianity, and rethink these experiences in modern terms. But when the humanists appeared upon the scene, with their Gospel of salvation

34. *Loc. cit.*

35. Walter Lippman, *A Preface to Morals,* (N. Y., Macmillan, 1929), p. 33.

by scientific research and cooperative effort, the dilemma of liberalism became acute."[36] Humanists would choose fundamentalism before they would the half-heartedness of modernism. "Better a clear-cut Fundamentalism than this sadly inadequate Modernism . . . The Modernists have fallen between two stools in trying to sit on both. A new faith for the new age is what we want, and Humanism is that faith."[37]

The humanist seriously tries to follow science throughout. He believes in a universe of science — a well-regulated mass of energy, impersonal, mathematically precise, natural. It is quite unscientific, therefore, for liberalism to talk of "God unfolding in a process in history." Science knows only of pointer-readings, not God. The universe appears to be quite indifferent to all final causes.

Such frankness may render existence a problem indeed; but the humanist "does not attempt to solve the mystery by saying that a God created the universe out of nothing."[38] The humanist is persuaded that the term "God" did not begin by science. It is man-made, "resulting from man's tendency to ascribe something like human personality to things and forces which he does not understand."[39] The humanist asks the modernist to put his hand over his heart. "Would it not be better, if that is the case — more honest and less open to the charge of insincerity — frankly to give up the term 'God' and to work out our religious philosophy entirely in other concepts, at least until enough people have learned this important lesson so that the term might be redefined without danger of bewilderment?"[40] The humanist does not *deny* God's existence, for that would be as unscientific as to affirm it. "We may dis-

36. Horton, *op. cit.*, p. 3.
37. Charles Potter, *Humanism a New Religion*, (N. Y., Simon and Schuster, 1930), pp. 96-97.
38. Huxley *et al.*, *Humanism*, (Watts & Company, London), p. 7. "As to the nature of the universe, the Humanist regards the universe as the given and is not likely to speculate unduly on either the beginning or the end of things cosmic." Curtis Reese, *The Meaning of Humanism*, (The Beacon Press, Boston, 1945), p. 20.
39. Huxley *et al.*, *ibid.*, p. 6.
40. Burtt, *Types of Religious Philosophy*, p. 354.

cover God some day, and we may not."[41] God has only a functional value, and the postulates of science will do just as well.

When the modernist sallies forth in his *final* religious feelings, he forgets that he has left the pale of science. "A third presupposition of the Humanist is that knowledge at best is inferential, instrumental and relative; consequently he has no reliance on either revelation or intuition."[42] Science knows only of tentativity, not finality. "The humanist maintains that we must resolutely take our choice — either refuse to admit the distinctive assumptions and methods of modern science, remaining in the supernaturalism hallowed in Catholic or orthodox Protestant tradition; or else go boldly with science the whole way, withholding nothing from its impartial investigation, and adjusting our moral and religious attitudes unreservedly to whatever conclusions realistic inquiry may reach."[43] The humanist says that final realities have yet to be found. The modernist, however, *in the name of science,* says that he has found finality in Christianity. "Humanists hold that there is no short cut to valid ideals. no code that is a final authority. Ancient laws, however good they may have been in their time, have no binding effect today, except in so far as they meet the test of modern, experimental living."[44] The modernist is pretentious, while the humanist is honestly searching. "We grope our way towards the Good: we can strive for it, we can die for it: we do not absolutely and for certain know it. If we did we should have penetrated the great mystery by which on every side man's little life is surrounded. That the Humanist does not attempt or believe to be possible."[45]

---

41. Potter, *op. cit.,* p. 1.
42. Reese, *op. cit.,* p. 22
43. Burtt, *op. cit.,* p. 371.
44. Reese, *op. cit.,* p. 12. Mains expresses the liberal mind: "Christ is not only the contemporary of all ages, his ideals are immeasurably in advance of the best civilizations, the perfection of his personality is beyond that of all other men." George Mains, *Modern Thought and Traditional Faith,* (N. Y., Eaton and Mains, 1911), p. 203.
45. Huxley *et. al., op. cit.,* p. 14. Machen would ask the humanist how he knows there is an absolute Good to be striven for in the first place? *This* hope did not come by the scientific method.

The humanist, furthermore, thinks that Socrates is a far better guide in scientific morals than Jesus Christ. "Jesus had no appreciation of the value of intelligence as the most dependable human faculty for analyzing the perplexities into which men fall and for providing wise guidance in dealing with them . . . His theory of the world, which to his mind justified this confident faith, is squarely opposed to the scientific naturalism that a frank assessment of experience increasingly compels modern man to accept. Far from thinking of nature as an objective, law-abiding order, to which man must patiently learn how to adjust himself while assuming responsibility intelligently to transform those parts of it that are amenable to human control, he believed it to be directly subject in all its details to the purposive care of a personal being."[46]

Humanism is a hard-headed realism. "We can never get outside man. Beyond man is the unknown, the realm of mystery which cannot be expressed in human language or comprehended by human thought."[47] The thought of God's "providence" may be emotionally stimulating, but it is of no scientific value to the humanist. "Man is capable of dealing with his own affairs."[48] Religion simply has a pragmatic value. It is a devotion to the highest that we may scientifically affirm. "True religion, for any man or woman, is wholehearted absorption in whatever envisioned greatness empirically brings wholeness or selfhood and promises to be a constant, dependable source of continued growth toward the goal of perfect harmony, within and without."[49] The tenderhearted mind may turn back to the emotion of faith as soon as science declares that no God has been found in the universe; but not the humanist. With the loss of an absolute ideal, a prudent man will

---

46. Burtt, *Types of Religious Philosophy*, pp. 359-360. The actual validity of these observations is questionable, however. A more cautious study of the meaning of Christ's life and message would reveal their congeniality to man's highest ideals.

47. Huxley *et al., op. cit.*, p. 13.

48. J. A. C. Fagginger Auer, *Humanism States its Case*, (Boston, The Beacon Press, 1933), p. 9.

49. Burtt, *ibid.*, p. 358.

devote himself to the highest known value. And that is man. We may not know God; but we *do* know man. Religion, hence, is not destroyed when God remains an unknown factor. "Whatever may prove to be the cosmic situation, there are human needs to be satisfied; there are human loves to be fostered; there are human friendships to be cultivated, there are physical and mental wants to be met."[50] Religion should be properly man-centered. "Religion is the attempt to unify one's personality and relate it to the world without."[51] Religion is any attitude of devotedness which may assist one in making adjustment. "Religion is the natural functioning of a normal person in the effort to achieve a full, a free and a socially useful life in ordinary circumstances."[52] Believing that he must work out his own salvation without God working in him both to will and to do, the humanist does not faint. He believes one must simply work all the harder when he has no God to lean on. The humanist "is sure that some things are of value in and for themselves — human decency and human dignity; experiences of beauty and of love; inner peace and reconcilement; true knowledge and noble expression."[53] These must be preserved. If man does not safeguard them, no one in the entire universe will. The humanist, therefore, has no "moral holidays" in which to take his ease. Faith in God, in fact, may be a drag on man. "There is enough latent power in human personality to transform itself and the world if men would only free themselves from the sense of inferiority and insignificance and the fears which Theism has bred in them through centuries."[54] If we are to turn to science for guidance, the humanist declares, then let us turn. "Humanism challenges a man to quit leaning on the everlasting arms, and to stop singing: 'Helpless I am and full of guilt.' "[55]

---

50. Reese, *op. cit.*, p. 16.
51. Potter, *op. cit.*, p. 9.
52. Reese, *ibid.*, p. 17.
53. Huxley *et al.*, *op. cit.*, p. 8.
54. Potter, *op. cit.*, p. 32.
55. *Ibid.*, p. 41.

C. *The Contradictory Verdict of History.*

Liberalism's *coup de grace* was finally delivered, however, not by opponents of the consistency of modernism, but by history itself. "Worse than any formal disproof of the idealistic philosophy, was the sense that grew upon men, during the World War, that they were in the hands of a tragic destiny which their reason could not comprehend nor their best efforts master; that life was an essentially dangerous and incalculable enterprise which even the boldest spirit could not face alone, and which was entirely meaningless except as one joined some group of fellow wanderers and confronted fate together, like comrades in the trenches."[56] Modernism was firmly committed to an optimistic view of history. Time failed to vindicate the truth of such a perspective, however. When evolution appeared to be following schedule, the illusion of an immanent theology seemed plausible enough. "In a time when 'modern science' and 'modern civilization' seemed to be going on from strength to strength, and from triumph to triumph, it was most natural that theology should address to the 'modern mind' a plea for reconciliation and partnership."[57] But when the world was plunged into war and death through weapons supplied by science, the immanence hypothesis, that God was working out an inevitable progress in history, was less convincing. World War I, then, marks the historical turning-point in liberal optimism.

Pessimism has stalked the corridors of the nations from the hour of that holocaust. "There have been days of as great external calamity before. But I doubt if there have been days when men on such a large scale have been so conscious of a rapid descent from hope to hopelessness."[58] Inertia, paralysis of effort, and skepticism have replaced interest, hope, and con-

56. Walter Marshall Horton, *Contemporary Continental Theology,* (N. Y., Harper and Brothers, 1938), p. 89.

57. Horton, *Realistic Theology,* p. 8.

58. Bennett, *Christian Realism,* (N. Y., Charles Scribner's Sons, 1941), p. 10. "Then came the deluge. Since 1914 one tragic experience has followed another, as if history had been designed to refute the vain delusions of modern man." Niebuhr, *Faith and History,* (N. Y., Charles Scribner's Sons, 1949), pp. 6-7.

cern. "In a survey of attitudes of European students at the beginning of the Second World War, it was found that the most common attitude was one of cynicism combined with a strange inertia, a paralysis of effort."[59]

It was clear to all that the time had come for modernism to put its house in order. The liberal could either return to evangelical conservativism, or work out a new approach. Having cast its lot with experience and science over against the veracity of propositional revelation, the former alternative was rejected in favor of the latter. The product of its revision is *neo-orthodoxy*.

IV. The Emergence of Dialectical Theology

When the foundations of a culture become insecure, men tend to become more realistic in their convictions. Idealism refuses to satisfy when the hard facts are bloody and torn. "The tragedy of the World War brought with it disillusionment as to the power of social idealisms, and a deep sense of the futility of human exhortation."[60] The pangs of social-cultural despair gave birth to the child, dialectical theology. A tragic sense of life fathered a new theology.

The child first saw the light of day in 1919 when Karl Barth published his volume, *The Epistle to the Romans*. Barth was a disillusioned liberal. He could sense sharply the discrepancy between the optimistic, modernistic view of history, which he had been taught, and the tragic conditions in the world. Seeking something to hold to, he testifies, he just happened to ring the bell of a new theology. Just as one that blindly walks up the stairs of a church belfry and quite accidently, to keep himself from falling, seizes the bell rope and awakens the town, so Barth rang the bell of the new theology with his commentary. In America a siren was sounded by Reinhold Niebuhr with his publication, *Moral Man and Immoral Society*, in 1932.

---

59. Bennett, *ibid.*, pp. 8-9. "At a time when central Europe was in the torment of defeated confidence, heartbreaking deprivation, and exasperating disunion, and staggering aimlessly under an impossible burden of debts and reparations, the 'tragic sense of life' must inevitably grip the German mind." Aubrey, *Present Theological Tendencies*, p. 76.

60. Aubrey, *op. cit.*, p. 74.

With these two radical departures from an idealistic, liberal view of social progress, the new theology was on its own.

A. *General Characteristics of the New Theology.*

Since the basic error of the liberals was immanence, it is logical to expect that the basic thesis of the new theology is transcendence and discontinuity. Discontinuity of man with God replaced old continuity. "Where liberal theology saw the goodness of God as continuous with the highest human goodness and the fulfilment of life as gradual sanctification and as the conservation of value, neo-orthodoxy is more concerned with the discontinuity between God's goodness and human sin, and visualizes the relationship of the eternal to history as a dialectic one in which God as the End fulfils man's desires and expectations only by disappointing them in their corrupted form."[61] The reason for discontinuity is obvious. Man can have faith in history only if God is moved out of the involvements of history's sinfulness. There must be a power over and above history if we are to have hope in eternity, on the one hand, and a reason for striving in history, on the other. The rejected liberal conviction, that God is not a sovereign Judge over history, is emphatically restored in dialectical theology. Barth charges the liberals with having made God in their own image. He himself defines God as absolutely transcendent, the wholly other, the *deus absconditus*. Anything less than wholly other is but an oversized man. The liberals had just worshiped themselves. "God, the pure and absolute boundary and beginning of all that we are and have and do; God, who is distinguished qualitatively from men and from everything human, and must never be identified with anything which we name, or experience, or conceive, or worship"[62] — that is the God of Barth. Barth uses superlatives piled upon superlatives to safeguard God's otherness. "In all this, Barth has been haunted by the ghost of Ludwig Feuerbach. Feuerbach was a

---

61. Mary Thelen, *Man as Sinner,* (Morningside Heights, N. Y., King's Crown Press, 1946), p. 131.
62. Karl Barth, *The Epistle to the Romans,* (tr. Edwyn C. Hoskyns, London, Oxford Press, 1933), pp. 330-331.

ruthless spirit . . . Men have, he said, made gods in their own images and in these images worshipped themselves. The history of theology is the history of delusion. There is no possible intellectual defense for any sort of God that is not Himself wholly taken into our own experience."[63] The straining of language runs all through Barth's works, as if he is deliberately laboring *ad nauseam* his reversal from continuity and immanence. "God is pure negation . . . He is the negation of the negation in which the other world contradicts this world and this world the other world."[64] Much of the obscurity of Barthian thinking arises from this persistent refusal to admit a univocal point of contact between God and man.

With God as the wholly other, special revelation in some form again was in order. But the dialectician refused to return to the orthodox view, since he believed that objective propositions are but another form of continuity. God's revelation must be arresting, shocking, engaging, confronting, convicting. A conservative, it was charged, could coolly and objectively carry a copy of the Bible in his hip pocket, believing that he "possessed" revelation. God must constantly intrude into our lives with a moment-by-moment revelation which cuts across our expectations and which yet meets the depth of our inner man. Revelation is exchanged in the encounter, the existential commitment. The test of revelation is not the application of the law of contradiction and whole experience to objective propositions, as in orthodoxy, but, rather, its existential tone. Revelation is a conversation between sinless heaven and sinful earth. God can confront a man wherever His "word" is heard. Revelation must thus always remain shattering in its message. It must simultaneously charge man with the tensions of condemnation and forgiveness if the dialectic between heaven and earth is to be maintained. "That is the reason why genuine theology must be dialectical. It is always a conversation between God and man."[65] Revelation can take

63. Cornelius Van Til, *The New Modernism,* (Philadelphia, The Presbyterian and Reformed Publishing Company, 1946), p. 39.

64. Barth, *op. cit.,* pp. 141-142.

65. Emil Brunner, *Revelation and Reason,* (tr. Olive Wyon, Philadelphia, The Westminster Press, 1946), p. 15.

root only when the heart has been plowed and broken by sensing its distance from God—metaphysically, ethically, and epistemologically. If there is the slightest token in man of that whereof he may boast, revelation is frustrated.

Mathematics, for example, is not existential. It does not confront us with a shattering decision. The message of the cross, however, meets us in the deepest moments of choice, conflict, crisis, catastrophe. Revelation, thus, is tainted with overtones of incomprehensibility when tested according to the canons of ordinary logic. If God is wholly other, His revelation cannot be a perfect accommodation to logic. Rational speculation is non-dialectical. "To wish to argue for revelation in rational terms means that we have not begun to understand what revelation is. That which can be based on rational grounds is, by its very nature, not revelation but rational truth. The truth of reason is that which we as rational beings can tell ourselves; the truth of revelation is that which, by its very nature, we could not tell ourselves, which . . . indeed is transcendent, communicated truth. Anything a human being can verify or deduce for himself by any process of argument, investigation, or proof, cannot possibly be revelation, and, vice versa, that which is revelation cannot be verified by any such process."[66].

The existential foundation of the new theology was laid by Sören Kierkegaard. He bequeathed to Barth, Brunner, and Niebuhr their dialectical framework. He was the master existentialist. Through the entire corpus of his publications there wends the one theme that man must mediate a passionate concern through his own person if he is to be saved. Objectivity is soul-destroying. Any laxity, morbidness, coldness, or pretension is sin. Sin is lack of concern. Sin is immediacy, complacency. Sin is a tensionless surrender to things as they are. Only in either/or decision is passion in man aroused. Both/and is of sin. In existential living onc passionately seeks to mediate in his own person the height of an absolute law of love, yet sensing all the time the inevitability of his own sinful-

66. *Op. cit.*, p. 207.

ness. Existential living, then, is inward tension in crisis, decision, passion. Character and salvation are created in the passionate, choosing moment of either/or decisions, those moments when life and death, happiness and unhappiness, health and sickness lie in the balance. "Without risk there is no faith. Faith is precisely the contradiction between the infinite passion of the individual's inwardness and the objective uncertainty. If I am capable of grasping God objectively, I do not believe, but precisely because I cannot do this I must believe."[67]

Existentialism senses a dimension in life beyond that of either cool reasoning or reading of Biblical propositions as "God's objective law." Existentialism believes that the individual himself must contribute something to the revelation transaction. He must respond to the confrontation as well as suffer it. Sin is the non-existential, the uncommitted part of man's heart. Sin is posited in every man as the precondition of all passion. But sin is truly revealed as sin only when a man senses his distance from God. Immanence blinds man to the rationale of revelation. When a man believes that he is congenially continuous with deity, he cannot be saved. He will never mediate in his own person the tensional relation between time and eternity. Revelation is relevant only where there is sin, and sin is possible only in the experience of an absolute distance between God and man. Neo-orthodoxy, thus, has earned for itself the title of making man *inevitably* a sinner. Sin posits itself. "Original sin" is called in as a formula to express this condition of man. Man is innocent only when he is ignorant of his state. Whenever he comes to himself, he is a sinner, for he immediately is overtaken by an existential feeling that he has fallen short of what is required of him.

Immanence and continuity, by confusing heaven and earth, destroy the tension between these two realms. Neo-orthodoxy has set these realms in a "dialectical" (dialogue) opposition. Eternity is always relevant to, and yet ever tensionally set against, earth at every moment of time. Eternity may never

67. Sören Kierkegaard, *Concluding Unscientific Postscript,* (tr. David Swenson, Princeton, Princeton University Press, 1944), p. 182.

be identified with earth, but earth may never declare independence from eternity.

B. *Continental and American Dialectical Emphases.*

Inasmuch as calamity struck on the Continent earlier, and with greater severity, it is only natural to expect that its forms of neo-orthodoxy would be more radical than the American. Investigation proves this to be so.

The argument which recently was carried on between Barth and Niebuhr in *The Christian Century* was not over either the *fact* of the revolt from immanence or the rejection of the liberal concept of continuity, for both agree that continuity is quite outmoded. The divergence emerges when each tries to define *how far* one should withdraw from immanence and continuity. Niebuhr claims that the Continent has gone too far.

Karl Barth leads the Continent in declaring for absolute discontinuity. "The Kingdom of God has not 'broken forth' upon the earth, not even the tiniest fragment of it; and yet, it has been *proclaimed*: it has not come, not even in its most sublime form; and yet, it is *nigh at hand.* The Kingdom of God remains a matter of faith, and most of all is the revelation of it in Christ Jesus a matter of faith."[68] Barth speaks of the "crisis," therefore. The crisis is the judgment under which history at every moment stands. Barth thinks that only in absolute discontinuity is there a final break with the sin of modernism. The only hope for men comes when they "suddenly awake to a realization that they are walking upon a ridge between *time* and *eternity* that is narrower than a knife-edge."[69] Barth is the perfect contradiction of liberalism, therefore. Immanence made God and man continuous; Barth rejects this. Immanence rests upon cool speculation; Barth relies on existential, whole thinking. Immanence made history and eternity continuous; Barth sets them in tensional contradiction. Barth, then, espouses the most radical discontinuity.

The other Continental leader of dialectical theology is Emil Brunner. He accepted the radical discontinuity of Barth for

---

68. Barth, *The Epistle to the Romans,* p. 102.

69. Barth, *The Word of God and the Word of Man,* (tr. Douglas Horton, Grand Rapids, Zondervan, 1935), p. 188.

a time. But then he broke. Brunner quickly began to sense the rational difficulties involved in denying a point of contact (*Anknuepfungspunkt*) between time and eternity, so he swiftly modified the radical otherness of eternity.[70] Brunner places a greater emphasis upon natural theology and the *imago dei* as the points of deliverance for revelation than does Barth. "Brunner apparently [is] seeking more and more, and Barth apparently [is] seeking less and less, contact for the gospel with the general consciousness of man."[71] Brunner served notice to Barth in his pamphlet *Nature and Grace.* Barth swiftly retorted with a forceful ultimatum, *Nein!* Barth charged Brunner with returning to the leeks and garlic of Egypt — liberal continuity.

It must be noted in this controversy, however, that Barth and Brunner both agree on the essential dialectical relation between time and eternity. Since their break has come only on minor interpretations of the extent to which this discontinuity may be taken, neither view is *essentially* related to historic orthodoxy, therefore.

It is evident, thus, that not "all the members of the Dialectical School are equally dialectical. Brunner, it seems to me, is not so dialectically inclined as Barth."[72] Brunner, in effect, stands in transition between the Continent and America; yet he is perfectly at home in neither. He taught at Princeton Seminary, and elsewhere in America, while Barth refuses to come to such an "undialectical" environment. And yet Brunner returned home finally where the magnet of dialectical thinking drew most powerfully. On the Continent he sees affinities with Barth, and in America he sees affinities with Niebuhr. Niebuhr says he is closer to Brunner, but that Brunner has de-

70. "So we find Brunner arguing for a large measure of continuity of the gospel with the general consciousness of man. The natural man is said in the activity of his conscience to display a certain knowledge of sin. And by the idea of the formal personality Brunner attributes to the natural man a capacity for the reception of the gospel." Van Til, *op. cit.*, p. 209.

71. *Ibid.*, pp. 189-190.

72. Walter Lowrie, *Our Concern With the Theology of Crisis,* (Boston, Meador Publishing Co., 1932), p. 44. "Barth would not have learned it from Kierkegaard, the great master of dialectic, unless he himself had had a preeminent disposition for it." *Ibid.*, p. 43.

feated his own case by conceding too much to transcendence. "In this debate Brunner seems to me to be right and Barth wrong; but Barth seems to win the debate because Brunner accepts too many of Barth's presuppositions in his fundamental premises to be able to present his own position with plausibility and consistency. Barth is able to prove Brunner inconsistent, but that does not necessarily prove him to be wrong."[73] Brunner, then, is too discontinuous to be classified with the American dialecticians and not discontinuous enough to go all the way with strict Continental, Barthian theology. Brunner, however, is still a Barthian, despite his minor differences. He belongs to the Continental, not the American, mind.

The American school of neo-orthodoxy sometimes travels under the name of "realism." It refuses complete identification with Continental neo-orthodoxy because its own retreat from liberal immanence is less ambitious. If Brunner conceded a *point* of contact, Niebuhr sees whole *areas* of contact. Niebuhr indeed follows Kierkegaard in defining the relation between time and eternity dialectically, but he recoils from Barthian extremes. Man is a sinner — but not *totally* a sinner. Otherwise, how could he ever know that he is a sinner? God is transcendent — but not a *wholly* other. Otherwise, how could man know God or how could God reveal Himself to man? Revelation is an offense to reason — but not *completely* so. Otherwise, how could man recognize truth when he saw it? God's law is above our expectation, but not *absolutely* so. Otherwise, how can we distinguish the voice of God from the voice of the devil? Natural theology cannot establish God's existence, but it is not *finally* blind. Otherwise, how could eternity be relevant to history or history be interpreted in the light of eternity? Niebuhr, therefore, indicts Barth for *talking* about God and expecting his hearer to understand what he means. If there is no univocal point between time and eternity, meaningful speech about God is impossible. "Though Karl Barth protests against all forms of analogical reasoning when dealing with the 'wholly other,' he neverthe-

73. Reinhold Niebuhr, *Human Destiny*, (N. Y., Charles Scribner's Sons, 1943), p. 64.

less avails himself of the analogy of the concept of personality when defining the character of the divine. He seeks to hide his analogic logic by inverting it. He declares that concepts of human personality are derived from the concept of divine personality . . . Barth's logic cannot hide the fact that, however imperfect human personality is in contrast to divine personality, he has taken the very concept of personality from human life and has applied it to the divine. From what other source could he have derived it?"[74]

Niebuhr has tried to remain more realistic in his synthesis between continuity and discontinuity than has Continental, crisis theology. He seeks to tack between the failures of the liberals and the extremes of the Barthians, while yet returning to both to convert each into a more realistic framework. Niebuhr refuses to reject the valid insights which liberalism has contributed to our culture. He has tried to unite the best in both Barth and liberalism. He may be called a "liberal realist" or a "realistic liberal."

John Bennett speaks of Niebuhr as "the soul of Europe hovering over American thought." American in his training and loyalties, and yet German by nature and Continental in sympathies, Niebuhr has achieved a remarkable synthesis of Continental pessimism and American liberal optimism. With the publication of his Gifford Lectures, *The Nature and Destiny of Man,* Niebuhr has emerged as the undisputed leader of American dialectical theology. "No contemporary American theologian has had such a wide influence as Reinhold Niebuhr in restoring a Christian revealed theology to its proper place within American Protestant theology."[75] Niebuhr has crystal-

74. Niebuhr, *op. cit.,* pp. 66-67, n.

75. Hammar, *op. cit.,* p. 61. "Niebuhr's theology is dialectical in the meaning that it preserves statements which, from a rational point of view, are contradictory, and in a state of tension, but his theology is not 'Barthian.' Niebuhr accuses German dialectical theology of being nearer Greek Platonistic dualism than the Christian paradoxes when vindicating the absolute difference between eternity and time. History and nature become meaningless in Barthian theology, as Niebuhr sees it, and even the very fact of the Incarnation ceases to be a historical fact, i.e. the absolute never becomes incarnate in time. In German dialectical theology Creation becomes a fall into sin, according to Niebuhr." *Ibid.,* p. 61.

ized American dialectical thought into a system. "In Niebuhr's Gifford Lectures the transition from criticism to positive statement may be said to have been completed."[76] The time is ripe, therefore, for a systematic and critical appraisal of this American synthesis.

---

76. Thelen, *op. cit.*, p. 1. "Niebuhr's thought, if studied as a whole, is extraordinarily balanced, though its dialectical form makes him in any one chapter, article, or speech seem extreme. This is aggravated by the fact that he thinks polemically. In this country Niebuhr has been the spearhead of a new tendency toward what is often called 'realism' among American religious thinkers. More effectively than anyone else in America he mediates to us insights that are common assumptions in European theology and he does so with moderation." John Bennett, *Christian Realism,* (N. Y., Charles Scribner's Sons, 1941), p. 48.

Part II

THE CONSTRUCTION OF DIALECTICAL THEOLOGY

II

Starting Point: Man

WHEN he was given the high honor of delivering the Gifford Lectures for 1939, at the University of Edinburgh, Reinhold Niebuhr, seeking a starting point for his system which would anchor the attention of his hearer in what he was yet to say about the Christian view of history, significantly commenced with a penetrating analysis of the nature of man. Such a point of contact was rich with response potentialities, for whereas men may become disconcerned with many things, they remain profoundly concerned with themselves. Niebuhr sensed that only after man has been shown how Christianity relates to his own threshold of value interests will he be in a mood to sympathize with overtures for self-commitment to Christianity.

I. The Double Environment

Assured of his steps, therefore, Niebuhr turned at once to an analysis of man's nature. And when he did, he uncovered something arresting. He found that whereas body and soul make up the obvious components of man's nature, few and far between were those minds which could harmonize these heterogeneous elements without either deifying one at the expense of the other or misinterpreting the exact way in which the two are compounded in the one personal unity. "How difficult it is to do justice to both the uniqueness of man and his affinities with the world of nature below him is proved by the almost unvarying tendency of those philosophies which describe and emphasize the rational faculties of man or his capacity for self-transcendence to forget his relation to nature and to identify him, prematurely and unqualifiedly, with the divine and the eternal; and of naturalistic philosophies to obscure the uniqueness of man."[1]

As a realist Niebuhr never wearies of reminding man of what he is. Since man is part of nature as a physical creature and part of eternity as a free spirit, he cannot consider himself explained accurately until these two environments are first recognized and related. Man must be measured within the tension of two worlds. Man is too high to be identified with this world, and too low to be identified with eternity. When either side of this double milieu is corrupted, some part of the essential man is either ignored or denied. Most errors in the interpretation of man reduce to a blindness at the point of the two worlds. "Man is not measured in a dimension sufficiently high or deep to do full justice to either his stature or his capacity for both good and evil or to understand the total environment in which such a stature can understand, express and find itself. One might define this total environment most succinctly as one which includes both eternity and time."[2]

A. *The Fact of the Double Environment*

Unwilling to state his case as sheer dogmatism, Niebuhr turns at once to an expatiation on the matter.

1. *Natural limitation.* The fact of the body is too self-evident a datum to be labored. Like the animals, man eats, runs, sleeps, and dies. And yet there develops through this seeming innocency of physical dependence an immediate complexity. (a) Being united with a physical frame, man is so hemmed in that he must abide by predestined natural limits during his earthly days. Man is lashed by nature's "vicissitudes, compelled by its necessities, driven by its impulses, and confined within the brevity of the years which nature permits its varied organic form."[3] The most other-worldly mystic must, at last, return at night from his dreaming and take soup for nourish-

1. Reinhold Niebuhr, *Human Nature,* (N. Y., Charles Scribner's Sons, 1946), p. 4.
2. *Ibid.,* p. 124.
3. *Ibid.,* p. 3.

ment and rest for physical renewing. There are myriads of ways in which man can overcome nature, but no absolute transcendency is ever achieved, since natural cohesions define the termination of man's potential powers of overcoming. Science may extend life, but senility knows no final cure. One cannot by taking thought add an inch to his stature. (b) "Nature supplies particularity."[4] Man is humbled by nature, since the body as a quantitative determinant can be piled, sorted, cased, ranked, classified, numbered. Medical experiments on animals can be transferred to man because of the marked way in which animals and man share the common dominator of particularity. This low estate does not finally exhaust man, however, for unlike the brutes which are only particular creatures at the most, man's particularity is converted into individuality and personality through freedom. (c) Bodily limitations introduce a complexity into anthropology which defies an easy solution. Man *is* body — he does not simply occupy body. A person who is realistically true to his whole experience will never say that the drives and impulses of his physical life are any less a part of his real self than the drives and impulses of his spiritual vitalities. All form the integral *Homo sapiens.* Whenever the lower impulses are corrupted, a satisfactory understanding of man as he really is has been shattered.

2. *Spiritual freedom.* The transition from limitation to freedom is made the moment one *admits* the fact of his own physical necessity. One cannot think about his own limitations without admitting his free capacity for thinking. Freedom is a fact. Man can do what no animal can: He can think about thinking. However, this second environment, like the first, is freighted with complexity. (a) Freedom's first manifestation is reason, or *nous.* Reason is the mysterious power in man which enables him to think discoursively. "Reason enables man, within limits, to direct his energy so that it will flow in harmony, and not in conflict, with other life."[5] Whereas the brute

---

4. *Ibid.,* p. 55.

5. Niebuhr, *Moral Man and Immoral Society,* (N. Y., Charles Scribner's Sons, 1947), p. 26.

must remain content within very narrow confines, man can seize the factors of his limitations and manipulate them until pressure points are relieved. (b) Freedom, however, is more than just the power of ratiocination. Man happens to possess a surveillance over reason itself. This faculty is spirit.[6] "Man is spirit who stands outside of nature, life, himself, his reason and the world."[7] Existentially, this facet to freedom is significant, for it provides Niebuhr with his greatest clue for understanding both the meaning of the warfare of good and evil in social life and the relevance of redemption wrought in man by Jesus Christ. Spirit is fullest freedom, endless imagination. Infinity is the parish of freedom. Spirit is man in his free height. When even reason itself staggers and faints, freedom of spirit continues its searching and wandering. For this reason rational coherence is always at the mercy of freedom, since individuality may convert pure coherence into pure irrelevance. Freedom is the reason why man is a problem unto himself. The significance of this will appear shortly.

B. *Perils in Explaining the Double Environment.*

Assured that it is infinitely easier to admit the fact of the double milieu than it is to explain the relation between the two sides without corrupting one or the other, Niebuhr skillfully exposes some of the deficiencies in non-Christian anthropology. Truth is always seen in sharper contours when contrasted distinctively against error.

1. *Love for the eternal in man.* Niebuhr concludes from the perennial vitality of idealism throughout history, that it is easy for man so to accent the freedom of his rational nature that natural involvement is either denied or, if admitted, reluctantly subordinated to the higher vitalities. The classical

---

6. The term comes, doubtless, from Kierkegaard, whom Niebuhr follows closely in his anthropology. The reader would err, however, if he interpreted this admission of spirit to entail the trichotomic view of man. "There is only one self. Sometimes the self acts and sometimes it contemplates its actions." *Human Nature,* p. 259. In interpreting the new realism of Niebuhr it will not do to convert existential insights into metaphysical truths.

7. *Ibid.,* p. 3.

tradition, for example, by which Niebuhr means Plato, Aristotle, and the Stoics, was so faithfully dedicated to the power of *nous* in man that no small depreciation of physical involvement resulted. The classical tradition made the easy mistake of identifying the real with the rational man, concluding in the first place that reason makes man continuous with the gods and discontinuous with the animals, and in the second that degrees of rationality among men form a just basis for social stratification. The philosopher-king, having gained mastery over his passions through reason, stands at the farthest end of the social scale from the slave. Because of his addiction to irrationality, the slave is simply a piece of property.

When once the real man is the rational man, it is easy to conclude that the body is something foreign to man at his best. Greek thought ended up in a dualistic metaphysics, therefore, the vitalities of reason being good and the vitalities of the body being bad. There was no other conclusion to draw when once one side of the environment was corrupted. "The dualism has the consequence for the doctrine of man of identifying the body with evil and of assuming the essential goodness of mind or spirit."[8]

Niebuhr contends that the idealistic premise follows only when one is not true to the full content of his experience. An existentially sensitive mind is no less conscious of the reality of physical impulses as being part of his real self than he is that the potentialities of ratiocination properly are his.

Dualism is only the beginning of errors for idealism, however.[9] The tendency among those who identify the real with the thinking man, is to make finite reason so continuous with divine or cosmic reason that essential individuality is finally lost. Idealism's initial gains in sensing the height of man's freedom are quickly dissipated. "Idealistic philosophy al-

8. *Human Nature*, p. 7.

9. The reader should be reminded that Niebuhr uses the term "idealism" in the widest (and most ambiguous) sense. In this instance he has primarily in mind the absolute idealists. Personalists, for example, while idealists, would not fall under these strictures, since they are very careful to distinguish human from divine consciousness. Idealism and the retention of individuality are not necessarily incompatible — as Niebuhr would be the first to admit.

ways has the advantage over naturalism in that it appreciates this depth of human spirit. But it usually sacrifices this advantage by identifying the universal perspective of the self-transcendent ego with universal spirit. Its true self therefore ceases to be a self in the true sense and becomes merely an aspect of universal mind."[10] It is characteristic of idealism, therefore, to talk lightly of particularity. This is due to its initial error of underestimating man's involvement in flux. "Rationalism practically identifies rational man (who is essential man) with the divine; for reason is, as the creative principle, identical with God. Individuality is no significant concept, for it rests only upon the particularity of the body. In the thought of Aristotle only the active *nous,* precisely the mind which is not involved in the soul, is immortal; and for Plato the immutability of ideas is regarded as a proof of the immortality of the spirit."[11]

As Plotinus subsumed the individual under the One and as Hegel subordinated the subjective mind under the objective mind, so there is this general penchant in all rationalism and idealism to corrupt the limitations of man by an overstress on freedom. "Idealism conceives the self primarily as reason and reason primarily as God."[12] Gentile brought rationalism to its logical conclusion when he finally identified the individual with thinking itself. Man *is* thought. With this emphasis, the conversion of a vital man into a rational man was finished. "Idealism begins by emphasizing man's freedom and transcendence over nature but ends by losing the individual in the universalities of rational concepts and ultimately in the undifferentiated totality of the divine."[13]

A fruit of idealism's indifference to the real man is an underestimation of the significance of time. The real is the eternal. "Neither Greek nor Roman classicists had any conception of a meaning in human history. History was a series of cycles,

---

10. *Human Nature,* p. 75.
11. *Ibid.,* p. 7.
12. *Ibid.,* p. 76.
13. *Ibid.,* p. 22.

a realm of endless recurrence."[14] One grossly underestimates Niebuhr's anxiety at this point if he supposes, however, that a loss of interest in time in transcendental philosophies is but an academic question. Niebuhr is a moralist seeking a moral basis for social action. But if either the individual is made inconsequential by being swallowed up into eternity, or time is rendered insignificant by reason of its non-ideational character, then it is rather self-evident that no meaningful program of social justice for individuals in time can be plotted. If the individual is nothing, justice for the individual is nothing. And if time is nothing, justice for the individual in time is nothing. Whenever either individuality or time is corrupted, a respect for degrees of justice within history, which alone prevents social betterment from merging with social indifference, is destroyed. If it makes no difference in eternity how one conducts himself in time, then the nerve center of social vitality is severed. If the significant things are only eternal, flight from temporal responsibility is made plausible.

2. *Love for the natural in man.* No small company of thinkers, outraged by idealism's blindness, have turned to the consanguinity of man with the physical world beneath him as the real environment. With this shift in milieu an identification of the real with the natural man results, and the attending errors soon match the proportions of those against which naturalism first turned. "The naturalist portion of modern culture seeks to reduce the whole dimension of spirit in man to an undifferentiated 'stream of consciousness' if indeed it does not seek to reduce consciousness itself to purely mechanical proportions."[15] William James boldly speaks out against the idealist's love for metaphysical monsters. "Metaphysics or theology may prove the soul to exist; but for psychology the hypothesis of such a substantial principle of unity is superfluous."[16]

The loss of the individual in naturalism is self-evident. If man is once either confused or identified with the ma-

14. *Ibid.*, p. 10.
15. *Ibid.*, p. 70.
16. Quoted by Niebuhr, *ibid.*, p. 73.

terial order, what essential individuality could he possibly enjoy? Chemistry and physics are not respecters of individuals. Physical forces are sheer continuity. Individuality can only be a material accident. The form which matter takes and the essential properties of matter itself are two entirely different things. For this reason it is easy for a naturalistic emphasis to incubate forms of social injustice. "Naturalistic philosophies may (and in modern nationalism do) destroy individuality by emphasizing consanguinity and other natural forces of social uniformity as the only basis of meaning."[17] Not understanding the height of man as a free spirit, the naturalist quickly succumbs to the error of his trade. Time becomes everything in naturalism, as history is a self-explanatory movement. Lacking the vantage point of eternity over against history, however, the naturalist's this-worldly emphasis soon runs into the ground from want of coordination and perspective. If eternity does not define man's fullest potentialities for him, the easiest turn for philosophy or sociology is to sanctify one of man's partial expressions of truth or justice, defining it as a finality beyond which progress in either truth or justice is impossible.

Niebuhr detects great strands of naturalism (and romanticism) in the capitalistic, bourgeois pattern of modern life. The capitalist is engaged in his own crusade, a crusade not for the Holy Grail but for the holy enrichment of social life by the strengthening of natural comforts and securities for man. "The business man developed a form of economic power which depends upon individual initiative and resourcefulness rather than upon hereditary advantages; and which creates dynamic rather than static social relationships. It naturally sees human history as a realm of human decisions rather than of inexorable destiny."[18] The bourgeois mind is a self-reliant mind. With today's vision and tomorrow's vitality a complete emancipation of the individual from those ties which have hitherto fettered him will be effected. What the bourgeois mind overlooks, however, is the fallacy of attempting to define earthly potential-

17. *Human Nature*, p. 69.
18. *Ibid.*, pp. 65-66.

ities apart from an eternal norm. "Speaking in social terms one may say that he lost this individuality immediately after establishing it by his destruction of the medieval solidarities. He found himself the artificer of a technical civilization which creates more enslavening mechanical interdependencies and collectivities than anything known in an agrarian world."[19] The very technology which was erected to be the everlasting monument to man's freedom from limitations and bondage emerges as a new cause for the destruction of justice and security. When technological power outruns moral strength, and history is cut loose from the judgment and grace of eternity, the freedom of man suddenly converts these newly acquired material cohesions into occasions of power and conquest. Security and peace in a bourgeois civilization is chimerical, therefore. "Thus the bourgeois individual who emerges from the social cohesions, restraints and inertias of medievalism and imagines himself master of nature and history, perishes ingloriously in the fateful historical necessities and the frantically constructed tribal solidarities of the age of decay."[20]

Having lost contact with eternity, naturalistic social and economic patterns inevitably corrupt the individual. If the individual is only quantitatively distinct from the steel and wooden tools with which he labors, no unusual mental gifts are presupposed to see that man is not much more than just a tool himself. Just as the horse exchanges its labor for the security of oats, so man exchanges his talents on the assembly line for the security of a weekly pay check. But those who hire remain impersonally related to both horse and man. The employee is, at best, but a number or a thing, hired for the increase of certain monetary values through the exchange of service. While serving a church as pastor in Detroit, Michigan, Niebuhr almost became an American Marxian on the question of social inequalities. Both Marx and Niebuhr sensed the logical outcome of a capitalistic philosophy which believes that the hired individual is subordinate to the capital gained from his serv-

19. *Human Nature*, p. 22.
20. *Ibid.*, p. 67.

ices. Money, not a personal concern for justice, is the cohesive bond which keeps the employer-employee relationship intact. "Detroit produces automobiles and is not yet willing to admit that the poor automata who are geared in on the production lines have any human problems."[21] Firsthand observations turned Niebuhr from unfounded optimism to a cold realism. While Niebuhr rejected the violent means which Marx proposed to break up the capitalistic stronghold, he yet found in Marx a sympathetic mind.

3. *A love for the vitalistic in man.* Sensing the inadequacies in both naturalism and idealism, romanticism attempted a *tertium quid.* "Naturalism loses the individual because it does not view life in sufficient depth to comprehend the self-transcendent human spirit. This spirit is a reality which does not fit into the category of natural causality which is naturalism's sole principle of comprehending the universe. Idealism on the other hand discovers the human spirit in its height of transcendence over natural process, but loses it again because the uniqueness and arbitrariness of individuality do not conform to its pattern of rationality, which is its sole principle of interpreting reality . . . Confronted with annihilation through either abasement or deification it is natural that modern culture should have sought for another way out. It found this way in romanticism."[22] Romanticism sympathizes with the refusal of the idealist to reduce man to a series of pointer readings, for expressive freedom in man is too integral a vitality to be submerged under physical forms. But romanticism recoils from the pretension of the idealist that freedom and rationality are synonymous pursuits. The romanticists, coming in the name of a gospel of individuality, avers that freedom is misunderstood if it is uncompounded with an appreciation of man's involvement in the flow of those nonrational vitalities, such as emotion, feeling, and will, which expressively reflect the inner man. The ro-

---

21. Niebuhr, *Leaves from the Notebook of a Tamed Cynic,* (Willett, Clark & Colby, 1929), p. 112.

22. *Human Nature,* pp. 81-82.

mantic man is a vital man. He can be a *Uebermensch* if he will only assert himself in the fullness of his passionate inwardness.

The irony of this attempt to do justice to both the naturalistic vitalities of man and his freedom is that, while romanticism was framed for the salvation of the individual, it proved to be extremely vulnerable for the inroads of a new corruption. Romanticism, like naturalism, having dropped its rudder into the sea, now finds itself without means of steerage. When the romantic mind is divorced from eternity, an autonomous individual, who has no check on his aimless, vital expression, results. With chaos threatening in every direction, therefore, it was evident that a check had to be found if the collective resources of the social unit were to be preserved. But when a super will or super mind was found, it turned out that the romantic individual was no longer romantic, for he was quickly swallowed up in this new cohesive center. Here again, as in idealism, the shift was made from the individual to its larger expression, until in the end the larger unit became more important than the individual. "The process of this romantic destruction of individuality can be briefly summarized as follows: Individuality is directly related to the eternal source of meaning and given unqualified significance, while idealism ascribes significance to the individual only as he is related to a rational universal value of history. Sooner or later the romantic thinker must, however, recoil from the pretension of this purely individual self-deification; and all but Nietzsche do recoil. They seek to increase the plausibility and reduce the pretension of this self-glorification by looking for the 'larger individual'; which they find in the unique nation. This collective individual then supplants the single individual as the centre of existence and the source of meaning. In the pursuit of seeking something larger than a person as his centre, the romanticist meets the absolute idealist who is intent upon finding something a little more domestic and manageable than the Absolute as the source of value. Thus they both discover the nation, approaching it from different sides but agreeing in its deification."[23] Thus the cycle is complete.

23. *Human Nature,* p. 83.

II. The Christian Balance

By negating these competing anthropologies, Niebuhr is supplied with a positive apologetic for the Christian view of man. Idealism, while releasing the individual from the tyrannical impersonalities of nature, succeeds only by engulfing him in either the mind of the state or in cosmic reason. Naturalism appreciates man's natural involvement and exploits it, only to lose a consolidation of this gain because it has no way of absorbing that self-transcendent freedom of man which alone can unite him to the stabilities of eternity. If idealism thinks too highly of man's freedom and too lowly of his natural contingencies, naturalism is guilty of thinking too lowly of freedom and too highly of involvement. Romanticism counters with the pretension that it has set both vitality and freedom in a proper balance by grounding them in the emotional centers of the free man. But this insight is quickly surrendered to the higher vitality of the mind or will of the state, as in the voluntarism of Nazi Germany.

If the fallacy of its alternatives is that they become enamored of one side of man's nature or another, so that the individual is either set against himself or completely destroyed — and "the cultural history of modern man gives him no resource to modify or to defy this tendency"[24] — Christianity at least professes to have found a vantage lookout from which one can plot a proper estimation of both freedom and involvement without invalidating either. "Without the presuppositions of the Christian faith the individual is either nothing or becomes everything. In the Christian faith man's insignificance as a creature, involved in the process of nature and time, is lifted into significance by the mercy and power of God in which his life is sustained. But his significance as a free spirit is understood as subordinate to the freedom of God."[25] The elevation preserves freedom, and the subordination safeguards limitation and involvement.

---

24. *Human Nature*, p. 92.
25. *Ibid.*, p. 92.

A. *Christian Presuppositions*

Inasmuch as every anthropology is framed on the strength of certain initial presuppositions, it may be pedagogically wise to accent the meaning of Christianity by outlining the fundamental radicals upon which the system itself rests.

1. *Creation ex nihilo.* Niebuhr contends that the doctrine of creation is Christianity's first distinctiveness. Christianity rejects any tendency toward a closed system, be it a modernistic immanence where history is a self-contained and self-explanatory process or a transcendental idealism or rationalism where the absolute ideas complete the system. If history is closed, eternity cannot break through; and if eternity is frozen, history has no meaning. Creation *ex nihilo* keeps the relations between time and eternity fluid enough to allow for historical progress, and yet rigid enough to keep history tensionally responsive to absolute norms of obligation.

Niebuhr doubtless has been profoundly influenced in this return to a realistic view of creation by the impasse into which all purely rationalistic attempts to explain life have come, such as are outlined in Lovejoy's classic, *The Great Chain of Being.* Only the freedom of God in creation, believes Niebuhr, can forge a fluid link on this chain which gives final significance to both eternity and history. Lovejoy, after exhaustively ransacking Western thought to evaluate the attempt to throw a net of rational prediction over the universe, concluded that the project has been unsuccessful. Whether time is elevated to eternity or eternity lowered to time, the result is the same; for the instant time and eternity are geared together without a fluid coupling between them, that moment both individual decision and natural flux become inconsequential. A closed universe results. Time and process are too liquid to be made a part of the machinery of eternity. If, as in Spinoza, the nature and order of mind is the same as the nature and order of things, and if mind is an eternally necessary, rational order, then the universe, with all its ebb and flow, is immediately converted into a colossal figure in geometry in which contingency and decision mean nothing. A closed, rational system might be convincing if it were not for the fact that such phenomena as decision, change, and flux actually exist. There is no rationally predictive reason for temporal change. The universe is contingent. "The world of concrete existence then, is no impartial transcript of the realm of essence; and it is no translation of pure logic into temporal terms — such terms being themselves, indeed, the negation of pure logic. It has the character and the range of content and of diversity which it happens to have. No rational ground predetermined from all eternity of what sort it should be or how much of the world of possibility should be included in it."[26]

Christianity's fluid coupling between time and eternity, which breaks the tyranny of the rationalistic threat and yet saves history from meaninglessness, is the sovereign will of a creating God. Teleology, thus replaces absolute causal connectiveness in the Christian Weltanschauung.

The scientific method, claiming that there is a perfect causal chain in the universe which, when found, will give man an absolutely accurate predictive formula, speaks of *ex nihilo nihil fit;* while Christianity, willing to admit no more natural causation than reality itself can bear, formulates its faith as creation *ex nihilo*. "The Christian concept of creation *ex nihilo* calls attention to the fact that the temporal process is not self-explanatory."[27] On Christian terms neither the world nor man enjoys self-contained existence. Therefore, when questing for the meaning of both time and eternity, the will of a sovereign God must be examined.

If proof of the doctrine of creation is called for, Niebuhr responds that, while no scientific demonstration can be given — since creation is something which is beyond the pale of experiment — a *profound* proof is possible. It is the following: The doctrine, when granted, explains life's complexity while, when

26. A. O. Lovejoy, *The Great Chain of Being,* (Cambridge, Harvard University Press, 1948), p. 332.

27. *Faith and History,* p. 48. "God is not merely mind who forms a previous given formless stuff. God is both vitality and form and the source of all existence. He creates the world. This world is not God; but it is not evil because it is not God. Being God's creation, it is good." *Human Nature*. p. 12.

if it is denied, man is left with embarrassments and absurdities. The scientific difficulties with creation, therefore, are dismissed by Niebuhr as existentially inconsequential.

The creation story is only a myth, furthermore, not a scientific formula.[28] Its validity depends upon depth of insight into the universe, not upon the paltriness of scientific analysis. When evangelical Christianity seeks to defend the scientific claims of creation as recorded in the Bible, thus, Niebuhr senses a strain of literalism. "The creation myths of Genesis, undoubtedly related in some way to the Babylonian creation epic, do not depart from the general character of the creation myths of early religion."[29] The evangelical is too literal. He is trying to make a scientific truth out of what must remain a mythological truth.[30]

This epistemological clue to American realistic thought ought to be grasped by every student of Niebuhr. Actually, Niebuhr is still a liberal in his view of the Bible. The Bible contains, not God's plenarily inspired will for man, as in orthodoxy, but rather a salvation history (*Heilsgeschichte*) which is to be appropriated critically through depth experience. Older liberalism had found in the Bible a normative statement for valid religious experience. Neo-orthodoxy simply enlarges this epistemology to discover in the Bible a normative statement for valid existential tension. For both liberal and Niebuhr, therefore, the Bible is authoritative only at those points where there shines through a clarification of an experience gained earlier. For example, whole experience concludes that there is a "more" to reality than can be gathered on rational grounds. History is not self-explanatory. The Bible teaches

28. "Myth" is a regrettable word for Niebuhr to use. To preclude an early misunderstanding, therefore, the reader must be advised that the term does not mean "fable" or "tale." In Niebuhr's mind the myth is a changeless insight into the relation between time and eternity, which is clothed in a hypothetical, historical situation. As we shall show *infra,* the myth is neo-orthodoxy's answer to the question how it plans to tack between the Biblical seriousness of orthodoxy and the Biblical frivolousness of modernism. One must learn to take the myth earnestly, but not literally.

29. *Faith and History,* p. 47.

30. With the reader's consent no critical remarks will be said about the success of the myth until Niebuhr has been given further opportunity to expatiate on its profundity.

that this "plus" factor can be explained if we believe in creation. Therefore, creation is a profound mythological truth, for it preserves that fringe of non-rationality at the edge of history which gives significance to crisis decision within history. The creation story in Genesis may be a laughing error, scientifically; but it is a lasting existential insight into the relation between time and eternity; for when it is taken seriously one has in his possession the most satisfying clue to the meaning of life.

2. *The imago dei.* The doctrine of creation *ex nihilo* lays the groundwork for the second great presupposition of Christianity, that of the image of God. The image is not to be pressed into a psychological literalism any more than is creation to be forced into a scientific mold. The *imago dei* doctrine is less a precise psychological elaboration than the inward confession that the full height of man's freedom can be explained only in terms of a vertical relation to God. Spirit finds its final resting place in the infinite will of a personal God.

The *imago* is best understood, then, when one turns his attention to an examination of final freedom. Man can overtake himself to that point where the self stands over the self. The outside limit of this self-transcendence is the being of God alone. "I dive on this side and on that," says Augustine, one of the profoundest interpreters of the image, "as far as I can and there is no end. So great is the force of memory, so great is the force of life, even in the mortal life of man. What shall I do then, O Thou my true life my God? I will pass beyond this power of mind which is called memory; yea, I will pass beyond it that I may approach unto Thee, O sweet Light . . . And where shall I find Thee? If I find Thee without my memory then I do not retain Thee in my memory. And how shall I find Thee if I remember Thee not?"[31] Augustine's insight is great, not only because it sensed "that the human spirit in its depth and height reaches into eternity and that this vertical dimension is more im-

31. Quoted by Niebuhr, *Human Nature*, p. 156.

portant for the understanding of man than merely his rational capacity for forming general concepts;"[32] but also because, while profoundly influenced by the mystical tendencies of Plotinus, he refused to allow the individual to be swallowed up in the One. Freedom may point in the direction of the ultimate source of our being, but finite freedom must not be converted into an ultimate.

The doctrine of the image goes hand in hand with the generic myth of creation in that it reveals from the side of the individual the fact that the universe is not closed. Since there is no conceivable limit to man's freedom short of God's infinity, no extension of rational categories will finally tax man to the point where fullness of spirit has been exhausted.

A paradox of freedom immediately results, for a spiritual man is simultaneously self-determining and self-determined in his exercise of spirit. Kierkegaard, while he tends to employ unguarded words to express himself, has given what Niebuhr thinks is the most penetrating statement of the paradox in Christian literature. The following utterance is typical: "I choose the Absolute? What is the Absolute? I am that myself the eternal personality . . . But what is this myself? . . . It is the most abstract and yet at the same time the most concrete of all realities. It is freedom."[33] Man is at once self-determined by God and yet self-determining in his having chosen God at the final limit of his freedom. "Man is self-determining not only in the sense that he transcends natural process in such a way as to be able to choose between various alternatives presented to him by the processes of nature but also in the sense that he transcends himself in such a way that he must choose his total end. In this task of self-determination he is confronted with endless potentialities and he can set no limit to what he ought to be, short of the character of ultimate reality. Yet this same man is a creature whose life is definitely limited

32. *Ibid.*, p. 157.
33. Quoted by Niebuhr, *Ibid.*. p. 163.

by nature and he is unable to choose anything beyond the bounds set by the creation in which he stands."[34]

B. *The Benefits of the Christian Perspective.*

The essential difference between the Christian world view and that of its alternatives is that the very values which are either lost or corrupted by other systems, emerge triumphant in Christianity as foundation pillars.

1. *Christianity preserves a sane view of the whole individual.* "The consequence of this conception of the world upon the view of human nature in Christian thought is to allow an appreciation of the unity of body and soul in human personality which idealists and naturalists have sought in vain."[35] The real man, the whole man, is neither reason nor body. The whole man is a finite creature, made in the image and after the likeness of God. The creative act sets the denotative and connotative definition of man.

2. *Spirit is fully recognized and accented.* When a balanced view of the whole is achieved, the parts of man likewise fall into a balanced perspective. Against the naturalistic and romantic underestimation of man's vertical powers, Christianity "emphasizes the height of self-transcendence in man's spiritual stature in its doctrine of 'image of God.' "[36] Whatever gains idealism may boast, Christianity can duplicate, yet without falling victim to the fallacy of identifying man with the eternal mind or will. God created man. Man did not emanate from God. This initial act of sovereignty, therefore, immediately sets man over against the being of God in final differentiation. Man, while being like God, is not God; for God is eternal

34. *Ibid.,* pp. 163-164. Notice the large point of contact the image of God becomes for Niebuhr. At this point Niebuhr is once again closer to Brunner than to Barth. "It is significant that Karl Barth, who stands, of course, in the general Augustinian tradition but who is interested to prove that revelation from God to man has practically no points of contact with man except those which it itself creates, finds Augustine's definitions of the image of God in man very inconvenient and criticizes them severely." *Ibid.,* p. 158, n.

35. *Ibid.,* p. 12.

36. *Ibid.,* p. 150.

Spirit and man is created, dependent spirit. Finitude can never pass over into infinity. By keeping man next to God for meaning, man's full height is appreciated; but by making God the final limit to man's potentialities, man's individuality is retained. "God as will and personality, in concepts of Christian faith, is thus the only possible ground of real individuality."[37] The world may not be mystically absorbed into the person of the Creator, for two distinct realms of being are in question.

Natural revelation sets the problem for man, and special revelation solves it. Man senses by nature that he stands too completely outside of both nature and himself to be understood in terms of either reason or nature. But without special revelation to enlighten him as to the exact demands of eternity, either reason is underscored too strongly or too lightly; or nature is made either all or nothing; or reason and nature remain in an unbalanced, unexplained ratio. Special revelation breaks through historical limitations to tell us the mind of God on the meaning of both man and history. When such an insight is lacking, the easiest course of resistance is to convert a partial truth into a final insight, so that either the lower or the higher in man becomes the final man. The revelation of God in Jesus Christ saves the Christian from thinking either too highly or too lowly of himself, for the being of God defines both man's dignity and his limitations. "To understand himself truly means to begin with a faith that he is understood from beyond himself, that he is known and loved of God and must find himself in terms of obedience to the divine will. This relation of the divine to the human will makes it possible for man to relate himself to God without pretending to be God; and to accept his distance from God as a created thing, without believing that the evil of his nature is caused by this finiteness."[38]

3. *The creation doctrine recognizes that freedom is not the full story of man.* Man is body as well as spirit. Therefore, Christianity "insists on man's weakness, dependence, and finiteness, on his involvement in the necessities and contingencies

37. *Human Nature,* p. 15.
38. *Ibid.,* p. 15.

of the natural world, without, however, regarding this finiteness as, of itself, a source of evil in man."[39] It is characteristic of modernity to appreciate man's natural vitalities, but it is not characteristic that it can understand this insight and at the same time enjoy a perspective which preserves individuality. Too low a view of man's Godward potentialities destroys the gains already made. "The modern experience belongs in the category of pathos or irony rather than tragedy, because contemporary culture has no vantage point of faith from which to understand the predicament of modern man."[40]

Classical Greek thought came to a more logical impasse than modern thought. Sensing an incongruity between the freedom of man and his physical limitations, the Greek concluded that the body is evil and that the higher vitalities are in perpetual war against the lower. "Thus life is at war with itself, according to Greek tragedy. There is no solution, or only a tragic solution for the conflict between the vitalities of life and the principle of measure."[41] Modern philosophy simply ignores the problem of the Greeks, assuming quite without justification that the body of man is as good as his spirit. Modern man's good opinion of himself will not stand scrutiny, however, for modernity can neither tell how self-transcendence is related to the problem of individuality or how a good, naturalistic man can do evil. Christianity is able to skirt Greek pessimism and the setting of man against himself without falling into the opposite ditch of modern optimism. "Man's finite existence in the body and in history can be essentially affirmed, as naturalism wants to affirm it. Yet the uniqueness of man's spirit can be appreciated even more than idealism appreciates it, though always preserving a proper distinction between the human and the divine."[42] Christianity neither ends up on a pessimistic note, nor does it leave man without a hopeful source of explanation; nor, having found this ultimate, does it lose individuality in it through a new absorption.

39. *Ibid.*, p. 150.
40. *Faith and History*, p. 9.
41. *Human Nature*, p. 11.
42. *Ibid.*, pp. 15-16.

4. *These gains reflect further implications.* With a balanced view of man, one can set time and eternity in proper relation. Non-Christianity stumbles by making time either everything or nothing. The classical tradition, seeing the linkage between body and time, saw little meaning to time and history. History is, at best, but a meaningless cycle series. Modern man, however, sees everything in time and little in eternity. The Greeks were plagued with the problem of the one within the *many,* while modern thought is troubled with the problem of the *one* within the many. Classical thought had no perspective to appreciate history, and modern thought lacks a perspective to understand eternity. The one leads to other-worldliness, and the other to skepticism. Christianity is able to correct the one-sidedness of both. God's eternal plan, revealed in Jesus Christ, absorbs the Greek insight, while God's covenant in history covers the insights of modern man. History, contrary to the Greeks, is not meaningless; nor, contrary to the moderns, is it self-explanatory.

Another solution which Christianity can manage is that of evil in society and history. The fact of evil in history is self-evident, but only Christianity can explain it in relation to man's full height and depth. Christianity "affirms that the evil in man is a consequence of his inevitable though not necessary unwillingness to acknowledge his dependence, to accept his finiteness and to admit his insecurity, an unwillingness which involves him in the vicious circle of accentuating the insecurity from which he seeks escape."[43] The moral cycle runs as follows: Freedom seeks to pass beyond the limitations which creation places upon it, while the limitations counteract the venture. Lust then sets in and freedom resorts to more forceful means to attain the vision of lust. "What causes wars, and what causes fightings among you? Is it not your passions that are at war in your members? You desire and you do not have; so you kill. And you covet and cannot obtain; so you fight and wage war."[44] Christianity is realistic about man's sinfulness without using this as an occasion for

43. *Human Nature,* p. 150.
44. James 4:1-2.

disparaging his finitude. "Man is a sinner. His sin is defined as rebellion against God. The Christian estimate of human evil is so serious precisely because it places evil at the very centre of human personality: in the will. This evil cannot be regarded complacently as the inevitable consequence of his finiteness or the fruit of his involvement in the contingencies and necessities of nature. Sin is occassioned precisely by the fact that man refuses to admit his 'creatureliness' and to acknowledge himself as merely a member of a total unity of life. He pretends to be more than he is. Nor can he, as in both rationalistic and mystic dualism, dismiss his sins as residing in that part of himself which is not his true self, that is, that part of himself which is involved in physical necessity. In Christianity it is not the eternal man who judges the finite man; but the eternal and holy God who judges sinful man."[45]

For a final recapitulation: Christianity, as Niebuhr has conceived it, takes in all that is valid in its major alternatives, without falling prey to the fallacies attending them. Whereas idealism has tended to draw man into the vortex of the absolute mind, Christianity anchors man on earth through its serious understanding of his temporal involvement. And whereas both naturalism and voluntarism corrupt individuality, the one within the flow of matter and the other within a social center of will or decision, Christianity preserves man's life by denying that the limited can be understood independent of the limitless. The mind and will of God sanctify the limitations by relating them vertically to an endless freedom.

45. *Human Nature*, p. 16.

III

The Predicament of Man

THE next link in the chain of Niebuhr's crucial arguments is forged by a shift from strict anthropology to the proposed way the double environment finally is compounded with the actions and intentions of individual men in history. A realistic appreciation of the nature of man, thus, is followed by a crisp diagramming of the predicament of man. Niebuhr senses that the polar properties of the double milieu, time and eternity, combine as ingredients to form that magnetic pressure point within the spirit of man which initiates a friction between what man wishes he were and what natural forms remind him that he actually is. It is this inward stress and strain which gives relevance to both the relation between time and eternity as a dialectical problem and the concept of Christ as a dialectical solution. Niebuhr is eloquent here, inasmuch as he realizes how pointless it would be to exhibit Christ on the cross to men before they have come to comprehend the predicament which makes the cross their only hope.

I. Elements in Man's Predicament

Enigmatically enough, the very datum in man which defines his glory, namely, spirit, becomes in due course the catalytic agent which activates a misery and ignominy of man. A free man is gloriously a self-, time-, and space-transcending creature. But concomitant to this prerogative are the alternatives of both creation and destruction. Immense power can be used either for the increase of human values or for their steady decrease. The coverage of freedom embraces both as eventualities. Let us examine these antitheses in turn.

A. *Freedom to Create.*

As a creative spirit, man is at his best. By creativeness Niebuhr means the power which freedom enjoys to conquer defiances that inhibit human security. Through freedom, *e. g.*, man plotted the overthrow of those injustices and tyrannies which the vested interests in a feudal-agrarian economy sanctioned and defended. A greater release of individual response resulted. Through freedom man created tools of industry and learning which have gone far to snap the shackles placed on him by nature's contemptuous opposition. Freedom empowers man to envisage, arrange, and imagine. While nature dictates that man keep his place on the ground, hence, freedom responds by creating the powerful airship. Man, thus, is endlessly at work seeking new and higher levels of perfection and security.

The account of the trials and attempts of man to overcome limitations and to extend security we know as *history*. "The extension of human powers is the basis of the progressive character of human history. Every new conquest of nature and every new elaboration of human skills means that human actions and responsibilities are set in the context of a wider field. This is the creative side of human history."[1] If there were a proof needed that man is free to create, therefore, history is it. Whereas the brute is submerged in the herd or flock, depositing for posterity neither loss nor gain, man leaves behind a chain of cultural monuments which in turn serve as the foundation of the next generation of free men. "Man's ability to transcend the flux of nature gives him the capacity to make history. Human history is rooted in the natural process but it is something more than either the determined sequences of natural causation or the capricious variations and occurrences of the natural world. It is compounded of natural necessity and human freedom. Man's freedom to transcend the natural flux gives him the possibility of grasping a span of time in his consciousness and thereby of knowing history. It also enables him to change, reorder and transmute the causal sequences

1. Niebuhr, *Discerning the Signs of the Times,* (N. Y., Charles Scribner's Sons, 1946), p. 65.

of nature and thereby to *make* history."[2] History, in short, is the record (or fact) of man's attempt to overcome the tension created by both natural necessity and the potentialities of eternity created within the dynamic of imagination. Changeless principles form the guiding light in change, and natural necessities define the conditions within which change may or may not be actual. "History thus moves between the limits of nature and eternity."[3] The collective expression of men in social units leaves behind it the deposit of culture. Pots, temples, libraries, and forms of government give clues to the cultural type of a given social structure.

Memory forms the linkage between the present and the past, it itself being an integral part of the *imago dei* endowment of man. "Memory represents man's capacity to rise above, even while he is within, the temporal flux. It proves that time is in him as surely as he is in time. The most obvious definition of 'history' is that it is a record or memory of past events."[4] Since neither the past nor the present has flowed from logical necessity, only the vitality of memory can preserve the uniqueness of the meaning which characterizes time's flux. Memory serves the collective, cultural unit by keeping before it those rallying vitalities which define its loyalties. Memory serves the individual and the nation by acting as a bank to house the deposits of free possibilities made by the race of man before. No simple logical analysis of terms can provide man with the catalogue of possibilities and limitations of freedom mediated through the unified experience of the race. Memory briefs man in one sweep on the vital connections in history, thus making the march of the race before him live in the contemporaneity of imagination.

Memory does not necessarily shackle a man to the past, however, because freedom may remain sovereign over devotion to history. Properly used, memory may emancipate the individual from the involvements of the present by suggesting to him alternatives in choice. The past can offer

2. Niebuhr, *Human Destiny,* p. 1.
3. *Ibid.,* p. 2.
4. *Faith and History,* p. 18.

peace from present troubles, or it can serve as leverage for further gains in tomorrow's world. "Memory is, in short, the fulcrum of freedom for man in history."[5]

B. *Freedom to Destroy.*

As a destructive spirit, man is at his worst. By destructiveness is meant the power which freedom enjoys to overtake and defeat those forms which increase human security and justice. "The tragedy of human history," which the Greek dramatists saw so vividly but could not solve, "consists precisely in the fact that human life cannot be creative without being destructive, that biological urges are enhanced and sublimated by daemonic spirit and that this spirit cannot express itself without committing the sin of pride."[6] The same freedom which increases justice may also be a means by which justice is decreased. The electric motor may either drive the oxygen to nourish the dying or power the treads and turrets of a lethal tank to destroy the living. The organs of sex may be a means to increase life, or be converted into instruments for sheer lust.[7] "The human self is . . . able by its freedom to transmute nature's survival impulse into more potent and more destructive, more subtle and more comprehensive forms of self-seeking than the one-dimensional survival impulse of nature."[8] Memory supplies the mind with history's latitude of vital expression, giving it leverage to select those potentialities which will increase the efficiency of evil intentions. The criminal, therefore, is often as astute a student of history as is the philanthropist. The difference is that one ransacks the past to augment evil, while the other searches it to augment good.

While the terms of the predicament are clear now, the reasons for the necessity of the predicament are not; since some

5. *Ibid.*, p. 19.
6. *Human Nature*, pp. 10-11.
7. "The sex impulse is never purely as biological in man as in the brute. It is creatively related to the artistic impulse and lies at the foundation of the family organization, which in turn is the nucleus of larger organizations of the human community. But sex can also become the perverse obsession of man because he has the freedom to center his life inordinately in one impulse." Niebuhr, *The Children of Light and the Children of Darkness*, (N. Y., Charles Scribner's Sons, 1946), p. 61.
8. *Faith and History*, p. 94.

may conclude that the potentiality to create will somehow gain ascendancy in man and the predicament will disappear. Niebuhr immediately counters by reminding the optimist that the time-eternity, creation-destruction tensions in man are *normal* to man's nature. Freedom to create and destroy are correlatives. Extinguish either one and the other perishes. If man is truly free, the option of choosing either the increase or the decrease of values in history must attend him throughout his life. *The essential definition of man embraces the simultaneous alternative potentialities of freedom to create and freedom to destroy.*

The divergency of neo-orthodoxy from historic Christianity at this point should be carefully observed, therefore. Reformation Protestantism, following the teaching of the Apostle Paul in Romans 5:12ff, taught that a covenant of works was made with Adam in which the opportunity was given him as the federal head of the race to gain confirmation in righteousness. When Adam failed in his probation, he not only forfeited this privileged opportunity for himself and for the race, but he also received the consequences of an evil nature. The essential nature of man, therefore, does *not* require the potentiality to do evil. Had man passed his probation and gained confirmation in righteousness, he would have been free only to do good, while still remaining essentially man. In heaven, hence, when the righteousness of Christ, the last Adam, will have restored to man his lost confirmation in righteousness, the essential man will everlastingly enjoy only freedom to create. *The difference between orthodoxy and neo-orthodoxy here is serious and important. Orthodoxy determines its view of the nature of man from propositional revelation; Niebuhr determines his from the existential witness of the heart.*

Having decided that the *falling* (not fallen) man is the normal man, therefore, Niebuhr disdains any eschatological commitment which would give man freedom only to create, be it in orthodoxy and a millennial reign of the saints with Christ or in Marx subsequent to the revolution of the proletariat. "The social harmony of which Marxism dreams would eliminate the destructive power of human freedom; but it would also destroy the creative possibilities of human life."[9] One reason why Niebuhr refuses to concede that man can attain historical perfectability is that the dialectical relation between time and eternity would be corrupted. The significance of this will appear shortly.

II. The Emergence of Sin

The locus of all sin and evil in history is the point of tangency between what man as a free being imagines himself to be and what the verdict of natural necessity defines him actually to be. It is this point of friction which is the precondition in man for the relevance of Jesus Christ. Man knows in the height of his freedom what the terms of life would be like if he had final security, but such dreaming is always challenged by the defiance of nature. "What is insufferable to man is that his self-conscious existence should challenge the universe for a brief moment without being able to relate itself organically to it."[10] By virtue of his freedom man imagines himself far more greatly secure than the facts will justify. The result of this friction between what man desires and what can actually be obtained, is anxiety and discontentment, the preconditions of sin. Being both high and low, man can quickly gain either too high an estimation of himself by accenting the high or too low by accenting the low. An unwarranted megalomania results only when man obfuscates the double environment. "This ability to stand outside and beyond the world, tempts man to megalomania and persuades him to regard himself as the god around and about whom the universe centres."[11] Man could never be deluded into thinking so unwarrantedly highly of himself if he conscientiously took into account his full involvement in nature.

A. *The Setting for Sin: Anxiety.*

Niebuhr, following Sören Kierkegaard, is persuaded that the friction of the double environment makes relevant both the inevitable rise of sin in history and the dialectical interpre-

9. Niebuhr, *The Children of Light and the Children of Darkness,* p. 60.
10. *Reflections on the End of an Era,* p. 196.
11. *Human Nature,* p. 124.

tation of time and eternity as a solution. It is questionable, therefore, whether one can appreciate Niebuhr fully until he understands his historical lineage in Kierkegaard.[12]

Kierkegaard postulated two syntheses in man. The first may be viewed from the point of view of *faculty*. Man is body and soul carried away by spirit. Spirit is exactly as Niebuhr has defined it: the power of self-transcendence, "the power of a man's understanding over his life."[13] The second may be viewed from the point of view of *potentialities*. "As for the latter synthesis, it evidently is not fashioned in the same way as the former. In the former case the two factors were soul and body, and the spirit was a third term, but was a third term in such a sense that there could not properly be any question of a synthesis until the spirit was posited. The other synthesis has only two factors: the temporal and the eternal. Where is the third term?"[14] Analysis shows that the two syntheses turn out to be the same one, however, save that each is viewed from a different emphasis. "The synthesis of the eternal and the temporal is not a second synthesis but is the expression for the first synthesis in consequence of which man is a synthesis of soul and body sustained by spirit."[15] Spirit finds its freedom in the moment of decision, the moment being "an atom of eternity."[16] It is the "moment" which is the locus of anxiety (dread) for Kierkegaard, since the moment opens up to the individual the simultaneous attraction of seizing eternal potentialities and the fear of the dizziness which would attend their actual possession. Whenever freedom comes to itself, therefore, anxiety results. Anxiety is as concomitant to man's freedom as eating and breathing are to his body. Only anxiety can goad

---

12. Niebuhr professes Kierkegaard to be "the greatest of Christian psychologists." *Human Nature*, p. 44, n.

13. *The Journals of Sören Kierkegaard*, (tr. Alexander Dru. London, Oxford University Press, 1938), § 1177.

14. Kierkegaard, *The Concept of Dread*, (tr. Walter Lowrie. Princeton, Princeton University Press, 1944), p. 76. "Man is a synthesis of the infinite and the finite, of the temporal and the eternal, of freedom and necessity, in short it is a synthesis." Kierkegaard, *The Sickness unto Death*, (tr. Walter Lowrie. Princeton, Princeton University Press, 1941), p. 17. Kierkegaard's words are almost exactly the same as Niebuhr's.

15. *The Concept of Dread*, p. 79.

16. *Ibid.*

the spirit into its full stature. When anxiety perishes, vision and progress perish.

Kierkegaard defines this power of dread in man as "an attraction to what one fears, a sympathetic antipathy. Dread is an alien power which lays hold of an individual, and yet he cannot tear himself loose from it, and also does not will to; for one is afraid, but what one fears also attracts one."[17] Anxiety might be illustrated by the young philosopher who simultaneously is attracted by the desire to know all wisdom, while being gripped by the fear that death will overtake him before the task is accomplished. Anxiety accompanies man at every expression of his essential freedom. There is never a moment when it is not part of his psychological make-up. Anxiety is the "dizziness of freedom which occurs when the spirit would posit the synthesis, and freedom then gazes down into its own possibility, grasping at finiteness to sustain itself."[18]

Niebuhr, believing that Kierkegaard has given western culture its profoundest insight into the relation between man's precondition and his final sinning, uses similar terminology to express exactly the same thing. "Anxiety is the inevitable concomitant of the paradox of freedom and finiteness in which man is involved. Anxiety is the internal precondition of sin. It is the inevitable spiritual state of man, standing in the paradoxical situation of freedom and finiteness. Anxiety is the internal description of the state of temptation."[19] Freedom is always accompanied by a dizziness at seeing the yawning gulf between the attainment of freedom and the limitations imposed by necessity. Sin is the artificial attempt of man to overcome the discrepancy between this craving for security and the attainment of it. The essentiality of anxiety provides the backdrop for the essentiality of the Christian dialectic. Only the terms of the dialectic are able to meet man where he is and satisfy his full environment without corrupting either one side or the other.

---

17. Kierkegaard, *Journals,* § 402.
18. Kierkegaard, *The Concept of Dread,* p. 55.
19. Niebuhr, *Human Nature,* p. 182.

Anxiety is the setting for sin. It catapults the individual to that place where a temptation to overcome insecurities through unnatural means develops. Anxiety is not sin, but it lies perilously close to it. Without anxiety there would be no sin. "The truth is that man is tempted by the basic insecurity of human existence to make himself doubly secure and by the insignificance of his place in the total scheme of life to prove his significance."[20] The ways in which men seek to overcome the insecurities of the double environment are as infinite as spirit is free. The tyrant resorts to power and wealth. The scholar pretends that he has a final system. The theologian boasts of his infallible church. The working man thinks that he is indispensable to society. The child pretends that he is the leader of the others in the playground. All of these artificial efforts to overcome insecurity are failures in the end, however, since they remain essentially related to the nature of man. The tyrant rules others, but soon he is ruled by death. The final system of the philosopher is displaced by a new one. The theologian's pretension is blasted by the uncovering of damaging data. The man on the street dies in insignificance. The child sees his friends leave him and turn to another.

The climax to fear and anxiety is death. With incisiveness Niebuhr exposes the futility of Epicurus' attempt to explain away death as a nonentity. "Epicurus overlooked the significance of the fact that man should inevitably fear death while animals do not."[21] The double environment of man precludes his easy classification with the animals which likewise die. The serenity of the beast is not man's possession, because man is at home only within the tensions of time and eternity. "No beast comes to the melancholy conclusion that 'all is vanity'; for the purposes of its life do not outrun its power, and death does not therefore invade its life as an irrelevance. Furthermore it has no prevision of its own end and is therefore not tempted to melancholy. Man's melancholy over the prospect of death is the proof of his partial transcendence over the natural process which ends in death. But this is only a partial tran-

20. *Human Nature,* p. 192.
21. *Ibid.,* pp. 98-99.

scendence and man's power is not great enough to secure his own immortality."[22] Death punctures the pride of all men, being the arch under which the mighty and the weak alike must all pass.

B. *Sinfulness.*

In existential terms, sin is what results when man tries to find security for himself outside the tension of the dialectical relation between time and eternity. "Sin is, in short, the consequence of man's inclination to usurp the prerogatives of God, to think more highly of himself than he ought to think, thus making destructive use of his freedom by not observing the limits to which a creaturely freedom is bound."[23] The desperation of man to overcome his limitation is great, since the law of self-preservation within him is compounded with a powerful egoistic drive to be found in the esteem of others. Pride is accented most frightfully when social security lashes a man on to extremities. "Man, being more than a natural creature, is not interested merely in physical survival but in prestige and social approval. Having the intelligence to anticipate the perils in which he stands in nature and history, he invariably seeks to gain security against these perils by enhancing his power, individually and collectively."[24]

Whether sin assumes the form of inward pretensions to either power or knowledge, on the one hand, or the outward lusts of the flesh, on the other, Niebuhr detects a common denominator in all sin: *the claim to finality*. "Man is mortal. That is his fate. Man pretends not to be mortal. That is his sin."[25] Instead of admitting his insignificance in relation to the whole of things, man artificially seeks to overcome limitations through his own contrivances. "Evil is always the assertion of some self-interest without regard to the whole."[26] The terms of the double environment make sin inevitable, but

22. *Discerning the Signs of the Times*, pp. 128-129.
23. *Faith and History*, p. 121.
24. *The Children of Light and the Children of Darkness*, p. 20.
25. *Beyond Tragedy*, p. 28.
26. *The Children of Light and the Children of Darkness*, p. 9.

not necessary. The inevitability arises out of man's persistent refusal to remain within created limitations. "Sin is occasioned precisely by the fact that man refuses to admit his 'creatureliness' and to acknowledge himself as merely a member of a total unity of life. He pretends to be more than he is."[27]

Since the individual and the collective will comprise two egos, and since both are free to create and to destroy, there emerges two species of sinful expression.

1. *Individual egotism.* The sins of the individual are of two types: the sin of pride and the sin of sensuality. Since the former is the more basic, however, it is the more important existentially.

(a) *The sin of pride.* "Man falls into pride, when he seeks to raise his contingent existence to unconditioned significance."[28] This is perfectly clear. But since the expression of freedom itself is complex, the manifestations of pride are no less complex.

(1) *The pride of power.* There is a persistence within the ego to believe itself more secure than it ought. This pride is exhibited in both those who already enjoy social security and those who wish they did. When social forms persuade men that they are secure, an incredible blindness to the finite and limited nature of human existence results. Tyrants and dictators fondly imagine that their position exempts them from the ruthlessness of accident and death to which all others are constantly subject. And those who are socially insecure exert their lust for power under the guise of an innocent search for security. "It is the sin of those, who knowing themselves to be insecure, seek sufficient power to guarantee their security, inevitably of course at the expense of other life."[29] This crusade for security is compounded with spiritual and moral vitalitics which are exploited by the individual for his own

27. *Human Nature,* p. 16.
28. *Ibid.,* p. 186.
29. *Ibid.,* p. 190.

ends. For this reason the pride of the labor union which struggles for the increase of the standards of living among its men is less easy to detect than that of the secure employer who contends he is earning his money the hard way — a million at a time. Greed in technological advancement has encouraged all classes to believe they will enjoy a final triumph over nature, as if science will defeat death.

The expression of the pride of power does not end until competing human egos exploit one another. Both nature and other men become subservient to the lust for security in the individual. The result is the increase of injustice in society. "It may be taken as axiomatic that great disproportions of power lead to injustice, whatever may be the efforts to mitigate it."[30] "Security through power means insecurity for those who lack power."[31]

The will to power is not simply the result of ignorance. It always involves some deliberate effort upon the part of the insecure individual to overcome the insecurities of nature, society, and death. "Thus the greatest monarchs of the ancient world, the Pharaohs of Egypt, exhausted the resources of their realm to build pyramids, which were intended to establish or to prove their immortality. A common mortal's fear of death is thus one prompting motive of the pretensions and ambitions of the greatest lords."[32] Poverty, obscurity, the lack of social approval and recognition, and the want of everlasting life are all insecurities discovered by the free individual. The predicament of man results from his refusal to make peace with his limitations, preferring instead, to defy what providence has defined as part of finitude. "The fact that human ambitions know no limits must therefore be attributed not merely to the infinite capacities of the human imagination but to an uneasy recognition of man's finiteness, weakness and dependence, which become the more apparent the more we seek to obscure them, and which generate ultimate perils, the more immediate insecurities are eliminated. Thus man seeks to make

30. *Human Destiny,* p. 262.
31. *Beyond Tragedy,* p. 102.
32. *Human Nature,* p. 193.

himself God because he is betrayed by both his greatness and his weakness; and there is no level of greatness and power in which the lash of fear is not at least one strand in the whip of ambition."[33]

(2) *The pride of the intellect.* More pious, but no less sinful, is the pretense of the philosopher or scientist that he has in his possession a final insight into truth. "Intellectual pride is thus the pride of reason which forgets that it is involved in a temporal process and imagines itself in complete transcendence over history."[34] One can detect the pride of the intellect by its *ideological* taint. "Ideology is a compound of ignorance and dishonesty. The dishonest element in it, the tendency of men to justify self-interest by making it appear identical with the common good, is an expression of the person, and not of the mind. It betrays a corrupted will, which is a mystery with which rationalism does not deal."[35] The start of the intellect is for the "pursuit of knowledge" — an innocent venture. But its end is the pretentious claim that one has arrived at a "final system" of truth. "It pretends to be more true than it is."[36] The will of the individual contributes somewhat to the pretension by adding claims which go beyond the knowledge situation and embrace the lust for security of the individual himself. One of the proofs of this is the way thinkers are hurt when their theories are exploded. "Descartes' intellectual pride was something more than the ignorance of his ignorance. That was disclosed when he resented the reminder of a friend that his '*Cogito, ergo sum,*' the keystone of his philosophical arch, was derived from Augustinian thought."[37]

Being compounded with freedom, the intellect knows no theoretic ends to its claims. Man can always pass from facts to pretensions. Intellectual pride does not convert itself to social injustice as immediately as does the sin of pride, for hypocrisy and conceit may remain convert attributes of the

33. *Human Nature,* p. 194.
34. *Ibid.,* p. 195.
35. *Faith and History,* p. 161.
36. *Human Nature,* p. 194.
37. Ibid., p. 196.

deluded individual himself, never passing into social injustices. But once *my* truth is confused with *the* truth, the perfect precondition for the contest between egos is created.

Since the freedom of man admits the possibility of the individual's recognizing his own limitations, pride of intellect is never simply a matter of sheer ignorance. "The ignorance presupposes pride, for there is always an ideal possibility that man should recognize his own limits."[38]

While it is necessary to go into this question with much greater care at a later point,[39] it does seem that Niebuhr at this point exposes one of the initial embarrassments in the existential epistemology. If, for example, one's claiming final truth is a sin, then it is but a further sin to affirm either that Christianity is "the *final* truth about life and history . . . the *final* key to this historical interpretation,"[40] or to affirm the proposition, "All social injustice is immoral." Either it is a final truth that Christianity is true, or it is not; if it is, we seem to be sinning that grace may abound. And if it is not, then we lose our criterion to judge all other sin. *There is no easy escape from this dilemma.* It seems to be a case of sinning to stop sin. But does one diminish his guilt by simply announcing in advance his own consciousness of sinning? Existentially, the Christian appears to be worse off than the man who sins ignorantly, for the Christian knows whereof he acts.

(3) *Moral pride.* "Moral pride is the pretension of finite man that his highly conditioned virtue is the final righteousness and that his very relative moral standards are absolute."[41] Unconditional values which are announced as unconditional contain an ideological taint in morality. The subtlety of this pride is that it employs virtuous claims as a means to sustain sin. Witness the conflict which Jesus had with the moral leaders of Judaism. The Pharisees and scribes, refusing to submit their righteousness to the test of the law of God, went about establishing their own moral security independently. They collided with the light of God in Christ, therefore, lest their deeds

38. *Human Nature,* p. 198.
39. See pages 130ff. and 239ff.
40. *Human Destiny,* p. 211 (Italics mine).
41. *Human Nature,* p. 199.

be reproved. The pride of morality, being most subtle, is also most vicious. Lurking beneath the outward morality is a fleshly heart of pride. Self-criticism is wanting. Tolerance is unknown. "It is responsible for our most serious cruelties, injustices and defamations against our fellowmen. The whole history of racial, national, religious and other social struggles is a commentary on the objective wickedness and social miseries which result from self-righteousness."[42]

In Niebuhr's explanation of this form of pride, like that of intellectual, one cannot but sense that some link in his argument is missing. The way the sin of moral pride is laid out by Niebuhr it seems that its individuating principle is but the sheer and simple claim to finality. But does this not conflict with Niebuhr's own claim that in the selfless love (*agape*) morality of Jesus Christ one finds a *final* norm for man? *Here* is a pretense to finality in the area of morality which somehow seems to escape the charge of the taint of pride. It would seem, therefore, that the sin is not so much that a claim to finality *per se* has been made, but rather that the wrong type of a claim has been advanced. *If this is not valid, then Niebuhr has no more right than his opponent to make a claim to finality; for a principle which undermines everything undermines itself also.* Great clarification is needed at this point.

(4) *Spiritual pride.* "The third type, the pride of self-righteousness, rises to a form of spiritual pride, which is at once a fourth type and yet not a specific form of pride at all but pride and self-glorification in its inclusive and quintessential form."[43] All other prides are on the way to this final expression of egotism, but they arrive only when the individual finally leaps completely out of himself and tacitly claims self-deification. It emerges at that point when "our partial standards and relative attainments are explicitly related to the unconditioned good, and claim divine sanction."[44] It is simple to see that moral pride gives birth to spiritual pride when the individual identifies his partial insights with the will of the gods.

42. *Human Nature,* p. 200.
43. *Ibid.,* p. 188.
44. *Ibid.,* p. 200.

The hideousness which can result from the union of spiritual pride with the prides of power, intellect, and morals can be illustrated endlessly in history. The pretensions of the dictators in World War II, however, will suffice to exhibit the fact that "the worst form of intolerance is religious intolerance, in which the particular interests of the contestants hide behind religious absolutes."[45] In the name of a presumed oracular contact with heaven the war lords sought to make a plausible case for their tyranny over the other nations. The Japanese descended from the gods. The Germans were continuous with the Wagnerian myths. There is no bloodier controversy written than that which has transpired between religious factions. The reason is that the individual, supposing that he is on the side of the gods in what he believes, considers all else but trivial means to achieve the end of his faith. Fanaticism results.

While it is true that there "is no final guarantee against the spiritual pride of man,"[46] it is the virtue of the Christian gospel that it is a religion of revelation "grounded in the faith that God speaks to man from beyond the highest pinnacle of the human spirit; and that this voice of God will discover man's highest not only to be short of the highest but involved in the dishonesty of claiming that it is the highest."[47] The Christian is somewhat like Socrates — only more enlightened. He is the most virtuous of all men by confessing his utter lack of virtue. Whenever a man makes claims to self-righteousness in the name of Christianity, he falls under the same indictment as the pagan.

(b) *The sin of sensuality.* Because the sins of sensuality are more open to social inspection, and therefore more easily detected and criticized, it is easy for Christian pride to overlook its own self-insufficiencies by concentrating on the sensual transgressions of others. Niebuhr strikes back, showing that sensuality is subordinate to the more basic pride of egotism. "Very frequently the judge, who condemns the profligate,

45. *Ibid.*, pp. 200-201.
46. *Ibid.*, p. 202.
47. *Ibid.*, p. 203.

has achieved the eminence in church or state from which he judges his dissolute brethren, by the force of a selfish ambition which must be judged more grievously sinful than the sins of the culprit."[48]

Niebuhr is dissatisfied with the usual Christian explanation of sensuality as a "confusion consequent upon the original confusion of substituting the self for God as the centre of existence,"[49] for such a position cannot give a consistent and satisfying explanation of the relation between self-love and gratification. "Is sensuality, in other words, a form of idolatry which makes the self Gód: or is it an alternative idolatry in which the self, conscious of the inadequacy of its self-worship, seeks escape by finding some other god?"[50] Does the drunkard become drunk to gratify himself or to flee from himself? That is the problem. The answer which Niebuhr turns to is a compound of both alternatives. The individual seeks to gratify his own self-love for a while, but then discovers in the expenditure a frustration which leaves him for the moment bankrupt of alternative securities. To cover up this deficiency, partial self-satisfaction is converted to a means by which the individual seeks to escape his predicament. "The self is seeking to escape from itself and throws itself into any pursuit which will allow it to forget for a moment the inner tension of an uneasy conscience. The self, finding itself to be inadequate as the centre of its existence, seeks for another god amidst the various forces, processes and impulses of nature over which it ostensibly presides."[51] Sensualism is ambivalent. The drinker initially drinks to gain an accenting of his own ego; finally he drinks to escape from himself. The very freedom which opens up an avenue of security now becomes a whip to lash the individual into the retreat from the self. "Anxiety tempts the self to sin; the sin increases the insecurity which it was intended to alleviate until some escape from the whole tension of life is sought."[52] Self-love is first

48. *Ibid.*, p. 228.
49. *Ibid.*, p. 233.
50. *Ibid.*
51. *Ibid.*, p. 234.
52. *Ibid.*, p. 235.

extended, and then an attempt is made to rid the self of it. The final form of corruption of sensualism is the anodyne of escape from the tensions of life by making the flesh an end in itself. But as for the one who converts his whole life into the lust after sex, "It is a flight not to a false god but to nothingness."[53] The individual who tries to make a final alliance with the flesh will come to grief inevitably, for the elements in the union are incompatible. Spirit and flesh cannot finally marry.

While it cannot easily be gainsaid that Niebuhr has succeeded in making a profound contribution toward explaining the elements involved in the decisions of sensualism — especially when viewed from the perspective of the psychology of the one indulging — there are yet reasons to believe that his final conclusions are extremely deficient in Christian content. Niebuhr makes no convincing effort to relate sensualism to its *involving a transgression of the law of God.* Existentialism seems able to process only the profligate, the one who goes to excesses in the flesh; while the Bible indicts all who transgress the law, however selective their sins may be. It is conceivable on Niebuhr's conclusions, therefore, that one could decide for fornication with moderation and respectability, indulging in non-marital intercourse with the same restraint and imperturbability that he would if eating and drinking. Such self-controlled sensualism does not seem to fall within the existential criterion. The individual is moderate and restrained, making sex outside of marriage only a minor pastime. The act has but small sociological consequences, and the individual himself apparently feels no effects for the worse. Niebuhr, therefore, by departing from the Biblical morality that *sin is a transgression of the objective law of God,* seems able to process only coarse sensualism. This Biblical omission greatly reduces both the validity and the worthwhileness of Niebuhr's arguments. The Bible indicts even the most fashionable form of sensualism, making the law of God, not an existential situation, the final criterion of the worthiness or unworthiness of any act. This failure on Nie-

53. *Ibid.*, p. 237.

buhr's part will inevitably attend all who seek to explain sin *psychologically* rather than *theologically*.

With an inimitable skill, however, Niebuhr tacks deftly between a Freudianism which seeks to reduce the fears and shames in man to social conventions and a Puritanic asceticism which, after the Hellenistic tradition, views the sensual acts, particularly sex, as sinful *per se*. Neither in the relaxing of the tensions of the inner life nor in the dualism of asceticism is there a final solution, for one side outrages the spirit by reducing it to finite dimensions and the other promotes a morbidity which ends in dualism.

2. *Collective egotism.* Because the social unit is formed of many individual egos, the ingredients in collective pride remain the same. But the new collusion results in a form of unity which transcends the power and pretenses of the individuals whose minds and wills make up the whole. Individuals can hide behind the plausible pretensions of the state, and by so doing gain an outlet for their own pride on a more efficient basis. "Whenever the group develops organs of will, as in the apparatus of the state, it seems to the individual to have become an independent centre of moral life. He will be inclined to bow to its pretensions and to acquiesce in its claims of authority, even when these do not coincide with his moral scruples or inclinations." [54]

The advantage which the group ego has is that it can make claims which go beyond those which the individual in isolation would dare venture. There is a weight and momentum to the collective ego which provisionally supports its boasts of finality. "The group is more arrogant, hypocritical, self-centered and more ruthless in the pursuit of its ends than the individual."[55] The pretensions of finality and immortality go hand in hand with the collective mind. Hence, the self-love of the individual finds an outlet in the collective ego through governments, armies, and technological fortifications. Idolatry, the sin of making the finite an infinite end, therefore, is almost congenital to statism. Lacking any attending organs of free-

54. *Human Nature*, p. 208.
55. *Ibid.*

dom for self-criticism through self-transcendence, the state inevitably is devoid of those sensitivities of spirituality which preserve the tensions of holiness and progress in the individual. It reluctantly participates in self-criticism, yielding only when alert individuals within the state determinately exert themselves. "The nation is a corporate unity, held together much more by force and emotion, than by mind."[56] The national mind, not having the agility and refinement of the self-critical individual, is unable to distinguish between a healthy self-criticism and a dangerous form of inner conflict, therefore. "So nations crucify their moral rebels with their criminals upon the same Golgotha, not being able to distinguish between the moral idealism which surpasses, and the antisocial conduct which falls below that moral mediocrity, on the level of which every society unifies its life. While critical loyalty toward a community is not impossible, it is not easily achieved. It is therefore probably inevitable that every society should regard criticism as a proof of a want of loyalty."[57]

Inasmuch as the sin of man is his claim to finality — a pretension to having successfully defied finitude — it is rather evident why the collective mind is able to give greater plausibility to its own claims than is the individual. In the minds of those seeking power and security, the state is the nearest thing to God on earth. Within the collective ego the individual is given a framework of security which makes the delusion of final security even less apparent. "Collective pride is thus man's last, and in some respects most pathetic, effort to deny the determinate and contingent character of his existence. The very essence of human sin is in it. It can hardly be surprising that this form of human sin is also most fruitful of human guilt, that is of objective social and historical evil. In its whole range from pride of family to pride of nation, collective egotism and group pride are a more pregnant source of injustice and conflict than purely individual pride."[58]

---

56. *Moral Man and Immoral Society,* p. 88.
57. *Ibid.,* pp. 88-89.
58. *Human Nature,* p. 213.

The collective ego has a legitimate zone in which to make certain claims and pretensions, since it is the center of vitality and value which gives transcendent depth to the freedom of the individual. The state, *e.g.*, seems destined to outlive the individual. But the sin of the nation is that it makes claims which pass far beyond the bounds of its own finitude, ignoring the fact that sooner or later the collective mind, like that of the individual, will pass into the oblivion of history.

Niebuhr contends that neither the individual nor the state can understand its true limitations until it sees itself from beyond itself, *i.e.*, until the voice of God is heard speaking to and against the ego. But this religious perspective, which entails a dialectical relation between time and eternity, is gained only within Biblical presuppositions. The precise way this follows will be dealt with in due time.

III. Alternate Explanations for Sin

The common denominator which threads through all modernity, giving divergent anthropologies their negative point of contact, is the faith that the fountainhead of evil in history is not man himself. Man is good, fundamentally good, good to the inner core of his personality. When it comes to explaining how evil has come into history, therefore, the modern man stands ready to blame almost anything and everything — except himself. Not being able to understand his true contradiction, he cannot understand the place of evil in history. "The modern man is, in short, so certain about his essential virtue because he is so mistaken about his stature. He tries to interpret himself in terms of natural causality or in terms of his unique rationality; but he does not see that he has a freedom of spirit which transcends both nature and reason. He is consequently unable to understand the real pathos of his defiance of nature's and reason's laws. He always imagines himself betrayed into this defiance either by some accidental corruption in his past history or by some sloth of reason. Hence he hopes for redemption, either through a program of social reorganization or by some scheme of education."[59]

A. *Non-Christian Explanations.*

Non-Christian understanding of evil is partially convincing because it is partially true. But it is profoundly wrong because it misses the connection between the essential predicament of a free creature, the rise of sin through anxiety, and the refusal of man to stay within his limitations.

The easiest scapegoat for evil in history is to blame some source within history for the occasion of sin and evil. Just as Adam blamed Eve and Eve blamed the serpent, so others, refusing to see themselves as they are, excuse themselves on the ground that history itself has something in it which, if removed, would solve all our problems. Religious priestcraft, ignorant leaders, unbalanced governments, or sundry institutions or customs are the bane of history. If idols, prejudices, and outmoded mores and customs could be sloughed off, Utopia would be present. Holbach traces our problems back to the pretensions of theology, which in turn gives rise to political tyrannies. Helvetius blasts religion as both the cause of the lag in men and the enemy of all progress. These drags are interpreted as excess ballast which keeps the spirit of man from soaring on to that inevitable progress which would normally and naturally be his if left uninhibited. Epicurus and the naturalists blamed the rise of evil on the drift of man from nature. Bad governments, bad dictators, bad philosophies all receive their vote in the glut of modern excuses for our predicament. Marx interprets the problem of evil in the narrow terms of a distorted social balance, as if a final elimination of the strife between classes will likewise eliminate all evil. John Dewey blames the historical failure on man's refusal to apply the scientific method in all of life. Lags on every side of our culture follow from this "prescientific" fixation. Idealism blames the lack of good reason, good education as the cause of our difficulties. Away from nature and back to reason! is

59. *Human Nature*, p. 96.

the cry. Rational prudence is the solution to all our problems.

And so the gamut is run — from naturalism, which exhausts man in his natural existence, to idealism, which exhausts man in his rational existence. This welter of voices simply betrays the fact, however, that freedom and necessity have been misunderstood to the point where one side of man is glorified at the expense of the other. Modern man "considers himself the victim of corrupting institutions which he is about to destroy or reconstruct, or of the confusions of ignorance which an adequate education is about to overcome. Yet he continues to regard himself as essentially harmless and virtuous."[60]

The partial truth of each explanation is that it lights upon some singularly offensive way in which evil expresses itself, and thus "has the virtue of throwing light upon the character of particular social evils and may point the way to their mitigation or elimination. But none of them explains how an evil which does not exist in nature could have arisen in human history."[61] Why do men seek lucrative priestly offices? Why do men refuse the cohesions of nature? Why do men turn aside from the bliss of rationalism, social equalities, and the application of the scientific method? Why are governors bad? Why are leaders ignorant? Why are governments unbalanced? If man's distinctiveness lies not in his union of time and eternity at the point of the free spirit, why is it that man refuses to pursue either the natural cohesions which bind the animal world in harmony, on the one hand, or the rational cohesions which mark angelic rationality, on the other? The answer is that the naturalists do not understand the degree to which man is free over nature and the idealists the degree to which man is bound by natural necessity. Not understanding man's essential conflict, therefore, they cannot understand man's essential sinfulness. "Whether they found the path from chaos to order to lead from nature to reason or from reason to nature, whether they regarded the harmony of nature or the coherence of mind as the final realm of redemption, they failed

60. *Human Nature,* pp. 94-95.
61. *Ibid.,* p. 97.

to understand the human spirit in its full dimension of freedom. Both the majesty and the tragedy of human life exceed the dimension within which modern culture seeks to comprehend human existence. The human spirit cannot be held within the bounds of either natural necessity or rational prudence."[62]

The bourgeois culture, which is a child of modernity's self-confidence, is destined to rapid decay because it is not sufficiently integrated with those free spiritual vitalities which direct and draw man. The one-dimensional view of history, which immanence is enamored of, fails to supply the individual with a perspective from which to judge himself and his values. For this reason the ties in a capitalistic society are flimsy and easily extinguishable. The workers are not devotedly related to the employer, as in the medieval world where spiritual values were compounded with an agrarian-feudal economy; but only by the ties of the dollar. Such a monetary relation, therefore, is more transient and vulnerable. The optimism of the bourgeois man stands unfortified with a sound philosophy of life. The delusions of righteousness on the part of both employer and employee are without bounds. Neither understands that sin lies essentially in his own will. Each is aloof from any blame in the West's decline. "The modern oligarchy conducts a bank or a factory. He 'serves' mankind. All bloodshed is abhorrent to him. The lust of power and the imperial impulse may prompt his actions but they express themselves subconsciously rather than consciously. He is not fully conscious of life's brutalities. He may tenderly send his family to escape the winter's cold on the sands of Palm Beach while his workers starve to death amid the social confusion of an economic depression. His cities are filled with humanitarians who eat meat but regard the killing of animals with repulsion. His institutions of learning boast of academics, supported by rather generous crumbs which fall from the rich man's table, who invent schemes for saving modern civilization by transmuting it into a rational and moral accommodation of interest to interest in which all coercion and conflict will be avoided.

62. *Human Nature*, p. 122.

They are unconscious of the fact that they are dreaming of such a moral world in a leisure provided by privileges which have emerged out of a terrific conflict of power."[63]

B. *Christian Explanation.*

Niebuhr resorts to the formula of "original sin" to explain why evil in history belongs to man, and not to the ants, and how there is introduced into nature what can not be found in nature. Unlike others, the Christian asks "how it is that an essentially good man could have produced corrupting and tyrannical political organizations or exploiting economic organizations, or fanatical and superstitious religious organizations";[64] and the answer to which he comes is that there is a bias toward sin in man's very will. The essence of original sin "is man's unwillingness to acknowledge his finiteness."[65]

Niebuhr again appeals to the existentialism of Kierkegaard to unravel the problem of sin. The final authority which Niebuhr bows to is not the Biblical witness, but rather the psychological experiences which men pass through when they analyze their own acts of wrongdoing. The doctrine of original sin is, while logically absurd, psychologically profound. "Here is the absurdity in a nutshell. Original sin, which is by definition an inherited corruption, or at least an inevitable one, is nevertheless not to be regarded as belonging to his essential nature and therefore is not outside the realm of his responsibility. Sin is natural for man in the sense that it is universal but not in the sense that it is necessary."[66] Existentially, man sins inevitably, yet not by necessity. While moralists may deride this formula as logically meaningless, experience finds that it is a valid expression of the inward conflict of man in moral situations. Man is free in that he is responsible, but he is not free to do other than sin. This is the paradox. The objection to it as a logical option is summed up very well in the Kantian formula, "I ought, therefore I can." Logic claims

63. *Reflections on the End of an Era*, p. 11.
64. *The Children of Light and the Children of Darkness*, p. 17.
65. *Faith and History*, p. 118.
66. *Human Nature*, p. 242. For one of the ablest Pelagian responses to Niebuhr's doctrine of original sin, see Lewis, *Morals and the New Theology.*

that it is meaningless to hold a man responsible for the fulfillment of an ideal which *ex hypothesi* cannot be attained. Pelagianism, therefore, defines the will of man in such a way that sin is simply perversity. Pelagius sees no significance to the idea of responsibility without ability.

Existentialism rejects the claims of Pelagianism on the ground that they run counter to experience. "The truth is that, absurd as the classical Pauline doctrine of original sin may seem to be at first blush, its prestige as a part of the Christian truth is preserved, and perennially re-established against the attacks of rationalists and simple moralists by its ability to throw light upon complex factors in human behaviour which constantly escape the moralists."[67] It is quite true that we sense an element of open-mindedness in our moral choices, so that our lust for security grows partly out of our own cruel deliberations. "In other words actual sin is involved in the bias toward sin which issues in specific acts of cruelty."[68] But what the Pelagian cannot comprehend is the fact that one senses within him a defiance against the very limits which God has placed upon him, a defiance which is part of human nature but which cannot be accounted for on the simple moral formula that one creates his own ends through deliberate choices. This unconscious drive or inclination in man is "original sin." Actual sin, therefore, is not simply a matter of inward perversity, nor is it only the innocent expression of ignorance. Sin is both conscious and unconscious; it involves both a bias and a deliberation, however difficult it may finally be to learn the exact proportions of each in any specific act. "There is, in other words, less freedom in the actual sin and more responsibility for the bias toward sin (original sin) than moralistic interpretations can understand. The actual sin is the consequence of the temptation of anxiety in which all life stands. But anxiety alone is neither actual nor original sin. Sin does not flow necessarily from it. Consequently the bias toward sin from which actual sin flows is anxiety plus sin. Or, in

---

67. *Human Nature*, pp. 248-249.
68. *Ibid.*, p. 249.

the words of Kierkegaard, sin presupposes itself. Man could not be tempted if he had not already sinned."[69]

The result of juxtaposing voluntary and involuntary elements in the psychology of sinning is the paradox that man sins inevitably but nonetheless remains quite responsible for his acts. The paradox is logically offensive, but existentially coherent. Neither simple determinism nor simple indeterminism satisfies the Christian moralist. "The fact of responsibility is attested by the feeling of remorse or repentance which follows the sinful actions."[70] However much the individual may feel himself wanting in strength to do the right, he cannot honestly exculpate himself of guilt, since he senses "that some degree of conscious dishonesty accompanied the act, which means that the self was not deterministically and blindly involved in it."[71] It is never possible for a man fully to transmute his moral intentions into consistent living, inasmuch as the want of perfect faith in God in his nature sullies final holiness. But (as will be later developed) guilt, while leading to repentance, does not lead necessarily to despair, for the love and grace of God as revealed in Christ provide a perfect ground for peace of heart.

A dialectical tension of heart emerges which provides the final setting for the dialectical relation between time and eternity in Christ. The one self senses a division of the house. The self in contemplation rises to the full height of its freedom and perceives the meaning and responsibility of the right; while the self in action shamefully cringes to reflect upon its concrete omissions and commissions. These ways of experiencing the self must not lead to the error of believing that there is not a unity of the self. Individuality is lost if there is a final division of the self. The one free self sometimes turns toward its obligations, and sometimes towards its own act. "The self, even in contemplation, remains the finite self. In one moment it may measure its situation and discover its sin. In the next moment it will

69. *Ibid.*, p. 250-251
70. *Ibid.*, p. 255.
71. *Ibid.*

be betrayed by anxiety into sin. Even the distinction between contemplation and action must, therefore, not be taken too literally. For any contemplation which is concerned with the interests, hopes, fears and ambitions of this anxious finite self belongs properly in the field of action; for it is a preparation for a false identification of the immediate and the ultimate of which no action is free."[72]

One of the most glaring lacunae in Niebuhr's system protrudes here. Niebuhr tells us very clearly why *sinning* (on his definition of sin) is inevitable — it is because men persistently refuse to remain within their appointed limits. But what Niebuhr does not oblige to explain with persuasion is why this *refusing* is inevitable. He rejects the notion that there is a sinfulness in the race which has come down through Adam through natural heredity — "an Augustinian corruption," in his words. But may it not actually be that man is far more constitutionally sinful than existentialism is willing to concede? How else can we explain the refusal of man to remain within his limits? When an automobile continually breaks down, one soon suspects that there is a constitutional deficiency in the machine. What, likewise, of man?

In dialectical tension the one self must tack between the Pelagian insight that sin is achieved in freedom and the Augustinian insight that freedom itself is corrupted by sin. The simple humanistic formula of the plenary ability of man to fulfill the whole law has encouraged the pretensions of the Augustinians to become too literalistic about sin's necessity on the one hand, while the Augustinian tendency to make original sin a simple, inherited taint has given rise to Pelagian successes on the other. Unless the two elements are kept in balanced relationship, the dialectic will be destroyed. "It is obviously necessary to eliminate the literalistic illusions in the doctrine of original sin if the paradox of inevitability and responsibility is to be fully understood; for the theory of an inherited second nature is as clearly destructive of the idea of

---

72. *Human Nature*, p. 260.

responsibility for sin as rationalistic and dualistic theories which attribute human evil to the inertia of nature."[73]

The time has arrived for those seeking to understand Niebuhr's existentialism to shift from conventional to existential logic. The paradox of freedom "expresses a relation between fate and freedom which cannot be fully rationalized."[74] Aristotelian logic is the formal guard of truth; but the material of truth has to be extracted from experience. The "dialectical truth" that man is determined in sin by freedom and not by natural necessity is explicable only when the individual is prepared to be so loyal to reality that even logical consistency is at times waived. "Formally there can be of course no conflict between logic and truth. The laws of logic are reason's guard against chaos in the realm of truth. They eliminate contradictory assertions. But there is no resource in logical rules to help us understand complex phenomena, exhibiting characteristics which seem to require that they be placed into contradictory categories of reason. Loyalty to all the facts may require a provisional defiance of logic, lest complexity in the facts of experience be denied for the sake of a premature logical consistency. Hegel's 'dialectic' is a logic invented for the purpose of doing justice to the fact of 'becoming' as a phenomenon which belongs into the category of neither 'being' nor 'nonbeing.' "[75]

73. *Human Nature,* p. 262
74. *Ibid.*
75. *Ibid.,* pp. 262-263. A veritable nest of difficulties will emerge as a result of this sweeping methodological concession.

IV

The Inevitability of the Dialectic

SELF-AWARENESS of the terms of our predicament can avoid despair only when the individual succeeds in passing from a shallow pessimism to "the assumption that life is meaningful and that its meaning transcends the observable facts of existence."[1] Religious perspective converts the terms of the moral situation into a tension of interest and concern. "The dimension of depth in the consciousness of religion creates the tension between what is and what ought to be. It bends the bow from which every arrow of moral action flies. Every truly moral act seeks to establish what ought to be, because the agent feels obligated to the ideals, though historically unrealized, as being the order of life in its more essential reality."[2]

I. The Necessity of Religion

The religious man refuses to believe that the moral tension of his life is unrelated to a personal Being who is both the author of moral ideals and the judging and forgiving agent in his sinful predicament. Without religion man has no depth of perspective. He is a creature straddling two dimensions while yet trying to interpret himself in terms of but one. Without the attraction of time-, space-, and self-transcending ideals the free individual cannot be drawn out maximally; but unless these ideals simultaneously indict man's historical achievements as well as draw them out, the free individual cannot be restrained in his sin of megalomania. Without ideals to encourage action, social indifference or anarchy may result. But ideals which do not indict the sin-

1. Niebuhr, *An Interpretation of Christian Ethics,* (N. Y., Harper and Brothers, 1935), pp. 7-8.
2. *Ibid.,* p. 8.

fulness of historical relativities may tempt man to pride or tyranny. Only dialectical religion is able to preserve man from fear by inoculating him with faith in eternity's plan, on the one hand, while yet keeping him humble and dissatisfied by exposing historical partiality, on the other. "The value of religion in composing the conflict with which the inner life of man is torn is that it identifies man's highest values, about which he would center his life, with realities in the universe itself, and teaches him how to bring his momentary impulses under the dominion of his will by subjecting his will to the guidance of an absolute will."[3] Religion grounds man in a stability which gives peace, while at the same time teaching him to remain historically dissatisfied with himself. The ideals exhaust man's freedom, while at the same time indicting the sin in all historical relativities. Religion cradles the tension of the dialectic. "It is the nature of religion that it can serve both to sanctify the partial and relative and to reveal the partiality and relativity of every specific historical project. The yearning after the absolute is what lifts humanity above the brute level."[4]

Those who are hasty to condemn religion, therefore, preferring instead a one-dimensional view of history, do not "understand that they are dealing with a more fundamental problem than anything created by this or that religion; that it is the problem of the relative and the absolute in history."[5] The logical conclusion of all one-dimensional thinking — whether that one dimension be solely time or solely eternity — is moral skepticism. The threatened end products of the destruction of a moral imperative which simultaneously guides and condemns history are called the "twin evils" of freedom: tyranny and anarchy. "These twin evils, tyranny and anarchy, represent the Scylla and Charybdis between which the frail bark of social justice must sail. It is

3. Niebuhr, *Does Civilization Need Religion?* (N. Y., Macmillan, 1941), pp. 22-23.
4. *Reflections on the End of an Era*, p. 185.
5. *Human Destiny*, p. 220.

almost certain to flounder upon one rock if it makes the mistake of regarding the other as the only peril."[6]

The procession of history itself proves these perils of freedom. Culture tacks dangerously between the lawless threat of revolution and the rigidity of a dictatorship. If men have no norms to stabilize their freedom, anarchy threatens; while if the norms do not condemn pretensions, tyranny threatens. The anarchist thinks that he is free from responsibility, and the tyrant supposes that he has fulfilled all responsibility. Neither can face the essential predicament of man and establish hope. Only a faith *beyond* history can give man assurance, thus avoiding moral flux; and only a faith *against* history can give man humility, thus avoiding moral totalitarianism.

II. Corruptions of the Dimension of Depth

Just as Niebuhr strongly opposed the tendency of anthropologists to lodge the essential man either in history or out of history, insisting that the double environment alone can satisfy man's complexity, so he here opposes the tendency of philosophers and moralists to retreat either too far from, or draw too near to, history. History may lead to eternity, but eternity must likewise lead back to history.

A. *Other-worldliness.*

The ease with which a person can lose himself in eternity may be illustrated in the rise of Neo-Platonism. Plato recoiled from Protagorian skepticism because he believed that if man is the measure of all things, then judgments can be classified only as useful, not true. One must presuppose the existence of eternal forms if the relativities of history are to have universal validity. His solution was the world of Ideas. These patterns in heaven were the greater reality, since the world which they inform is but their shadow. When once the sweet wine of the universal, the changeless, and the eternal had been tasted, however, drunkenness with eternity quickly followed. Plotinus identified all reality with the

6. *Ibid.,* p. 258.

One. Soon the changing particulars in history clung perilously near the bottom of the ladder of being. When Plotinus mystically united himself with the One, the great chain of being was closed and all particularity was momentarily swallowed up. The body, which Plotinus found an embarrassment, was absorbed in the union.

The objection to other-worldly soarings in both classical rationalism and classical idealism is summed up in what Niebuhr calls an "ahistorical spirituality."[7] The solution to the predicament of man is presumed to come through an escape from history. "The common characteristic in all of these approaches is that a rigorous effort is made to disassociate what is regarded as a timeless and divine element in human nature from the world of change and temporal flux."[8] Neither tyranny nor anarchy can be avoided by a withdrawal from responsibility, however, inasmuch as man happens to be in history, not eternity alone. When man becomes devoted to an eternity which stands unrelated to history, it matters little how one conducts himself in history. This is anarchy. Tyranny follows in another way: If the individual is nothing in relation to the One, the dictator is armed with a perfect basis for his pretension that he descends from the One, and that his cause and that of the One are the same — regardless how ruthless his moral program might be. The claims of the Japanese emperor in World War II illustrate this. From yet another side one can trace this corruption. With eternity unrelated to time, group relations are left without unambiguous standards as guides. When abandoned in indecision, the floundering multitudes are again a perfect prey for the whip of the dictator.

Because he believes that dialectical Christianity actually avoids these perils, Niebuhr is just as concerned to expose the errors of undialectical other-worldliness in Christianity as he is to contest philosophical mysticism. He properly senses that one can do no greater disservice to the truth than

7. *Faith and History,* p. 16.
8. *Ibid.,* p. 16.

to state it badly. Certain wings of Christianity bear this guilt.

1. *Lutheran tendencies.* Niebuhr's personal integrity is exhibited once again as he exposes some of the excesses of the very atmosphere in which he was reared. It takes a fine adjustment of the mirror of God's law to see one's own faults.

After recognizing and applauding the singular way in which Luther grasped the doctrines of justification by faith and the primacy of the law of love in the life of the Christian, Niebuhr counters quickly by exposing some of the quietistic strains in Lutheran moral theory. For one thing justification by faith becomes an occasion of defeatism in the life of the individual. Since God does it all, man does nothing. This severs the nerve of social action. But more seriously still, Luther did not see his way to an unambiguous understanding of the relation between the law of love in the individual and its counterpart, the law of justice, in the state. Goaded by a fear of anarchy, Luther uncritically delivered to the state a power unchecked by the law of justice. He lodged no norm of self-criticism in the ruler. "By thus transposing an 'inner' ethic into a private one, and making the 'outer' or 'earthly' ethic authoritative for government, Luther achieves a curiously perverse social morality. He places a perfectionist private ethic in juxtaposition to a realistic, not to say cynical, official ethic. He demands that the state maintain order without too scrupulous a regard for justice; yet he asks suffering and nonresistant love of the individual without allowing him to participate in the claims and counter-claims which constitute the stuff of social justice. The inevitable consequence of such an ethic is to encourage tyranny; for resistance to government is as important a principle of justice as maintenance of government."[9]

The tragedies of German civilization, as traced trenchantly in such works as McGovern, *From Luther to Hitler* and Lilge, *The Abuse of Learning,* bear out the frightful conse-

9. *Human Destiny,* pp. 194-195.

quences of a statehood not subject to criticism. Relative degrees of justice are unrespected, until in the end there is an absolute dichotomy between the will and word of a Hitler and the will and word of God's justice. Luther was quite "unmindful of the perils of tyranny which reside in every scheme of coerced order; nor did he see to what degree a government or state might represent the principle of order in domestic relations and yet represent the principle of anarchy in the relations of states to each other . . . The Lutheran Reformation is therefore that particular locus in the history of Christendom where the problem of justice is most nearly disavowed."[10]

Barthianism, Lutheran's modern expression on the Continent, "actually reduced Lutheran pessimism to a new level of consistency and made it even more difficult for the Christian conscience to express itself in making the relative decisions which are so necessary for the elaborations of justice in the intricacies of politics and economics."[11] Because of its uncritical view of the text of the Bible — for Niebuhr believes that Barthianism has returned to a Biblical literalism which removes our right to apply "the mind of Christ" critically to the Bible (the mind of Christ being *agape* love) — Barthianism cannot break through its other-worldliness to supply the individual caught in the meshes of history with "sufficient criteria of judgment and impulses to decisive action in moments of life when a historic evil, not yet full-blown and not yet requiring some heroic witness, sneaks into the world upon the back of some unobtrusive error which when fully conceived may produce a monstrous evil."[12]

Calvinistic emphasis, while guilty of never fully understanding the law of love, nevertheless succeeded in bringing

10. *Christianity and Power Politics*, pp. 50-51.

11. *Ibid.*, p. 58.

12. Niebuhr, "An Answer to Karl Barth," *The Christian Century*, February 23, 1949, p. 236. Niebuhr properly distinguishes between Barth, the man, who "himself has rendered a great service to the Lutheran world in recent decades by extricating the Lutheran conscience from the grip of another Pauline text — Romans 13:1: 'Let every soul be subject to the higher powers . . . the powers that be are ordained of God,' " (*Ibid.*, p. 235), and the Barthian system which leads to other-worldliness through the lack of a working criterion by which to evaluate the temporal.

criticism into statism in time to prevent the disastrous results which the Lutheran quietism invited. Later Calvinists came to see that the law of love as an individualistic ethic is not discontinuously related to the law of justice in the state. Since power must be balanced by power, the individual Christian retains the right of revolution.

2. *Pietistic tendencies.* By identifying an "inner light" with an "inner Christ," pietists and Christian mystics tend to lose the tensions of social responsibility. Meditation replaces social action. That is one evil. The other is that a threatening false perfectionism encourages the individual to believe that he is no longer subject to the relativities of history. New pride and self-righteousness are incubated. The individual has no rule by which to judge either himself or society. "The idea of an immanent Christ in man, just as a completely immanent *logos* in history, obscures the real dialectic between the historical and the eternal. It fails to recognize that the freedom of man in history, whether conceived in rational or mystical terms contains possibilities of both good and evil."[13]

3. *Eschatological corruptions.* The perfectionist impulse of the sects has tended to divert interest from present duties to the promises of things which are to come — "the blessed hope," "the other side," "the golden river." Rather than bringing the kingdom of God on earth through Christian action and preaching, therefore, the eschatological sects sit by and do nothing, waiting for God's catastrophic breaking through into history. Such an excessive futurism blinds Christians to here-and-now responsibilities, encouraging a pacifism which can neither anticipate the rise of both anarchy and tyranny or cope with them when they appear. The paradoxical result of this emphasis is, thus, that the very Christains who ought to be the first to work for justice in history are the very ones who turn from the assignment, leaving the work of social melioration to fall on the shoulders of unbelievers. "Thus the sceptics have frequently been the primary bearers of the social meaning of existence."[14]

---

13. *Human Destiny,* p 176.
14. *Discerning the Signs of the Times,* p. 89.

B. *This-worldliness.*

If the error of a love for eternity exhibits itself in a tendency either to neglect or misunderstand temporal responsibilities and possibilities, the obvious sin of its counterpart, a this-worldly optimism, is the unfounded faith that history can bear its own meaning without reference to eternity. The Renaissance ideal incarnates this latter tendency. "It is the impulse towards the fulfillment of life in history."[15] History is the only reality that counts; the sin of man is that he does not begin to tap the vitalities which are historically at his disposal. "The Renaissance as a spiritual movement is best understood as a tremendous affirmation of the limitless possibilities of human existence, and as a rediscovery of the sense of a meaningful history."[16] Faith that life can be fulfilled without antecedently defined limits, on the one hand, is compounded with the optimistic confidence that human capacities are self-sufficient for the work, on the other.

The Renaissance ideal grows partly from religious convictions. It draws its faith in both man and history from sources which pass far beyond scientific validation. It is a curious compound of Christian faith in the meaning of history and the classical faith in the inherent goodness of man.

The manifestations of the Renaissance ideal are legion, including such examples as the Baconian scientific ideal, philosophical rationalism, liberal immanence, Marxism, and Christian perfectionism. Each in his own way clings to the illusion that history can bear its own ideal.

The Renaissance motif, however, suffers from at least one false presupposition. It does not understand that it is impossible for man to be free to create in history without being free to destroy. "They hope for an ever increasing dominance of 'form' and 'order' over all historical vitalities, and refuse to acknowledge that history cannot move forward towards increasing cosmos without developing possibilities of chaos by the very potencies which have enhanced cosmos."[17]

15. *Human Destiny,* p. 160.
16. *Ibid.*
17. *Ibid.,* p. 169.

Marx, for instance, does not understand that a "classless society" is an historical impossibility. He remains blinded by an unjustified faith in the power of a collective revolt to overthrow existing forms and to usher in higher and more final forms of justice and tolerance. Marx forgets man's inevitable sinfulness. Science may increase our zone of securities in history, but it cannot be a final solution to our problems; for free men can always corrupt the forms of scientific advance by converting them into tools of destruction. The Renaissance optimism, in short, is unrelated to a realistic view of the nature of man. "It was enamored of the tremendous possibilities of the human mind, saw human history as a realm of infinite potentialities, but forgot that it is a realm of evil as well as good potentialities."[18]

Liberal Protestantism, with its doctrine of the immanence of God in history and the inevitablity of human progress, falls under Niebuhr's strictures with vengeance. The lofty calculations of the modernist outrun all historical possibilities. No exhibition of the kingdom of God in history can finally be free from the tendencies of men to convert their insecurities into premature securities. "The inability of any age, culture or philosophy to comprehend the finiteness of its perspectives and the limit of its powers always produces a presumptuous claim of finality."[19] Liberalism is partially responsible for the present bitterness and skepticism in the minds of many. By narcotizing men into thinking that history can contain its own solution, human equilibrium is shattered when war and destruction displace peace and construction. "The difficulty of religions which limit their hopes to historic possibilities is that they tempt men to despair when the possibilities are not fulfilled."[20]

Liberal immanence is morally unarmed. It has no effective way to cope with either tyranny or anarchy. If history *does* sustain one's optimism, pride and conceit may emerge. The individual is not taught the relativity of historical advances. As

18. *Christianity and Power Politics*, p. 52.
19. *Human Destiny*, p. 167.
20. *Discerning the Signs of the Times*, p. 80.

it becomes more plausible that the kingdom of God is coming to earth, the pride of moral achievement grows concomitantly. And if history *does not* sustain one's optimism, fear and uncertainty result. The individual is left without anchorage. Defeat in history should prompt us "to faith . . . in the very realization of our limited power and wisdom,"[21] but it can do so only when eternity condemns as well as supports the relativities of time. When we have no means of judging ourselves from beyond ourselves, we may be tempted to give finality to that which ought only to merit partiality. A bad religion may be worse than no religion.

III. The Dialectical Synthesis

The controlling insight in all of Niebuhr's thinking is that, while history has the seeds of infinite progress in it, a cross section of history at any point will reveal the sullying forces of sin. "Briefly this means that on the one hand life in history must be recognized as filled with indeterminate possibilities. There is no individual or interior spiritual situation, no cultural or scientific task, and no social or political problem in which men do not face new possibilities of the good and the obligation to realize them. It means on the other hand that every effort and pretension to complete life, whether in collective or individual terms, that every desire to stand beyond the contradictions of history, or to eliminate the final corruptions of history must be disavowed."[22] If man does not have imperative norms to serve as ideal limits of freedom, the individual will lack a sense of direction in living; but if these ideals do not simultaneously sanctify man's partial achievements, while condemning any attempt to give finality to a partiality, they will either lead men to undue pessimism on the one hand or undue optimism on the other. Both ideal and achievement must be suspended in a dialectical relation: at every moment eternity must set the ideal of man, while judging the relativities of history as partial, yet inadequate. A "combination of this-

21. *Ibid.,* pp. 88-89.
22. *Human Destiny,* p. 207.

worldly and other-worldly hopes is the only adequate religious expression of the human situation."[23]

A. *The Meaning of Dialectic.*

Dialectic, etymologically, means "discourse." The Greeks thought of dialectic as the art of disputation, the drawing out of new truth through the tensions of dialogue (Socrates), first principles (Plato), and syllogisms (Aristotle). Kant applied the term to the futile effort of man to apply the categories of the understanding beyond the data presented in the sensuous intuition — a very specialized sense which does not concern Niebuhr. In Hegel the concept crystallized. Hegel sought, through the analysis of categories, to discover a logical connection between thought and experience. Since the real is the rational and the rational the real, it follows that one category, when analyzed, must lead to a second, and that to a third, *ad infinitum,* until all reality is known. *Being,* for example, leads to *non-being,* for pure being is nothing; and non-being, when analyzed, is the becoming of being: so that *becoming* is a third category which emerges from the analysis of the two initial terms, being and non-being. Being is called the *thesis;* non-being is the *antithesis;* and becoming is the *synthesis.* This analysis goes on indefinitely.

Two important facets to the Hegelian insight must be noted. *First,* the process of the dialectic is without end. The Spirit is everlastingly seeking freedom. *Second,* the ideality of the process, though endless, bears along with it norms which are relevant to historical process at every point. The Spirit always seeks freedom, yet it is in history that the expression occurs.

Marx turned Hegel upside down, converting the lofty logical terms of the dialectic into a this-worldly economic tension. The capitalistic owners of goods form the "exploiting class" while the proletariat forms the "exploited class." These together make up the thesis and antithesis of the dialectic. The revolution is the sublimating force (*Aufheben*) which brings about the new synthesis, the classless society. "Just as the contradic-

23. *Discerning the Signs of the Times,* p. 74.

tory elements which compose material reality bestow upon it an immanent motion towards development and the production of new species, so do the opposing classes which make up the social organism generate a conflicting motion which perpetually results in the production of new types of society. These conflicts between class and class are known to us as 'revolution,' periods of violence which invariably characterize the transition of society from one system of organization to another. They are ruthless unique means by which the oppressed are able to free themselves from the yoke of the oppressor."[24]

Niebuhr divides his sympathies in Marx. Marx is profound in that he understood both the endless possibilities of man in history and the realistic means which must be employed to achieve the end of wider justice. Like the Renaissance Marx believed in man; but unlike the Renaissance he saw the sinful strain in man which made the expediencies of force and revolution necessary. But Marx was extremely naive when he thought that by the simple manipulation of economic tensions a classless society would become an historical actuality. He forgot that each synthesis is but a step on the way to a final goal, not the goal itself. History is always freighted with both justice and injustice. Eras are distinguished only by their *degrees* of justice and injustice. Marxism will never suffer from the fate of liberalism, which "is completely lost when its neat evolutionary process toward an ethical historical goal is suddenly engulfed in a social catastrophe";[25] but it must suffer from a blindness resulting from thinking that historical perfection is an easy attainment. Because it supposes that tomorrow may usher in the frictionless society, if violence is but laid to the roots of capitalism today, it is critical of everything but itself and the means it sanctions. Marxism "rightly conceives the social character of all existence" but "its dream of a frictionless harmony and identity between individual and community is an illusion."[26] Communists are excited today over the live possibility of the conversion of the entire

24. Charles McFadden, *The Philosophy of Communism,* (Benziger Brothers, 1939), p. 101.
25. *Reflections on the End of an Era,* p. 135.
26. *The Children of Light and the Children of Darkness,* p. 58.

world to Marxism, thus ushering Utopia into social and economic relations; but the very terms of the freedom of man cry against the right of any social philosophy to defend such an optimism. "The weakness of the Marxian apocalypse is that its naturalism betrays it into utopian fantasies. Whenever naturalism appropriates the mythical symbols in religion of the unconditioned and transcendent, to make them goals in time and history, it falsely expects the realization of an absolute ideal in the relative temporal process . . . Utopianism must inevitably lead to disillusionment."[27]

While Niebuhr sees no inherent moral objection to the use of violence in social revolution, it must not be supposed for a moment that he approves of Marx's methods. The right of revolution is safeguarded by a basic axiom of morals. With Kant, Niebuhr sets down the dictum that "nothing is intrinsically immoral except ill-will and nothing intrinsically good except goodwill."[28] The decision to employ violence can be made only upon the basis of whether it results in more or less justice over all. Violence is morally justified if it proceeds from a good will; but it is morally dangerous because it may be unattended by the checks of self-criticism which keep it from descending to ill-will and revenge. Marxism lacks these moral checks. It does not know enough about the relation between time and eternity to sense that the communistic doctrine itself is a relativity which stands under judgment. For this reason, and others, Niebuhr breaks with Marx on the violence of the means. Violence, like the right of impeachment of a president, is morally justified; but it should be used exceedingly cautiously. All other forms of mediation must be exhausted first.

The trouble with Marx is that his religious insights become the occasion to justify, not judge, both the means and the end of the communistic ideal. Religion is good, however, only when it serves as a perspective from which one may segregate both the absoluteness of the ideal and the relativities of all historical achievements. Marx has bad religion. "Nations

27. *An Interpretation of Christian Ethics*, pp. 18-19.
28. *Moral Men and Immoral Society*, p. 170.

and classes, cultures and civilizations are usually able to use religion, not to reveal the imperfection and partiality of their life and values, but to give the prestige of the absolute to what is relative and tentative."[29] Marx forgets the dialectic.

B. *Christianity Dialectically Stated.*

The *thesis* of the Christian ethic is the absoluteness of the moral ideal and the endless possibilities for the fulfillment of brotherhood in history. "In the religion of Jesus the perfection of God is consistently defined as an absolute love by comparison with which all altruistic achievements fall short."[30] This is *the wisdom of the cross.* In the life and death of Jesus Christ the outside ideal of man is defined. This is the Renaissance side of the Christian ethic. The *antithesis* is *the foolishness of the cross.* Original sin makes the fulfillment of the rule of *agape* love impossible, for pride encourages man to pretend far more for himself than the facts will justify. This is the Reformation side of the Christian ethic. It contains a realistic pessimism which balances the initial Renaissance optimism. The *synthesis* is *the power of the cross.* Through faith and justification resources of grace are made accessible to the individual who remains within the pincers of the dialectic.

IV. The Dialectical Relevance of the Christ

With this clarification before us, let us now seek to enlarge upon the exact way in which the completed dialectic requires the Christ concept. The need for backdrop scaffolding is especially grave at this point, inasmuch as there are few who perceive the exact reasons why Christ is the chief cornerstone in a working moral edifice. If Niebuhr is obscure at this point of transition, it might cost him success in communicating Christianity.

A. *The Generic Argument.*

In briefest compass Niebuhr's general argument for the Christ concept is as follows: Because a free man stands out-

29. *Reflections on the End of an Era,* p. 10.
30. *Does Civilization Need Religion?* p. 54.

side of history, his full explanation requires a pattern or mind which likewise stands outside of history. History is one-dimensional; it suggests, therefore, more than it can explain. If history is to have meaning, such a meaning must not be identified with the process itself; for that which exemplifies a pattern is numerically different from the pattern. If, *e.g.*, an act has meaning, the act is one thing and the meaning which it exemplifies is another. There is a numerical difference between the blueprints used in constructing a building and the finished building itself. Translated religiously, Christ is the mind or blueprint which gives moral finality to our ideals. Christ is the moral solution to the predicament of man. Christ is the heaven-sent clue to clarify the meaning of history. "Christianity enters the world with the stupendous claim that in Christ . . . the expectations of the ages have been fulfilled."[31] Christ is the mind of God for men. Christ is the wisdom of eternity. History does not contain its own explanation.

What the world of Ideas was for Plato, therefore — a system of ultimates which supplied epistemological and metaphysical ultimacy to philosophic inquiry — thus Christ is to Niebuhr: *A moral absolute which stands outside of history to exhaust the freedom of man but sufficiently in history to clarify history's possibilities and limitations.*

The free reaches of man are such that only within the dimensions of a religious perspective of depth is satisfaction in the whole man conceivable. Man's freedom responds to ideals, which response in turn gives rise to history. History moves between nature and eternity. The Christ is the eternal in time, a breaking through of the everlasting mind of God which gives both meaning and consummation to process.

One looks for a Christ, therefore, only when he understands his own height and depth, on the one hand, and the ingredients of both nature and eternity which form the tensions of history, on the other. History is meaningful only to the one who looks within history for significant clues to its structure and end. "A Christ is expected wherever history is thought of as a realm

31. *Human Destiny*, p. 35.

of fragmentary revelations of a purpose and power transcending history, pointing to a fuller disclosure of that purpose and power."[32]

B. *Corruptions of the Expectation.*

Because man's nature and destiny are such closely related subjects, it is not possible for one to proceed consistently from a false view of man to a true view of his destiny. It is not surprising to learn, therefore, that Niebuhr sets up exactly the same catalogue of corruptions here as he did earlier when examining the nature of man. "A Christ is not expected whereever the meaning of life is explained from the standpoint of either nature or supernature in such a way that a transcendent revelation of history's meaning is not regarded as either possible or necessary."[33]

1. *Blindness to the transcending element.* Niebuhr denies the ability of a materialistic philosophy to account for man from within the process of flux itself. The freedom of man, which expresses itself everywhere in life and climactically in the fear of death, points clearly to the fact that an eternity-minded individual is the creator of history. History, therefore, moves outside of the forms of nature which hedge in the lower animals. Because man is transcendent, history is itself transcendent. "The effort of classical naturalism to reduce history to the proportion of nature is, in short, abortive. It annuls the very meaning of life by its disavowal of history."[34]

In a very significant way Niebuhr's conclusion that Christianity is "beyond rationality" is, therefore, profound. The most regrettable part of the formula lies in the words used; for if the natural man is encouraged to believe that Christianity is sustained by categories which are discontinuous with rational coherence as we know it in social life, he will laugh, not repent. What Niebuhr seems to mean — despite the fact that he ex-

32. *Human Destiny,* p. 5.
33. *Ibid.,* pp. 4-5.
34. *Ibid.,* p. 11.

presses himself in a way which suggests that Christianity is *irrational* — is that when man has exhausted all possible clues to history from within history itself (when, in short, science has had infinite time to do its final and perfect work), the meaning of history yet lies "beyond" in the sense that inaccessible data are needed before justice can be done to man's transcendence over history. These needed data become accessible, or at least significant to the heart, only when the individual repents and converts. Christ becomes truth to men of contrite hearts, those who have already come to the outside limits of their own strength. Armed with this new perspective from eternity a man now sees that Christ is the final meaning to history, by giving balance and completeness to what materialism and scientific inquiry left truncated. Full coherence now results out of what was formerly inchoate.

2. *Blindness to the involvement.* "If classical materialism reduces history to the proportions of natural sequence and temporal process, classical idealism and mysticism seek to flee the world of history precisely because they find no more meaning in history than classical naturalism finds. But they find something in man which classical naturalism does not find; and by that something man is to be emancipated from history. That something is either the intellectual principle of his soul, or something even more transcendent than his mind. Classical idealism and mysticism in short understand the transcendent freedom of the human spirit; but they do not understand it in its organic relation to the temporal process."[35] Because the power of self-transcendence in man inevitably leads him to the search for an eternity which transcends the world, there is always a temptation for man to forget the clay from which he was dug. Other-worldly philosophies tend to conclude that history and process, which man happens to stand in, possess neither being nor meaning. All is eternity. The obvious fallacy in this emphasis is that man happens to be involved in historical process, whether he elects it or not.

---

35. *Human Destiny*, p. 11.

Those who know not the Christ, therefore, incline toward one form of corruption or another. "The only alternatives are either to reduce the meaning of life to the comparative meaninglessness of the natural order, or to emancipate life from this meaninglessness by translating it into the dimension of pure reason, which is to say, pure eternity."[36]

C. *Time-eternity Links.*

Extremely crucial elements in Niebuhr's moral philosophy are the concepts of *myth* and *symbol.* Ethical fruitfulness is measured by the ability of norms to maintain a tension between what is and what ought to be, between the historical and the transcendental; for unless both of these elements are adequately balanced in one theory, one side of man will be either misunderstood or overestimated or underemphasized. This means that eternity is the absolute and history the relative, and anything in history which is a pointer to the eternal can be no more than a symbol of the eternal. To identify anything in history with eternity is as foolish as it is dangerous. It is foolish because it is impossible for the same thing to be limited and unlimited at the same time, perfect and imperfect; and it is dangerous because it breaks the dialectical relation between time and eternity. It sets the wedge for man to corrupt moral progress by sanctifying as finalities in history what ought rather to be judged by finalities in eternity. The quality of ethical norms is judged by the following criteria: "The degree to which the transcendent truly transcends every value and achievement of history, so that no relative value of historical achievement may become the basis of moral complacency; and the degree to which the transcendent remains in organic contact with the historical, so that no degree of tension may rob the historical of its significance."[37] The symbol is the link between the realms of time and eternity and may be finally identified with neither.

Niebuhr never wearies of indicting both orthodox evangelicalism and modernistic immanence for corrupting the symbols

36. *Human Destiny,* p. 15.
37. *An Interpretation of Christian Ethics,* p. 9.

of religion from one side or another. Orthodoxy corrupts the dialectic by taking the symbols literally, while liberalism does despite to Christianity by frivolously dismissing Biblical symbols in favor of the ephemeral moral criteria of a bourgeois, commercial age. Orthodoxy is enslaved by the expressions of an age which is past; liberalism is enslaved by the expressions of the age which is present. "In each case religion fails because it prematurely resolves moral tension by discovering, or claiming to have realized, the *summum bonum* in some immediate and relative value of history."[38]

Niebuhr believes that the devotion of liberalism to modern science is partially intelligible when we remember that science has crushed forever the literalistic pretensions of orthodoxy, thus opening up the possibility of the new symbolism. Liberalism simply forgot to subject science itself to the space- and time-transcending moral absolute which stands over all historical contingency.

Symbols are rallying points for the religious myth. The myth is a story, the origin of which is generally forgotten, which serves to explain the basis of a religious practice or belief. Mythologies convey an artistic attempt to capture from the experience of both the race and the individual what is contemporaneously true for all. The myth is an artistic attempt to give depth to history, a way to explain the collective insights of man's interaction with eternity. If eternity is reduced to history, then the meaning of history has been corrupted and what remains is bad science. "Meaning can be attributed to history only by a mythology."[39] Orthodoxy has vitiated the usefulness of the myth by trying to literalize it into a metaphysical truth, while liberalism has cavalierly by-passed the symbols as prescientific nonsense. "Orthodox Christianity . . . cannot come to the aid of modern man, partly because its religious truths are still imbedded in an outmoded science and partly because its morality is expressed in dogmatic and authoritarian moral code."[40] Liberalism "failed to realize that mythi-

38. *Ibid.,* p. 10.
39. *Reflections on the End of an Era,* p. 123.
40. *An Interpretation of Christian Ethics,* p. 4.

cal descriptions of reality, though always inexact in describing detailed and historical fact, have the virtue of giving men a sense of depth in life. Pure science is always secular and horizontal in its references, and cannot express the vertical tendencies in culture which refer to the ultimate source of meaning in life."[41] An existentially significant insight into life must "combine the exact data of the scientist with the vision of the artist and must add religious depth to philosophical generalizations."[42]

It takes an individual with a full-heart insight into life and death, history and eternity, to appreciate the myth. One can just as easily corrupt the myth by perfunctorily subjecting it to either scientific or philosophic analysis as he can spoil a beautiful poem by critical and literalistic analysis. Poetry and art presuppose that the individual has a sympathy for the finer things in life. Joyce Kilmer wrote the beautifully expressive poem, *Trees* — "A tree which may in summer wear, a nest of robins in her hair" etc; but any unimaginative analyst can distort the words to show their literal untruth. But no person with a heart, no person with a feeling of depth in life, can do it. In like manner, the "mythical symbols of transcendence in profound religion are easily corrupted into scientifically untrue statements of historic fact."[43] Science is confined to the surface of life. It can analyze, bottle, slice, and classify, but it cannot give a deeply satisfying interpretation of reality. This is inevitable because science has no heart. "The religious myth, on the other hand, points to the ultimate ground of existence and its ultimate fulfillment. Therefore the great religious myths deal with creation and redemption. But since myth cannot speak of the trans-historical without using symbols and events in history as its forms of expression, it invariably falsifies the facts of history, as seen by science, to

41. *Christianity and Power Politics,* pp. 183-184.

42. *Reflections on the End of an Era,* p. 122. Niebuhr exhibited early signs of having the poetic prerequisite for appreciating the myth. "Religion is poetry. The truth in the poetry is vivified by adequate poetic symbols and is therefore more convincing than the poor prose with which the average preacher must attempt to grasp the ineffable." *Leaves from the Notebook of a Tamed Cynic,* p. 32.

43. *An Interpretation if Christian Ethics,* p. 12.

state its truth."[44] Crude mythologies, those advanced by immature mentalities which have not been subjected to the critical mind of the race, are prescientific. Profound mythologies are super-scientific, dealing with "vertical aspects of reality which transcend the horizontal relationships which science analyzes, charts and records."[45] Science and philosophy can uncover genuine clues to the meaning of history, but only "the myth alone is capable of picturing the world as a realm of coherence and meaning without defying the facts of incoherence. Its world is coherent because all facts in it are related to some central source of meaning; but is not rationally coherent because the myth is not under the abortive necessity of relating all things to each other in terms of immediate rational unity."[46]

By means of symbols the Christian mind facilitates both the understanding and the communication of the myths. Niebuhr speaks of the future as "the symbol of the unpredictable possibilities of eternity which may appear in time."[47] The "wrath and judgment of God are symbolic of the seriousness of history."[48] In the myth of the resurrection the body symbolizes "the contribution which nature makes to human individuality and to all historical realizations."[49] Biblical symbols are an attempt upon the part of the religious mind to point to ultimate meaning from the perspective of the conditioned and the finite.

The corruption of the symbols comes when one either literalizes them as pure history or dismisses them as historically irrelevant. Once more we perceive the same theme running through Niebuhr's theology of history: time and eternity must be kept in dialectical tension. The *locus classicus* on this question is the following: "If the symbol is taken literally the dialectical conception of time and eternity is falsified and the ultimate vindication of God over history is reduced to a point in history . . . On the other hand if the symbol is dismissed

44. *Ibid.*, pp. 12-13.
45. *An Interpretation of Christian Ethics*, p. 26.
46. *Ibid.*
47. *Human Nature*, p. 289.
48. *Human Destiny*, p. 211.
49. *Human Destiny*, p. 296.

as unimportant, as merely a picturesque or primitive way of apprehending the relation of the historical to the eternal, the Biblical dialectic is obscured in another direction. All theologies which do not take these symbols seriously will be discovered upon close analysis not to take history seriously either. They presuppose an eternity which annuls rather than fulfills the historical process. The Biblical symbols cannot be taken literally because it is not possible for finite minds to comprehend that which transcends and fulfills history . . . The symbols which point towards the consummation from within the temporal flux cannot be exact in the scientific sense of the word."[50]

D. *The Expectation of a Christ.*

The precondition for the expectation of a Christ is a personal awareness that existence introduces greater problems than man alone can solve, and that though history contains a partial explanation of itself, it does not yet contain the final answer. Christ is needed as a "symbol of the relevance between the divine and the human."[51] "A Christ is expected wherever history is regarded as potentially meaningful but as still awaiting the full disclosure and fulfillment of its meaning."[52]

When men look for Christ they expect in history something which will be the final explanation of history. The Christ must exhibit a "transcendent perfection which clarifies obscurities of history and defines the limits of what is possible in historic development."[53] A man can look for a Christ, however, only after he has come to himself, only after he understands the full height of his freedom and the full depth of his involvement in the forms of nature.

V. The Redemptive Relevance of the Christ

Since Niebuhr is a moralist seeking a moral solution to the predicament of modern man, and since morality is a study

50. *Human Destiny*, p. 289.
51. *Ibid.*, p. 112.
52. *Ibid.*, p. 4.
53. *Ibid.*, p. 86.

which turns upon the maintenance in the individual of a peculiarly sensitive relation to his own heart, it is only natural that the epistemological relevance of the Christ is finally displaced by his redemptive relevance. It is the heart which needs redeeming.

A. Locus of the Proof for God: The Heart.

The reason why the religious man can see God everywhere, while the secular pagan sees God nowhere, is because the former, unlike the latter, has come to that place of submissiveness where he is able to perceive in his own freedom a "sense of being confronted with a 'wholly other' at the edge of human consciousness."[54] Through a sensitive heart God communicates *general revelation.* General revelation clarifies God's nature as Creator and Judge. Through Christ comes *special revelation.* This clarifies God's nature as Redeemer. God is Redeemer, however, only to those who already know him as Creator and Judge.

1. *God as Creator.* "To believe that God created the world is to feel that the world is a realm of meaning and coherence without insisting that the world is totally good or that the totality of things must be identified with the Sacred."[55] Through the myth of creation the great chain of being is broken and history is given that fringe of non-rationality which makes contingency possible. As Creator, God is both transcendent and free. His existence must be postulated if one is to give a satisfactory account of the world itself. Natural causation can never explain why there is *this* causal series rather than another. "This irrational givenness must be regarded either as merely chance or caprice, or the order of the world must be related to a more ultimate realm of freedom."[56] In existential terms, one becomes satisfied with the faith that the Creator exists when he remembers that he is not the author of himself. We have a "sense of dependence upon a

---

54. *Human Nature,* p. 131.
55. *An Interpretation of Christian Ethics,* p. 26.
56. *Human Nature,* p. 134.

reality greater and more ultimate than ourselves."[57] This is not a demonstration of God in the strict sense of the term, inasmuch as it is a perception of ultimates which only faith can grasp. But it is a proof adequate for one who sees existence through religious glasses. "There is, in other words, a gain for an adequate cosmology, if man uses concepts in his interpretations of the cosmos which he won first of all in measuring the dimension of his own internal reality."[58]

Niebuhr claims exemption from the sundry criticisms which have been hurled against the metaphysical statements of the cosmological argument, on the ground that he is leaping to God's existence through faith, not progressing step by step through a logical demonstration We *feel* our dependence. God is related to the world, therefore, not as an immense gear within the world, as in pantheism, or as an impersonal force of attraction on the edge of the world, as in Aristotelianism. "If he were first cause (a rational conception) he would be either one of the many observable causes in the stream of things, in which case God and the world are one; or he would be the unmoved mover, in which case his relation to the world is not a vital or truly creative one. To say that God is the creator is to use an image which transcends the canons of rationality, but expresses both his organic relation to the world and his distinction from the world."[59] God does not stand related to the world as the form of the triangle is to the triangle. The inevitable result of such an arrangement is a Spinozistic world in which progress and contingency are impossible.

The myth of creation is valid for all men everywhere by virtue of the fact that "the individual faces the eternal in every moment and in every action of his life."[60] Without faith in creation the dialectical relation between time and eternity would be broken, for a sense of dependence upon God must be presupposed if the moral obligation of love is to be absolute. "The experience of God is not so much a

57. *Ibid.*, p. 131.
58. *Ibid.*, p. 134.
59. *An Interpretation of Christian Ethics*, p. 26.
60. *Human Destiny*, p. 312.

separate experience, as an overtone implied in all experience. The soul which reaches the outermost rims of its own consciousness, must also come in contact with God, for He impinges upon that consciousness."[61]

In its broadest outlines this methodological procedure is very healthy, and it reminds one of the method employed by the Reformers themselves. "Our poverty conduces to a clearer display of the infinite fulness of God. Especially, the miserable ruin, into which we have been plunged by the defection of the first man, compels us to raise our eyes towards heaven, not only as hungry and famished, to seek thence a supply for our wants, but, aroused with fear, to learn humility."[62]

2. *God as Judge.* General revelation, which is "the testimony in the consciousness of every person that his life touches a reality beyond himself, a reality deeper and higher than the system of nature in which he stands,"[63] is powerful in its witness that man is morally related to God as Judge. We have a deep and abiding awareness "of being seen, commanded, judged and known from beyond ourselves."[64] We feel guilt, shame, and remorse in our acts. Existentially explained, the free individual is making contact with a stratum of reality which claims a right to confront and judge men from beyond themselves. The flow of vitalities within us when we are thus confronted points conclusively to the fact that a personal Judge is being dealt with. The experience is parallel to the feeling an individual has when he confronts other human beings. Repentance toward God is like apologizing to a friend, save that the guilt toward God is infinite. "This word spoken from beyond us and to us is both a verification of our belief that we are dealing with a different dimension than animal existence; and also a revelation of the actual and precise character of the person with whom we are dealing."[65]

---

61. *Human Nature,* p. 127.
62. Calvin, *Institutes of the Christian Religion,* I. 1. 1.
63. *Human Nature,* p. 127. Niebuhr speaks of general revelation sometimes as "private revelation." For all practical purposes, however, they are the same.
64. *Ibid.,* p. 128.
65. *Ibid.,* p. 130.

Conscience functions within the tension of man's freedom. While eternity defines man's moral ought, conscience indicts the same man for not mediating the terms of this ought within history. If we deny conscience, we deny our freedom to contact eternity; but when we admit it, we are guilty. "The significance of the Biblical interpretation of conscience lies precisely in this, that a universal human experience, the sense of being commanded, placed under obligation and judged is interpreted as a relation between God and man in which it is God who makes demands and judgments upon man."[66] God is "the Holiness before whom 'all our righteousnesses are as filthy rags.' "[67] The universality of the feeling of guilt prepares the way for the universality of the redemptive relevance of Jesus Christ.

3. *God as Redeemer.* The final solution to the predicament of man, together with the completion of the dialectical relation between time and eternity, cannot be enjoyed until the knowledge of God as Judge passes to God as Redeemer; for without hope there is no final antedote to pessimism and despair, preconditions of anarchy or tyranny.

It is not possible to discover this final key from within nature, however, inasmuch as nature points to the problem without affording a solution. The solution is found within the area of special revelation, the self-disclosure of the Christ. The locus for this disclosure is history and the Bible.

Niebuhr thinks of himself as a "Biblical realist," tacking between the so-called literalism of evangelicalism and the flippancy of modernism. The Bible is not God's objective revelation, true in the whole and in the part, as in orthodoxy; for science, according to Niebuhr, has forever smashed plenary inspiration. The Bible is a very fallible document penned by very human authors. Niebuhr, thus, is fully congenial to destructive higher criticism.[68] While refusing to go as far as the

---

66. *Ibid.,* p. 129.
67. *Beyond Tragedy,* p. 56.
68. It is the "second Isaiah" which speaks this and thus, *e.g., Human Nature,* p. 138. Niebuhr has not broken in any essential epistemological way with liberalism. He has simply enlarged the "kernel" of Biblical truth to include *Heilsgeschichte.* But both the kernel-husk theory of the Bible and the tendency to divorce theology from history remain.

liberal who supposes that the Bible is just man's search for God in written form, Niebuhr halts far short of historical Protestantism. The Bible contains truth only at those points where it supports both the dialectical interpretation of history and the existential assurances within the race and the individual. The Bible is the locus of the symbols, the repository of the myths of the Christian religion. It "is by no means man's increasingly adequate definitions of the person of God, interpretations to which modern liberal thought has sometimes reduced Biblical revelation. It is rather the record of those events in history in which faith discerns the self-disclosure of God."[69]

Niebuhr finds in the Bible an account of a divine self-disclosure which not only recognizes the problem of man but which likewise provides a profound existential solution. Man is under a moral obligation, an obligation which comes from God. The abiding relation between God and his people is defined in a *covenant.* By the covenant God sovereignly makes clear both moral demands upon his people and the moral solution to evil. In the covenant sin is taken seriously. God turns his face from sin. His wrath lies upon all unrighteousness. "The serious view which the Bible takes of this sin of man's rebellion against God naturally leads to an interpretation of history in which judgment upon sin becomes the first category of interpretation. The most obvious meaning of history is that every nation, culture and civilization brings destruction upon itself by exceeding the bounds of creatureliness which God has set upon all human enterprises."[70]

God's self-disclosure passed through steps, however, until a final climax was reached in Jesus Christ, where the problem of the relation between God's justice and mercy is solved; for in Christ God takes the sins of the world into himself, effecting a final forgiveness. "Christian faith regards the revelation in Christ as final because this ultimate problem is solved by the assurance that God takes man's sin upon Himself and into Himself and that without this divine initiative and this

69. *Ibid.*, p. 136.
70. *Ibid.*, p. 140.

divine sacrifice there could be no reconciliation and no easing of man's uneasy conscience. This revelation is final not only as a category of interpreting the total meaning of history but also as a solution for the problem of the uneasy conscience in each individual."[71] Let us trace the steps involved in this Messianic disclosure.

B. Stages in the Messianic Self-Disclosure.

Niebuhr interprets the history of redemption in the Bible on the pattern of evolution, an evolution, however, with the divine transcendence superintending it.

1. *Egoistic-nationalism.* "On the egoistic-nationalistic level Messianism looks forward to the triumph of the nation, empire or culture in which the Messianic hope is expressed."[72] The collective life is defined as the locus of God's redemptive interests, while the problem of the group is the fact that the collective ego is too finite to realize its ambitions. The triumph of the group over its enemies is always expected; but it is never quite clarified exactly how it will be achieved. The Messiah must come to vindicate the nation.

In its most subtle form, however, the Messiah is looked to as the one who will vindicate the believer over against the unbeliever. This is the Christian corruption of egoistic — nationalistic Messianism. From this indication, hence, Niebuhr is a universalist. Reasons will be given *infra* to support the evangelical conviction that universalism itself severs the dialectical tension between time and eternity.[73]

2. *Ethical-universalism.* When we cease speaking of the triumph of *our* nation, *our* people, *our* brotherhood by extending to ourselves the same knowledge of God as Judge which we apply to others, we are then in a position to speak in terms of the broader problem of the triumph of good over evil in history. "The momentary triumph of evil in history is seen as a threat to the meaningfulness of history and this threat is overcome by the hope of the coming of a Messianic king who

71. *Human Nature,* p. 143.
72. *Human Destiny,* p. 18.
73. See pages 196ff.

will combine power and goodness."[74] What is needed to complete the hope of the righteous here is the entrance of one who unites in his person both the goodness and the power to make good its triumph in history. "How could history finally culminate in a reign of perfect righteousness except by a divine king who would combine justice with absolute power?"[75]

The profundity of this form of Messianism is that it recognizes that evil comes from the power of will over will in history, not from natural forms alone. This insight arms it with a realistic view of history which far surpasses egoistic-nationalism. "Its strictures are directed particularly against unjust 'rulers' and 'elders.' It recognizes that injustice flows from the same source from which justice comes, from the historical organization of life."[76] Its eyes are open to the fact that the free possibilities of men include the simultaneous alternates of both good and evil. The agencies which promote justice also organize power for injustice.

The blindness of ethical-universalism is that it does not understand the impossibility of mingling power with goodness; since the administration of power in society always involves particularism. "The God who is both powerful and good by reason of being the source of all power, and not some particular power in history, cannot remain good if he becomes a particular power in human society. Perfect goodness in history can be symbolized only by the disavowal of power."[77] Power is the expression of human interest. The solution to history cannot be found by power in history. It can be found only in eternity. History is only able to contain the symbols of the solution. If it is ever asked to bear the solution the dialectic is corrupted.

3. *Religio-ethical Messianism*: *Prophetic Messianism.* It was left to the later Hebrew prophets to understand that the sovereignty of God extends to all men, on the one hand, and that the universal guilt of all men destroys the claim of any to self-righteousness, on the other. The prophets end with this note:

74. *Human Destiny,* p. 19.
75. *Discerning the Signs of the Times,* p. 140.
76. *Human Destiny,* p. 21.
77. *Ibid.,* p. 22.

Either God saves us or we are all lost. "This means that prophetism has the first understanding of the fact that the real problem of history is not the finiteness of all human endeavors, which must wait for their completion by divine power. The real problem of history is the proud pretension of all human endeavors, which seeks to obscure their finite and partial character and thereby involves history in evil and sin."[78] Faith in God begins in real earnest when men understand that the divine judgment is directed against the whole human enterprise, and that there is none righteous, no not one.

Prophetic Messianism simply needed completing, not supplanting, for it introduced a true problem which it itself could not truly solve. It properly understood the judgment of God against all men, but it did not know how God could save Israel and still remain just. The Hebraic forms of Messianism, however high they rose, did not break sufficiently with their nationalism to understand the implications of their own religious insight that all men lie under God's condemnation. The relation of the degrees of guilt in men to God's wrath was not clear. Israel believed that she deserved judgment — but less judgment than the more wicked nations. Israel chafed under the problem of evil. There was an abiding self-righteousness in her which blinded her to the final way in which God was to redeem men. "It was certain that the hidden sovereignty of God would guarantee the ultimate triumph of good over evil in history. But it was not certain how the divine mercy is related to the divine wrath and how the perplexity of a total history standing in defiance of God would be resolved."[79] How could men be saved?

At this point the Old Testament ended. The problem which was raised was never solved. Not until the eastern star heralded the birth of Jesus Christ did God show men the exact way in which he would provide his own solution. God's plan of salvation "did not become clear until the One appeared who rejected all concepts of Messianic dominion and became a 'suffering servant.' "[80]

78. *Ibid.*, p. 25.
79. *Ibid.*, p. 33.
80. *Ibid.*, p. 22.

Part III

THE CHRISTIAN DIALECTIC

V

Thesis: The Wisdom of the Cross

THE CROSS of Christ forms the final apex of Christian wisdom because of its rich and comprehensive exhibition of both the glories and the defeats of selfless love in history, on the one hand, and the unexpected way in which it clarifies and solves the problem which prophetic Messianism raised, but never met, on the other.

I. Original Righteousness

A. Law and Vital Expression.

Since man is free, he refuses to remain content within the boundaries of natural forms with the animal. Man does not enjoy what Niebuhr idoneously calls "bovine serenity." But because man creates destinies for himself which outrun nature's cohesions, some law or rule must stand over him. Law has both a goading and a restraining power. On the one side law defines the outside perfection of human nature, while on the other it clarifies that point to which an individual may go without infringing on the rights and securities of a neighbor. The goading dynamic of law seeks to draw man out maximally by defining the exact conditions attending perfect morality. The restraining dynamic of law seeks to limit freedom so that it does not transgress the social rights and securities of others. The one side of the law defines positive righteousness, while the other defines the conditions of trangression.

Being both in and out of nature, man has two different laws to define the positive nature of righteousness. "The essential nature of man contains two elements; and there are correspondingly two elements in the original perfection of man. To the essential nature of man belong, on the one hand, all his natural endowments, and determinations, his physical and social impulses, his sexual and racial differentiations, in short his character as a creature imbedded in the natural order. On the other hand, his essential nature also includes the freedom of his spirit, his transcendence over natural process and finally his self-transcendence."[1]

1. *The natural law.* The purpose of the natural law is to define for the free individual "the proper performance of his functions, the normal harmony of his impulses and the normal social relation between himself and his fellows within the limitations of the natural order."[2] There is no easy way to determine what, if anything, ought to be included in natural law, however, inasmuch as there can be no adequate understanding of man's natural involvement apart from his limitless possibilities as a free creature. Mindful of this, Niebuhr makes practically no attempt to draw up a catalogue of what comprises final components of the natural law. He feels that while there is a provisional justification in dealing with man as a creature whose natural order must be defined, it will yet do more harm than good to become either too final or too specific in this detailing. The widest possible opening should be left here in order that man's infinite possibilities for development might not be prematurely throttled.

However, since few have grasped this issue as profoundly as Niebuhr, and since the natural law is a perfect prey for the moralists seeking to impose final legislations upon man, it is easy to understandstand why Niebuhr spends more time indicting corruptions of the natural law than in stating the positive terms of that law for Christians. All forms of finality in natural law fall under the same charge — whether the form be Stoic natural order, Roman Catholic divine laws, liberal laws of reason, Lutheran *Shoepfungsordnung* (order of creation), or Marxist laws of economics — "The effect of this pretended finality of 'natural law' is obvious. It raises 'ideology' to a

1. *Human Nature,* p. 270.
2. *Ibid.*

higher degree of pretension, and is another of the many illustrations in history of the force of sin in the claim of sinlessness."[3]

Exhibit A of the fallacy of pronouncing a premature finality within the natural order is Roman Catholicism. Its roots reach back into the Catholic theory of the fall and its tenuous distinction between the *donum supernaturale* and *pura naturalia.* "The primary mistake of Catholic theory is precisely the sharp and absolute distinction which it makes between the two. It speaks of an original righteousness which was lost in the Fall and a natural justice which remains essentially uncorrupted by the Fall. This distinction obscures the complex relation of human freedom to all of man's natural functions, and the consequent involvement of all 'natural' or 'rational' standards and norms in sin. There is therefore no uncorrupted natural law, just as there is no completely lost original justice."[4] This neat little division gives plausibility to the belief that man's present involvement can be defined with finality. Catholicism does not fully understand how both the reason used in defining this position and the motives of the church in sanctioning it are themselves involved in individualistic and collective egotism. The "rational" and the "natural" are inevitably compounded with the personal interest and the final security of the church. For this reason Catholicism has very little difficulty in seeing "rational necessity" in all those forms of cultural patterns which keep men subservient to both the church herself and her attending corrupt feudal-agrarian economy. Such reasonableness is advanced purely under the name of God's law, of course; but it never is really that pure. It is always part of the complex program of the church to enhance the security of her own vested interests.

Birth control illustrates this Catholic fallacy perfectly. It is well known that the most effective evangelistic agency that the church has is the marriage bed. Through the promotion of larger families, Roman authorities believe that they will inevitably gain the hegemony in a given social

3. *Human Destiny,* p. 253.
4. *Human Nature,* pp. 280-281.

structure. The church, therefore, takes an "uncompromising" stand against contraceptives. Forgetting the basic moral axiom that there is no good but a good will, all use of contraceptives is defined as intrinsically immoral. In the name of God the church takes its "holy" stand against the practice. What Catholic divines overlook, however, is the following: *First,* they are blinded to the extent to which their crusade is accelerated by their own unconscious pride to defend the security and privileges of the church. They do not know that "reasonable" actually means "increasing the prestige of Catholicism." They forget their own personal interest in the matter. *Second,* they do not understand that natural involvement cannot be treated as a separate order, for man is not an animal. Sexual relations are "governed on the one hand by the natural fact of sex differentiation and on the other by the spiritual fact of human freedom."[5] If a man's heart is right, the sex act may sublimate physical union into an occasion to enrich the spiritual ties which unite husband and wife. Intercourse may remain basically a means of procreation, but its potentialities in a free individual are not exhausted there. Man differs from the animals in that the natural is always compounded with the supernatural. The Catholic theory of "rhythm" is but a legalistic attempt upon the part of Roman moralists to cover up what is obviously a deficiency in their own code.

An interesting problem emerges at this point. Niebuhr is a master at showing the excesses and extremes of his opponents. And every generation needs its gadfly. But one looks in vain in the corpus of Niebuhr's works for any compelling reason why the same charges which are hurled against certain expressions of the natural law cannot be applied *mutatis mutandis* to all other forms; until in the end one is left with an absolute relativism. Niebuhr is conscious of this danger of going too far, for he quickly advances the following concession: "There are of course certain permanent norms, such as monogamy, which, contrary to the relativism of such Protestant sceptics as Karl Barth, are maintained not purely by Scriptural authority but by the cumulative experience of the race.

5. *Human Nature*, p. 282.

About these universalities, amidst the relativities of standards, a word must be spoken presently."[6] The fact of the case is, however, that one looks very much in vain for this "word which must be spoken presently." Niebuhr nowhere succeeds in showing precisely why even monogamy may be regarded as a final natural law. The experiences of the race can only establish what has been true up to date; they cannot normatively set down what *ought* to be true tomorrow. One can only wait and see what tomorrow may bring forth. Because he has given the lion's share in his epistemology to empiricism, Niebuhr cannot avoid skepticism within the natural law. Everything is provisional and tentative. Indeed, he professes to escape this skepticism, but he nowhere rigorously justifies his pretension. The truth is that on an existential epistemology no defense is possible.

Niebuhr's reference to Barth is reminiscent of the recent literary fracas between Continental and American existentialists. Niebuhr and Barth contest neither their basic existential epistemology nor the veraciousness of Kierkegaard's psychologized version of sin. On such ultimates they stand firmly united against evangelicalism both at home and abroad. Niebuhr charges Barth with returning to the fleshpots of a literalism. In the February 23, 1949 issue of *The Christian Century,* for example, Niebuhr, in the course of giving an answer to Karl Barth, charges the latter with being unable to separate what is "time-bound" in the Bible from what is "the mind of Christ." Barth professes to take Paul seriously when he says that women ought to be in submission to their husbands and to the church, but Niebuhr indicts this as foolish literalism. Paul was just "a child of his times" here. His view "may have been influenced by the second creation story, according to which God fashioned Eve from Adam's rib. It is certainly colored also by the traditional standards regulating the relation between men and women in every pre-technical culture."[7]

---

6. *Ibid.,* pp. 282-283.
7. "An Answer to Karl Barth," *The Christian Century.* February 23, 1949, p. 235.

We shall not presume to speak for Barthianism on this question — for Barthian presuppositions themselves flow so basically from Kierkegaard that Niebuhr's charge against them is justified — but the evangelical, who repudiates Kierkegaardian existentialism in favor of an objective authority in the Scriptures, has grounds for rebuttal. Niebuhr's Biblical inaccuracy is unbelievable. He gropes for a plausible reason to explain why Paul taught that women must be refused the offices of elder and bishop, when the apostle himself has explained the basis of the doctrine with lucidity: "I permit no woman to teach or to have authority over men; she is to keep silent. *For Adam was formed first, then Eve; and Adam was not deceived, but the woman was deceived and became a transgressor.*"[8] The judgment on womanhood goes back to the story of the fall in Genesis. Nothing could be clearer but that Paul stands quite outside of the Kierkegaard-Barth-Brunner-Niebuhr tradition that "every man is Adam" and that the first Adam, thus, was not the federal head of the race. What existentialism does not adequately face and answer is the question why, if the federal headship of Adam is "time-bound," the federal headship of Christ is not equally so? If we do not need an historical Adam, why do we need an historical Christ? Each can be floated on the existential experience of a personal confrontation with eternity. Let Christ remain on the "edge of history," not in history, like the Logos in Heraclitean thought — an abstraction which defines the flux of everything else but which itself is not in flux. Reasons will appear in due time to support the evangelical conclusion that once the existential experiences of the race may veto Scriptural authority on such crucial doctrines as the historicity of the fall and the federal headship of the first Adam, it can likewise do the same with either the doctrine of the second Adam or that of God's taking our sins upon and into Himself. An undercurrent of skepticism runs through the entire theology of Niebuhr.

2. *The law of the spirit.* "The virtues which correspond to the second element in his nature, that is, to the freedom of his

8. I Timothy 2:12-14.

spirit, are analogous to the 'theological virtues' of Catholic thought, namely faith, hope and love."[9] These virtues exhaust the definition of *justitia originalis,* for they so define man's responsibilities in freedom that there is no thinkable point of progression beyond them. The terms of freedom themselves entail faith, hope, and love. Niebuhr explains the generic characteristics of these virtues as follows: "Faith in the providence of God is a necessity of freedom because, without it, the anxiety of freedom tempts man to seek a self-sufficiency and self-mastery incompatible with his dependence upon forces which he does not control. Hope is a particular form of that faith. It deals with the future as a realm where infinite possibilities are realized and which must be in a realm of terror if it is not under the providence of God; for in that case it would stand under either a blind fate or pure caprice . . . Love is both an independent requirement of this same freedom and a derivative of faith. Love is a requirement of freedom because the community to which man is impelled by his social nature is not possible to him merely upon the basis of his gregarious impulse. In his freedom and uniqueness each man stands outside of, and transcends, the cohesions of nature and the uniformities of mind which bind life to life. Since men are separated from one another by the uniqueness and individuality of each spirit, however closely they may be bound together by ties of nature, they cannot relate themselves to one another in terms which will do justice to both the bonds of nature and the freedom of their spirit if they are not related in terms of love."[10]

Since "the greatest of these is love," it is understandable why Niebuhr devotes the largest measure of his efforts to clarifying both the nature of love itself and its essential relation to freedom. Through love the individual is no longer an object which can be used and manipulated for private ends. Love establishes the I-thou relationship, elevating the feelings between persons to the level of spirituality.

---

9. *Human Nature,* p. 271.
10. *Ibid.*

Love is the final law of freedom, and it is expressed definitively by Jesus Christ: "Thou shalt love the Lord thy God with all thy heart, and all thy soul, and all thy mind. This is the first and great commandment. And the second is like unto it, Thou shalt love thy neighbour as thyself." Niebuhr pithily comments on these words as follows: "Here something is commanded and demanded. That means law. But what is commanded is a state of heart and mind, a harmony between the soul and God ('Thou shalt love the Lord thy God'), a harmony within the soul ('with all thy heart, and all thy soul, and all thy mind"), and a harmony between the self and the neighbour ('thy neighbour as thyself') which, if attained, would exclude all commandment."[11] This law states a possibility/impossibility. If the law were not in some sense possible, it would be irrelevant; but if it were an easy possibility, it would not stand as an imperative yet to be reached.

(a) *Harmony toward God.* "The first of these three requirements is the most basic one, just as unbelief or mistrust is the basic and primal sin." [12] Faith in God's providence and hope in the future are preconditions of both inward peace and social harmony. Because history will not lend itself to a simple rational interpretation, the existing individual can be settled in his own person only after he has gained faith in the providence of God over history. Anxiety cannot be eliminated until the individual discovers the center and source of his own meaning in God over history.

Anxiety is not easily overcome, however, inasmuch as assent to the ideal, and a fulfillment of its obligations, are two entirely different things. "Freedom from anxiety, in other words, is an ultimate possibility which man as sinner denies in his action. Even the man of faith does so, insofar as he is a sinner. It belongs to the perfection before the Fall. The sinful self is anxious about itself and it yet knows that it ought not to be."[13] When a man has faith in God he may find the expulsion of anxiety very difficult; but at least he finds the work of trying

11. *Human Nature,* p. 286.
12. *Ibid.,* 289.
13. *Ibid.,* p. 290.

both meaningful and rewarding. Love for God retires the individual from inordinate self-concern, that he might turn to the task of promoting harmonious living.

(b) *Harmony within.* Because the radical cause of anxiety is one's uneasy feeling that the self has neither center nor end, it follows that an established fellowship with God may create internal harmony by relieving anxiety; for God now becomes both center and end of the self. Strife in the individual grows out of the fact that the will lacks the power to make good what it intends. This strife can be mitigated only when the individual reorganizes his inward tensions within the dynamic of the ideal of love. Through a resignation in doing and loving the things which God does and loves, the individual is harmoniously at home with himself. "The perfect harmony of the soul with itself is thus a derivative of its perfect communion with, and love of, God. Where the love of God transcends obedience, the soul is centered in its true source and end without reservation."[14]

Simply because a sinner cannot attain unto perfect righteousness in his own person it does not follow that love's ideal character as *justitia originalis* cancels out as irrelevant. A man who comes to himself morally acknowledges that this law ought to be fulfilled in himself and that he really ought to have no need for being reminded of it in Christ. "The sense that an obedience which is less than love is not normative even though it is universal, is the *justitia originalis.* It is the sense that there ought not be a sense of ought; it is the 'thou shalt' which suggests that there are no 'thou shalts' in perfection."[15]

(c) *Harmony towards others.* Faith in God likewise retires man from that competition of egos which blinds him to the obligation of procuring the needs and securities of others. Only the lover can see beyond the object to the inner person. Love operates where freedom meets freedom, spirit meets spirit. The lover converts the *I-it* (person-object) into an *I-thou*(person-person) fellowship. "Real love between person and person is

14. *Human Nature,* p. 293.
15. *Ibid.*

therefore a relationship in which spirit meets spirit in a dimension in which both the uniformities and the differences of nature, which bind men together and separate them, are transcended."[16] Love sees all the accidents of "geography, race, time, place and history"[17] which tend to disrupt the harmony of man with man; but it overlooks them, for it is more concerned with spirit than with body.

The person-person relationship is possible, however, only when an individual himself has first been loved by God. Not until men feel their own unworthiness before God together with their need of His love and forgiveness toward them, will they be in that selfless condition of humility where they are willing to place the security of the neighbor before their own. "We are demanded to forgive those who have wronged us, not because a forgiving spirit will prove redemptive in the lives of the fallen, but because God forgives our sins."[18]

"The Christian love commandment does not demand love of the fellow man because he is with us equally divine (Stoicism), or because we ought to have 'respect for personality' (Christian liberalism), but because God loves him. The obligation is derived, in other words, not from the obvious unities and affinities of historic existence, but from the transcendent unity of essential reality."[19]

B. *Evaluation.*

There is probably no side to the theological system of Niebuhr which strikes a truer note than this high and wholesome emphasis upon *agape* love as exhausting both the height of man's freedom and the outside revelation of God's law in Jesus Christ. One can only draw back and admire the magnificent way that Niebuhr has succeeded in relating the Christian doctrine of love to some of the most complex facets of the human situation. It is a rare individual who manages to remain true to so exalted a moral imperative throughout

16. *Ibid.*, p. 294.
17. *Ibid.*, p. 295.
18. Niebuhr, "The Ethics of Jesus and the Social Problem," *Contemporary Thinking about Jesus*, Thomas Kepler, ed. (N. Y., Abingdon-Cokesbury Press, 1944), p. 286.
19. *An Interpretation of Christian Ethics*, p. 213.

an entire system of thought. Surely he who deviates from the expression of the law of the spirit in love is, to the extent of that deviation, forsaking Christianity. "Beloved, let us love one another; for love is of God, and he who loves is born of God and knows God. He who does not love does not know God; for God is love." (I John 4:7-8)

II. The Locus of Original Righteousness

In an equally skillful (but far less convincing) way Niebuhr relates the terms of perfect love to the feeling of the individual in history that he not only stands obligated to this law but that he miserably falls short of it.

A. *The True Existential Locus*

In his customary way of preferring the insights of Kierkegaard to those of both the Lord Jesus Christ and the apostles whenever the Danish theologian's position supports the dialectic, Niebuhr unhesitatingly breaks from historical Christianity on the locus of original righteousness. Orthodoxy, in all of its forms, has been united on the crucial doctrine that our first parents, Adam and Eve, were *historically sinless,* and that not until they fell from that estate did the tension of sin emerge. "How did God create man?" "God created man, male and female, after his own image, *in knowledge, righteousness, and holiness,* with dominion over the creatures."[20] A temporal interval separated the enjoyment of holiness in history from its forfeiture in the fall. "Did our first parents continue in the estate wherein they were created?" "Our first parents, being left to the freedom of their own will, fell from the estate wherein they were created, by sinning against God."[21] The entire Biblical revelation is committed to the doctrine that man was created upright in history, and that he forfeited this uprightness by breaking the commandment of God not to partake of the fruit of the garden. The Scriptures assume without embarrassment that there *was* a real historical Adam and that this Adam was the literal federal head of the race. The entire redemptive program is structurized in reference to the one act of the one man, Adam.

20. *The Westminster Shorter Catechism,* Question 10.
21. *Ibid.,* Question 13.

Jesus Christ believed it. The apostles believed it. And the church universal has always believed it.

But Niebuhr, following Kierkegaard's insight that freedom, not history, is the true locus of original righteousness, does not. And with customary personal integrity he is not ambiguous in the statement of the fact that he does not. There is nothing clearer in all existentialism than the uniformity of its break from orthodoxy at this point. Neo-orthodoxy is the construction of the minds of erstwhile liberals. Barth, Brunner, and Niebuhr were all schooled as liberals. And the tragic events of history, together with a discovery of Kierkegaard, have forced them from immanence to transcendence. But one of the liberal presuppositions which no member of this school has been able to slough off is the hypothesis that science and higher criticism have forever smashed the doctrine of the plenary inspiration of the Bible. In this sense liberalism and neo-orthodoxy are identical. Each negates evangelicalism for trying to make the Biblical narratives themselves objectively veracious whether any man ever accepts them or not. A crucial question of epistemology separates the historical Christian mind from the existential mind, therefore. *The evangelical says that inward experience is to be explained in terms of the Biblical revelation, whereas existentialism says that the Biblical revelation is to be explained in terms of our inward experience.*[22] A *toto caelo* difference separates these two epistemologies. If one tries to plot the difference between orthodoxy and neo-orthodoxy in any less broad dimension than this, he has not yet grasped the issues which provoke the conflict between the two systems. As far as the evangelical is concerned when a person takes Jesus as the *Lord* of his life, Jesus then becomes his sovereign authority everywhere. And when there is a con-

---

22. The evangelical is swift to fortify his position, however, by insisting that, rightly interpreted, the experience of the self as transcendent and the contents of Scripture are *not* disharmoniously related; and that whenever an ostensible collision appears between them the fault lies either in a hasty interpretation by the self of the nature of the data discovered in its freedom or a hasty interpretation of the nature of the data in the Bible. Careful exegesis of the Bible and the witness of our whole experience come out harmoniously. For a modest attempt to show how this is plausible, see my *An Introduction to Christian Apologetics.*

flict between what the race may say and what the Son of God does say, the orthodox soul knows where to put his vote every time. He deems it blasphemy to call his blessed Lord "a child of his times" on matters which are apparently existentially inconsequential. Christ is either the Son of God, possesssing endowment from the Father for his office commensurate with heaven-sent dignity, or He is an impostor. If He is Immanuel, *God with us,* then He is sovereign over even the existential witness; for He is either God of all or He is not God at all. And if He is not God in the flesh, when he claimed that He was, then He is not even a worthy authority where He *happens* to say things which coincide with our existential experiences.

Niebuhr unashamedly speaks out on matters into which angels long to look. Professing that he will be true to his whole experience, regardless where he is led, he turns away from the Biblical account of Adam as the head of the race, preferring instead Kierkegaard's *The Concept of Dread,* where the existential case is made out for Adam's inclusion in the race. The upshot of the matter in neo-orthodoxy, therefore, is that both the primal righteousness of man and the locus of the fall, being removed from the garden of Eden, are made marching, contemporaneous experiences of all men. Original righteousness is our possession now — yet it is possessed only by the self-as-transcendent, never by the self-as-historical.

Man existentially contacts original righteousness at that high moment in freedom when eternity impinges in with direction and conviction. The voice of obligation shouts down the corridors of memory in the conscience of both the race and the individual. There is a recollection of having possessed righteousness — but a possession not so much of a fulfillment as an obligation to fulfill. All men possess this memory. The memory of what ought to be is the moral salt which keeps man's self-respect and dignity pitched on a high level. "No man, however deeply involved in sin, is able to regard the misery of sin as normal. Some memory of a previous condition of blessedness seem to linger in his soul; some echo of the law which he has violated seems to resound in his conscience. Every effort to give the habits of sin the appearance of normality betrays something of the frenzy of an uneasy conscience."[23]

To assist in making the point as clear as possible, Niebuhr resorts to the analogy of the locus of health in the individual who is sick. Is not health out of history as possession, but in history as memory? The same is the case with primal perfection: The self which is transcendent makes contact with original righteousness, but part of what it learns is that the historical or empirical self is quite devoid of this righteousness as a present possession. "The self in the moment of transcending itself exercises the self's capacity for infinite regression and makes the previous concretion of will its object. It is in this moment of self-transcendence that the consciousness and memory of original perfection arise. For in this moment the self knows itself as merely a finite creature among many others and realizes that the undue claims which the anxious self in action makes, result in injustices to its fellows."[24]

Whenever memory-possession is confused with empirical-possession, the dialectic is broken to the extent of that confusion. One remains decisively dialectical only when he lodges *justitia originalis* "in a moment of the self which transcends history, though not outside of the self which is in history."[25] The self in freedom and memory is the self-as-transcendent.

This "double self" theory is subject to such an easy misunderstanding that Niebuhr goes to special pains to make himself clear. There are not two selves, actually. The difference between the self in history and the self out of history lies only in the variegated activities of the one self which is both free and limited. "There are obviously not simply two selves in conflict with each other. But in every moment of existence there is a tension between the self as it looks out upon the world from the perspective of its values and necessities and the self as it looks at both the world and itself, and is disquieted by the undue claims of the self in action."[26] Freedom and in-

23. *Human Nature*, p. 265.
24. *Ibid.*, p. 277.
25. *Ibid.*, p. 279.
26. *Ibid.*, p. 278.

volvement happen to be complex affairs. There is no easy way of stating the relation between man as he ought to be and man as he is, without conveying the impression that there are two different selves. "The 'I,' which from the perspective of self-transcendence, regards the sinful self not as self but as 'sin,' is the same 'I' which from the perspective of sinful action regards the transcendent possibilities of the self as not the self but as 'law.' It is the same self; but these changing perspectives are obviously significant."[27]

A rather curious implication of this existential reinterpretation of the locus of original righteousness is Niebuhr's undaunted insistence that "this universal testimony of human experience is the most persuasive refutation of any theory of human depravity which denies that man has any knowledge of the good which sin has destroyed."[28] The reason why this claim is really curious — although it gives the reader the impression of being a really profound insight — is that only a man of straw is refuted. Niebuhr's argument is as follows: If man were *totally* depraved, he would not even know it; but because he has this trans-historical memory of original righteousness, man knows of his depravity, and thus is not totally depraved.

The fact of the case is that there is no classical statement of Reformed theology which defines total depravity to exclude this negative point of contact in man. Total depravity is a vertical reference, having nothing directly to do with either man's awareness of what he ought to be or of his ability to do social good. *Before God* man is without affection. That is the point. The total man is without natural affection before God. Romans 3 makes that quite clear. This means that even the acknowledgement of the law of love in life is an act which itself is quite without natural affection for God.

Niebuhr fails to give any reformed instances to back up his serious charges. He speaks of Lutheranism as defining away the *imago dei* in man completely; but he then counters with the admission that Luther taught "that the law, and man's uneasy

27. *Human Nature*, pp. 278-279. (Original is in italics).
28. *Ibid.*, p. 266.

conscience, are the first point of contact between God and man."[29] He again quotes from the Formulary of Concord as the most extreme statement of total depravity. But the Formulary itself states specifically that the total depravity concerns *"divine and spiritual things."*[30] What shall account for this theological superficiality in Niebuhr? The conscience, rather than refuting total depravity, is one of the very means by which man discovers his depravity. Depravity is a vertical question: *Coram deo* man is without affection and righteousness.

B. *Corruption of the Existential Locus*

Niebuhr is an admirable opponent in a theological debate. Whereas many of the theologians of crisis likewise follow Kierkegaard in the belief that every man is Adam and that there is no historical locus to the fall, Niebuhr alone seems to have the merit of coming right out and unequivocally declaring his break from historic orthodoxy here. There is no terminological jargon in Niebuhr which one has to make his way through to gain the point. With crisp language he states his case. One may not finally agree with what Niebuhr defends, but he cannot help respecting the fine and clear way in which he states himself.

Niebuhr charges orthodoxy with the "literalistic error of insisting upon the Fall as an historical event."[31] Orthodoxy — both in its Protestant and its Catholic forms — is attempting to pass from a mythological to a scientific truth, and, claims Niebuhr, ends up with poor theology and bad science.

Niebuhr acknowledges that the basic cause of the orthodox heresy is the Scriptures. The Bible seems to teach clearly that there was an historical locus to original righteousness. The "Biblical myth must be regarded as the primary source of the Christian belief in a chronological period in which man had a perfection which he has since lost."[32] But why have men been so foolish as to take the Bible literally, when it is only valid as a

29. *Human Nature*, p. 274.
30. *Ibid.*, p. 268 n.
31. *Ibid.*, pp. 267-268.
32. *Ibid.*, p. 268.

document containing religious myths? That is the problem. In answering it Niebuhr does not suggest either that good exegesis requires it or that Christianity would be incoherent without it. Rather, he dismisses the cause with the unbelievably superficial suggestion that primitive mentality gravitates in the direction of literalism. Man "regards the innocency of his childhood as a symbol and a reminder of his true nature."[33] Here, again, one can detect the spotty worth of Niebuhr's dialecticism. Sometimes it is profound, sometimes naive. Here it is obviously very artless.

Niebuhr attempts to prove that the literalistic view of the fall seriously corrupts the dialectic in the following two ways: First, it has encouraged evangelical theologians to define man as having completely lost the image of God by severing continuity with a literal historical righteousness. Second, it has encouraged Catholic theologians to make the perilous division in the image as *donum supernaturale* and as *pura naturalia,* so that it is licit to claim that there is some part of man which is not involved in the inevitability of sin. "In Catholicism the Fall means the loss of something which is not essential to man and does not therefore represent a corruption of his essence. In radical Protestantism the very image of God in man is believed to be destroyed." [34]

While Catholicism and radical Protestantism (Barthianism) will have to speak for themselves, the evangelical is quick to remind Niebuhr that classical reformed theology has *not* historically led to the abuse of denying the image of God completely in the fallen man, and therefore cannot significantly be charged with corrupting the dialectic. The "original corruption, whereby we are utterly indisposed, disabled, and made opposite to all good, and wholly inclined to all evil"[35] *pertains only to divine and spiritual things.* It does not even consider the context of relative social performances by common grace, on the one hand, or the contact of the free man with the rule of his duty in moments of transcendence, on the

33. *Ibid.*
34. *Ibid.*, p. 269.
35. *The Westminster Confession of Faith,* Chapter VI, iv.

other. Man has lost *moral excellency.* He has retained *moral agency.* The Reformed doctrine of the image may have to be proved true on other grounds, but surely Niebuhr is out of bounds when he avers that the Biblical doctrine of an historical locus of original righteousness *necessarily* corrupts the dialectic. It is just as antecedently plausible that man's memory of original righteousness reaches back through the race to an historical reference as well as to an ahistorical. The free self simply recognizes the witness of conscience; the self-as-transcendent is never told in such an experience whether original righteousness lies only at the *edge* of history or whether it lies *in* history likewise.

III. The Second Adam

Perhaps the greatest disappointment that one encounters in studying Niebuhr is the regrettable way in which a sharp division is made between *Christ the abstract wisdom of history,* the revelation of the mind of the eternal God for man, and *Jesus the historical person who walked in Jerusalem.* There is not the slightest question but what Niebuhr takes a high view of *agape* as the revelation of the mind of God. As wisdom and truth, Christ is heaven-sent. But on the question of the person of the Jesus of history, Niebuhr fails to pass beyond his erstwhile liberalism. There actually is only a *quantitative* difference between the person of Jesus and the person of, perhaps, Gandhi. Niebuhr has become so enamored of his mythological reinterpretation of Christianity that he cannot restrain momentum when Christ and the cross are discussed. While he may not personally intend to dismiss the absoluteness of the Jesus of history from his theology, the Jesus of history at best remains inconsequentially related to his system. Christ becomes a pure abstraction. Christ is only a symbol. "Christ is the symbol both of what man ought to be and of what God is beyond man."[36] The "Christ" and the "Jesus of history" are somehow related, but Niebuhr never succeeds in showing just exactly what this relation is.

---

36. *Beyond Tragedy,* p. 23.

George Hammar brilliantly sums up this same concern: "Niebuhr succeeds brilliantly in restoring the 'myths' of the Creation and the Fall into sin, but these 'myths' have not only a trans-historical content, they are in essence *non-historical.* A slight suspicion therefore easily arises that Niebuhr's concept of 'myth' refers not only to something trans-historical but also to something non-historical. Is then the 'myth' of Christ also non-historical as the Creation and the Fall into sin? That is the decisive critical question of Niebuhr's theology. No doubt Niebuhr would deny that he rejects the idea of the incarnation. He wants to restore Christology, not dissolve it. Even in *Reflections on the End of an Era* we saw him reject Barthianism exactly because it lost the Incarnation as an event in history. Nevertheless Niebuhr's 'mythical' interpretation of the Christian dogmatic tradition forces him to do away with the Incarnation. If his 'mythical' thinking really has reference to something non-historical, then Niebuhr must be forced to reckon, on the one hand, with a relative historic Jesus and, on the other, with an absolute transcendent Christ . . . Niebuhr clearly states that the relation between Jesus and Christ does not differ from the relation between '*all* life and history and the transcendent,' i.e., Jesus is a *general* revelation of the transcendent Christ! While the non-historical Christ is absolute as God, Jesus is relative as man is!"[37]

This objection rests on the firmest of evidence. And the evangelical would remind all theologians consistently pursuing a mythological path with Niebuhr, that the cost of rejecting the first Adam as the federal head of the race is the loss of the second Adam as the federal head of the saved. If a premature obedience to science entails the price of losing Jesus Christ in history, the capital investment is too dear. *Why gain something insignificant at the cost of losing the only thing which finally counts?*

A. *Christ and Messianism.*

---

37. *Christian Realism in Contemporary American Theology,* pp. 241-242.

Christ caught up the prophetic insight that all Israel was sinful, converting its terms into the offensive doctrine that only he who says he is blind actually sees, and only he who acknowledges his sin is without sin.

Christ collided head-on with the official legalism of his day. "Legalism is a kind of arrested and atrophied religion of history. In Hebraism it rests upon the idea that the God, who delivered Israel out of the land of Egypt, made the decalogue a part of the covenant between Himself and the nation. This legalism is therefore type and symbol of every form of legalistic religious consciousness which binds the counsels of God prematurely to a law which is contingent to time and place."[38] Christ comprehended that man's freedom to transcend historical forms renders laws ineffectual to account either for the "complexities of motive which express themselves in the labyrinthine depths of man's interior life"[39] or the infinite degrees by which man "can screen evil motives by outward conformity to the law." [40] The only rule which can satisfy is a law which finally exhausts the outside freedom of man, inasmuch as lesser laws may themselves become the vehicle of new prides and pretensions.

Although Niebuhr detects overtones of nationalism in Christ's ministry, for "Christianity does not finally purge itself of nationalistic particularism until St. Paul asserts the right to preach the gospel to the Gentiles," [41] he nevertheless believes that the most consistent witness of Jesus was a rejection of nationalism. The doctrine that all men are equally one in God was offensive to the clandestine Jewish mind.

When Jesus finally announced the terms of His solution to the problem raised by the prophets, however, the offense reached its climax; for while Israel looked for a Messiah to save her and deliver her from all opposing enemies, she did not anticipate that the deliverance would come in such a morally demanding way.

38. *Human Destiny,* p. 39.
39. *Ibid.,* p. 40.
40. *Ibid.*
41. *Ibid.,* p. 42.

In showing how Christ solved the Messianic problem, Niebuhr, disregarding the many times in which Christ warned that God would effect a final separation between the sheep and the goats in eternity, settles upon the parable of the last judgment to establish his doctrine of universalism. "The symbolism of the parable, the picture of the Messianic judge separating the sheep from the goats, the righteous from the unrighteous, is a recurring motif of apocalyptic literature. Jesus accepts it and on one level of his own interpretation it would appear that history culminates in the Messianic vindication of the righteous and the destruction of the wicked. But a significant new note is added. The righteous are humble and do not believe themselves to be righteous. They accept the judge's commendation with the confession, 'Lord, when saw we thee an hungered, and fed thee? . . .' While the righteous are contritely aware of their unworthiness of this vindication, the unrighteous are equally unconscious of their guilt."[42] Jesus makes the provisional distinction between sheep and goat, thus respecting the degrees of good and evil in history; but in the *final* judgment there are no righteous. This puncturing of the pride of the Jews was the first reason why he was an offense to his own.

The second basis of the offense came after Jesus announced the terms of his Messianic office. While men looked for power and self-vindication in history, seeking to take Christ by force as their king, Jesus quietly announced that he had come to suffer. "To declare, as Jesus does, that the Messiah, the representative of God, must suffer, is to make vicarious suffering the final revelation of meaning in history. But it is the vicarious suffering of the representative of God, and not of some force in history, which finally clarifies the obscurities of history and discloses the sovereignty of God over history."[43] The meaning of this will be detailed *infra*.

Niebuhr breaks radically with the liberal interpretation of the cross, where Christ's sufferings are supposed to leave a moral deposit in history which gradually gains control over

42. *Human Destiny*, p. 43.
43. *Ibid.*, p. 45.

evil until finally the kingdom of God is on earth; and accepts in its place the idea "that vicarious love remains defeated and tragic in history."[44] Looked at simply from the historical perspective the cross is a tragedy. But it is a glorious triumph from the divine point of view because it contains the final revelation of the relation between God's justice and mercy, bringing to a climactic denouement the solution to prophetic Messianism. "The synthesis of Jesus, according to which the suffering servant is not merely a character of history, but is the representative of the divine, transcends both the simple optimism of the first interpretation and the purely tragic implication of the second conception. It is God Who suffers for man's iniquity. He takes the sins of the world upon and into Himself."[45] God does not finally reject those who do evil in history (for Niebuhr sees no place for the doctrine of hell as a symbol of anything), but rather bears in his own person the evil committed. Not only was this doctrine offensive to those who first heard it, but it has been offensive to all generations since. Even those who find wisdom in it struggle within themselves constantly. Their own pride and lust for self-vindication collides with the resounding voice of Jesus, "There are no righteous."

B. *The Wisdom of God.*

Niebuhr perceives a profundity in the epic of Christ's life and death which both outreaches and passes the optimistic liberal visions that Christ is only a way of life, an example for men, which all are to follow if they are to attain to the highest good. He senses that Christ really understood the essential factors of the existential predicament of man. To interpret Christ simply as a symbol of divine goodness, as liberalism does, is to confuse relative goals in history with eternal ideals, on the one hand, and to neglect the real ingredients of sinfulness on the other. "Such interpretations of life and faith do not proceed from a radical or profound analysis of the problem of life. They assume that the problem of life is to discover

44. *Ibid.*
45. *Ibid.*, p. 46.

the highest form of goodness; to learn what is 'worthy of man's highest devotion.' They do not understand life in its two-fold character of involvement in finiteness and transcendence over it; or the further complication of the corruption of sin which is the consequence of premature and self-sufficient efforts to escape from the weakness, dependence and insufficiency of the human situation."[46]

The wisdom of Christ lies in the fact that it dealt with history as if what was characteristic of history at one point is likewise characteristic of it at all points. The essential predicament of man involves the inevitable presence of sinfulness, even to the end of history. One does not see a wisdom in Christ until he himself becomes dialectical. "Whenever the complexities of history's relation to eternity are not known to be characteristic of history on every level of its development, the Christian claim that God has been revealed in Christ cannot be taken seriously."[47]

Christ is the wisdom and truth of God because He revealed "the purpose and the will of the divine sovereign of life and history."[48] The wisdom of Christ which culminates in the cross, gives life and history meaning; for it testifies to the fact that there is a power and a resource beyond history which will bring history its end. The finality of Christ's insight is not a sentimental thing, as liberal Christianity would have it. It is not simply the announcement that God is merciful. Christ does not negate the prophetic insight that God is full of wrath and justice. "The *wisdom* apprehended in Christ finally clarifies the character of God. He has a resource of mercy beyond His law and judgment but He can make it effective only as He takes the consequences of His wrath and judgement, upon and into Himself."[49] God voluntarily accepted in His own person the consequences of sin. History is serious. Christ came to suffer.

C. *The Meaning of the Second Adam.*

46. *Human Destiny*, p. 53.
47. *Ibid.*, p. 54.
48. *Ibid.*
49. *Ibid.*, p. 55.

The first Adam, which is a complexity of the transcendent self's meeting eternity and the empirical self's sensing its shortcoming in the light of that rule, is completed and explained by the second Adam. The point of contact between time and eternity is love. Man knows how to give good gifts to his children (Matthew 7:11), and God knows how to give the good gifts of rain to the just and the unjust (Matthew 5:45). In all of man's dealings in love, therefore, an echo of the divine can be heard. Men are evil, but they are not completely evil. As a point of contact between God and man, therefore, love serves perfectly. "Man is a creature who cannot find a true norm short of the nature of ultimate reality. This is the significance of the historic doctrine of Christ as the 'second Adam.' The same Christ who is accepted by faith as the revelation of the character of God is also regarded as the revelation of the true character of man. Christ has this twofold significance because love has this double significance. 'God is love,' which is to say that the ultimate reality upon which the created world depends and by which it is judged is not an 'unmoved mover' or an undifferentiated eternity, but the vital and creative source of life and of the harmony of life with life. But the essence of human nature is also love, which is to say that for man, who is involved in the unities and harmonies of nature but who also transcends them in his freedom, there can be no principle of harmony short of the love in which free personality is united in freedom with other persons."[50] Because the second Adam completes the love which man knows, He is thus continuously related to that love. For this reason Christ is both a surprise and an expectation. The revelation must be more than we know in history, or God would not be speaking; but it must be continuous with what we know through natural revelation to constitute the height of the law of our own spirit, or that voice would be irrelevant. "The Christian doctrine of Christ as the 'second Adam,' as normative man, is thus a doctrine which hovers between natural and revealed religion. It belongs to natural religion in the sense that any rigorous analysis of the moral life of man will, partially disclose the

50. *Human Nature,* pp. 146-147.

tangents towards the eternal in all morality. It belongs to revealed religion because it is not possible, without faith, to follow these implications through to their final logical conclusion."[51] History gives tokens of the virtue of love, but history cannot finally vindicate love. Only eternity can both set the ideal and guarantee the power of love's vindication.

Niebuhr pays tribute to Nygren's monumental work, *Agape and Eros,* for the profound way the distinction between disinterested love in the New Testament and the concept of mutual love in classical thought is set down. But he objects to Nygren's conclusion that *agape* is not a genuine point of contact in history antecedent to the coming of Christ after the flesh. "He makes the contrast too absolute. Non-Christian conceptions of love do indeed seek to justify love from the standpoint of the happiness of the agent; but the freedom of man is such that he is not without some idea of the virtue of love which does not justify itself in terms of his own happiness. It is significant that Jesus does not regard the contrast between natural human love and the divine *agape* as absolute."[52] Niebuhr stands on very solid ground here, and he does an incalculable service in pointing this fact out. "Albert Schweitzer," for example, "under a sense of responsibility for the needs of Africans and under a sense of guilt for the white man's sins against the colored race, decides to expiate that guilt by casting his lot with the Africans on the edge of the primeval forest . . . illustrates the freedom of spirit which transcends the limitation of nature."[53] No healthy-minded evangelical could object to this high view of man's potentialities within common grace. The only implication to be guarded against is the supposition that natural acts of love can in anyway obviate the need of Christ's atonement on the cross as God's way to forgive sins. God saves by grace, not by human merit.

Niebuhr is willing to concede the formula that Christ is the second Adam on the ground that Christ's life and death

51. *Human Destiny,* pp. 75-76.
52. *Ibid.,* p. 84 n.
53. *An Interpretation of Christian Ethics,* p. 79.

exhibit a very consistent expression of what man knows in his freedom to be continuous with the law of his spirit. Christ is the absolute fulfillment of man's outside nature. Christ is "the symbol of the norm of man's historical existence."[54] Christ is "the norm of human nature" the "final perfection of man in history."[55] Christ has exhausted the full meaning of what it means to be a man. Therefore, he is fully the second Adam; he is the norm by which God will finally judge man at the end of history.

D. *The God-man.*

Christ is "the Son of God" as well as the second Adam because he "discloses the ultimate mystery of the relation of the divine to history. This revelation clarifies the meaning of history; for the judgment of God preserves the distinction of good and evil in history; and the mercy of God finally overcomes the sinful corruption in which man is involved on every level of moral achievement by reason of his false and abortive efforts to complete his own life and history."[56] Christ is the Son of God because "His ethical doctrine contains an uncompromising insistence upon conformity to God's will without reference to the relativities and contingencies of historical situations."[57] Niebuhr rejects the moralistic liberal view of Schleiermacher that Christ's perfection consisted simply in His "God-consciousness." It was more than an intention. It was a life. "The animating purpose of his life is to conform to the *agape* of God. His life culminates in an act of self-abnegation in which the individual will ceases to be a protagonist of the individual life; and the life ends upon the Cross."[58]

After making these, and many other, admissions which suggest on the surface that Niebuhr stands within the framework of consistent reformed theology, a reversal sets in and he calls back everything he has said.

---

54. *Faith and History,* p. 197.
55. *Human Destiny,* p. 68.
56. *Ibid.*
57. *Ibid.,* p. 73.
58. *Ibid.,* p. 74.

In prefacing his remarks about the incarnation, Niebuhr commits a rather common theological blunder. He suggests that orthodoxy tries to give metaphysical plausibility to the doctrine of the sinless perfection of Christ by leaning "heavily upon the doctrine of the Virgin birth."[59] By the virgin birth Christ is supposedly removed from ordinary generation, so that the taint of hereditary corruption does not become his. But Niebuhr confuses Biblical with Catholic doctrine. The Bible nowhere even hints that Christ was virgin born that He might be preserved from the stain of Adam's sin. Christ was sinlessly preserved simply because it was the will of His Father to prepare for him a nature which was without sin. The virgin birth was a sign that something wonderful was taking place in this birth, a sign to wake the world up to the glories of Christ's coming. It was not a mechanical device to preserve sinlessness. Niebuhr's theological inaccuracy here is apparent.

All that Niebuhr will concede concerning the person of Christ is that the symbol of the God-man provides a framework which makes "the doctrine that Jesus was both human and divine *religiously and morally meaningful* and dispenses with the necessity of making the doctrine metaphysically plausible."[60] Having proceeded to Jesus Christ through the existential witness of the free soul, rather than through Biblical revelation, Niebuhr claims (quite without final justification) that he is free from the necessity of giving a metaphysical explanation of the God-man doctrine. If existential epistemology can ignore metaphysics, it assumes to itself a convenience which no rigorous philosophy of religion has hitherto dared do. Metaphysics has been deemed very important.

The church universal has always understood the person of Jesus Christ in metaphysical terms. The two natures of Christ are united *"inconfusedly, unchangeably, indivisibly, inseparably;* the distinction of natures being by no means taken away by the union, but rather the property of each nature being pre-

59. *Human Destiny*, p. 73.
60. *Ibid.*, p. 70. (Italics mine).

served, and concurring in one Person and one Subsistence, not parted or divided into two persons, but one and the same Son, an only begotten, God the Word, the Lord Jesus Christ."[61] Niebuhr indicts this as the "wooden-headed literalism of orthodoxy."[62] With obsequiousness Niebuhr bows to both his liberal training and Kierkegaard, for in both traditions a metaphysical statement of the incarnation is viewed as absolutely paradoxical and a final offense to reason. Niebuhr can only conclude that, while Jesus symbolizes both the second Adam and the Son of God, He was yet a sinner. Niebuhr has already conceded the Kierkegaardian insight that a "man could not be tempted if he had not already sinned";[63] so he has no other course but to conclude either that Christ was not a true man or that He was a sinner. He obviously elects the latter — although he submerges his admission behind many pious words. If Christ were not tempted, He did not have a human nature; and if He were tempted, then He has already sinned. Niebuhr has no other alternative to rest in after having trod the dialectical path this far. Jesus is *not* literally God in the flesh. "Since the essence of the divine consists in its unconditioned character, and since the essence of the human lies in its conditioned and contingent nature, it is not logically possible to assert both qualities of the same person."[64]

At this point the evangelical mind recoils with shock. While the evangelical can bear up under the sub-*agape* charge of being called a wooden-headed literalist, he cringes within to hear that his blessed Lord, whose shed blood has redeemed him from sin, is, like himself, a sinner. To charge Christ with sin is pure blasphemy, and it borders perilously on the edge of the unpardonable sin against the Holy Spirit. With all the fanfare which Niebuhr gives to the procession of events in history leading up to Christ, the person of Jesus trails along as a pathetic anticlimax. The historical Jesus, is, as another has put it, like a very small boy beating a very small drum at the end of a very long parade. The glory is in the dialectical rela-

61. *The Symbol of Chalcedon.*
62. *Beyond Tragedy,* p. 28.
63. *Human Nature,* p. 251.
64. *Human Destiny,* p. 70.

tion between time and eternity. The person of Christ is an afterthought.

The amazing thing about Niebuhr's rejection of Christ's metaphysical divinity, and the concomitant doctrine of sinlessness, is that it does not seem to trouble him much. The issue is by-passed with almost an air of aloofness. Christian faith seems to be so busy living within the terms of the dialectic that "it has not tried with too much consistency to fit every action of the historical Jesus into the symbol of this perfection."[65] In other words, the Jesus of history appears merely to be a convenient locus to pin the Christ symbol to, for He was simply more consistent in his *agape* living than others. But one must note that if Socrates had been more consistent in his life and a little more successful in his oracular contacts with eternity, he could just as well serve as the symbol of our faith. Our faith then would be the "Socratic faith," and our hope, not the cross, but "the flask of hemlock." Jesus was just more consistent in his conformity to the will of God than was either Socrates or Gandhi; but He, not less than they, was a sinner. "It is not possible for this reason to assert the sinlessness of every individual act of any actually historical character."[66]

Niebuhr scythes down everything in the words of Christ which does not neatly conform to his antecedently conceived dialectic. Jesus was literalistic in His view of the Old Testament, of His metaphysical continuity with God, of His claims to sinlessness, of His eschatology, and a whole host of other non-dialectical commitments. He thought of a literal heaven and hell, a literal entering of God into history, a literal end to history. Jesus was "a child of his times" in everything but his revelation of love. "Jesus, no less than Paul, was not free of these historical illusions. He expected the coming of the Messianic kingdom in his lifetime."[67] Faith is able to wade through all of Christ's sins and errors, however, and see in Him a token of how God is finally going to solve the problem of sin. Faith takes what is worth-while out of the life of Christ and

65. *Human Destiny,* p. 73.
66. *Ibid.*
67. *An Interpretation of Christian Ethics,* p. 57.

discards the rest. Whatever is sub-*agape* in Christ is the husk, while whatever is dialectical is the kernel. Here the old wine of liberalism is simply poured into the new bags of dialectical thought.

The evangelical would be quick to take note, however, that while he believes that Niebuhr's view of the person of Jesus is sheer blasphemy, he yet retains a profound respect for the intellectual honesty and the personal integrity of the man himself. There are few who are as courageous as he is to defend what is believed to be the truth. Most theologians who agree with Niebuhr on the person of Jesus are too timid to come right out and say so. Niebuhr at least is not.

There are probably three fundamental reasons why Niebuhr can not accommodate the metaphysical doctrine of Christ into his existentialism.

1. *Logical nonsense.* Even if the issue of God literally entering history were not a problem of Christianity, Niebuhr would still argue against it on the formal ground that it is pure nonsense. "By stating this double facet of Christ in ontic terms, a truth of faith, which can be expressed only symbolically, is transmuted into a truth of speculative reason. Christ is, according to these statements of faith, both God and man . . . All definitions of Christ which affirm both his divinity and humanity in the sense that they ascribe both finite and historically conditioned and eternal and unconditioned qualities to his nature must verge on logical nonsense. It is possible for a character, event or fact of history to point symbolically beyond history and to become a source of disclosure of an eternal meaning, purpose and power which bears history. But it is not possible for any person to be historical and unconditioned at the same time."[68]

No attempt will be made here to defend the evangelical point of view. One need only read a volume such as John Lawton's *Conflict in Christology,* especially the chapter on "The Divorce of Theology from History," to gain an appreciation of some of the difficulties which attend any alternative to the evangelical formula.

68. *Human Destiny,* pp. 60-61.

2. *Corruption of faith.* Niebuhr stands in the Kierkegaardian tradition that there must be a "leap" in faith, a "risk" of some kind.[69] As an outcome of making faith an inward apprehension of what outwardly appears to be scientifically or logically incomplete, therefore, Niebuhr indicts a metaphysical statement of the incarnation with the charge that it sullies the inwardness of faith. "The logical nonsense is not as serious a defect as the fact that the statement tends to reduce Christian faith to metaphysical truths which need not be apprehended inwardly by faith."[70] No comment is needed here. If metaphysical clarification is not needed in explaining the person of Christ, why ought it to be needed in explaining either the nature of man or the dialectical relation between time and eternity? Let silence reign.

3. *Dialectically superfluous.* If history contains its own ideal, then the freedom of man has lost assurance that the eternal norm for history stands at the edge of history and outruns all historical forms. The Christ is useful to man, therefore, only as an ideal which becomes tangent to history, but not as an absolute in history. "The interpretations which define the sinlessness and perfection of Christ in either metaphysical or legalistic terms can have no real illumination for human conduct. If only a God-man, who transcends the conditions of finiteness absolutely, can define and delineate the norm of human existence, the contrition which contemplation of such a norm may prompt is quickly transmuted into complacency. For we must live our life under the conditions of finiteness; and

69. Niebuhr objects to Kierkegaard's tendency to make faith an *absolute* leap, however. "The final truth about life is always an absurdity but it cannot be an absolute absurdity. It is an absurdity inasfar as it must transcend the 'system' of meaning which the human mind always prematurely constructs with itself as the centre. But it cannot be a complete absurdity or it could not achieve any credence. In this sense Kierkegaard goes too far . . ." *Human Destiny*, p. 38 n. Kierkegaard would doubtless respond to Niebuhr that "absolute absurdity" is a far more existentially provocative basis for "the inwardness of faith" than Niebuhr's partial rationalism and partial symbolism. Kierkegaard, of course, is right. If the "leap" is the essence of faith, then the wider the leap, the more faith one has; so that the man who can believe absolute nonsense is the true believer. Niebuhr is trying to take a value of existentialism without going all the way with its implications for epistemology.

70. *Ibid.*, p. 61.

may therefore dismiss any ideal or norm as irrelevant which does not have to meet our conditions."[71]

This third charge simply bristles with difficulties. *First*, it is theologically inaccurate. The orthodox formula of the sinlessness of Christ does not defend a God-man "who transcends the conditions of finiteness absolutely." A cursory examination of any of the classical reformed creeds will show that the full humanity was defended as well as the full deity. The metaphysical formula defends a Christ who was tempted in all points like as we — yet, contrary to Niebuhr and in harmony with Biblical revelation, *without sin*. Niebuhr cannot see this because he understands more about Kierkegaard's *The Concept of Dread* than he does about the Biblical insight that sin is a transgression of the revealed law of God. Christ was in perfect harmony with the law of God even though He was a free individual within history. His freedom did not make Him sinful. If this is a "legalistic" interpretation of the Bible, then so is it likewise legalistic to appeal to the Bible for the revelation of how God is going to solve the problem which was raised by the prophets. May one assume for himself a privilege in method which he denies to others?

Second, the charge that orthodoxy leads necessarily to complacency is without foundation. Indeed, neither the Scriptural writers nor the mind of the church have ever taught that any man actually could match Christ's sinlessness. The everlasting uniqueness of Christ lies precisely in the fact that as the second Adam He alone has fulfilled the whole law of His Father. If man could imitate Him, he would never need Christ as Savior. But man cannot imitate Him. Man is born in sin and conceived in iniquity. However, that does not make the norm irrelevant; for one seeks to mediate the terms of an absolute law out of the motive of a love for Christ. Complacency is avoided on the ground that redeemed men respond to their blessed Redeemer with the earnest intention to fulfill all righteousness. The reference is vertical.

Third, the conclusion that freedom would be offended if history were to bear its own ideal is absurd. Freedom is con-

71. *Human Destiny*, p. 74.

cerned only with the nature of the ideal, not whether it lies either in history, on the edge of history, or solely in eternity. Freedom can just as well look back to find its outside norm as it can to look forward. The locus of the ideal is not what determines its validity.

Furthermorè, would not the Christ be a far more plausible basis for judgment at the end of history if history actually had borne that perfection in Jesus? If Jesus Himself did not attain unto perfection, how, then, can He serve as a ground for judgment? *Let him who is without sin cast the first stone!*

E. *Where is the Blood?*

Whereas the Bible regards the shedding of blood as the basis for God's forgiveness of sins, Niebuhr does not seem to see even a symbolic worth in the blood. The Biblical witness here is clear. "Without the shedding of blood there is no forgiveness of sins" (Hebrews 9:22). "The blood of Jesus his Son cleanses us from all sin" (I John 1:7). Niebuhr sees only the cross, never the blood. The reason for this is, doubtless, that he was forced to conclude that it was a sinner who hung on the cross. How can Jesus atone for sins when He Himself stands indicted by the Christ?

The "wisdom of the cross," therefore, really turns out to be Niebuhr's own wisdom — together with a generous sprinkling of insights from Kierkegaard and Tillich. Existentially, men are saved by their perseverance within the tensions of the dialectic, and not by the precious blood of the Lord Jesus Christ. But is this not simply another form of good works? The reader must judge for himself whether this soteriology is Christian or not. The evangelical unequivocally says that it is not. The Bible, which is our only source of Christian knowledge, declares without ambiguity that men are saved by the blood of Jesus Christ through imputed righteousness, not by the simple moral process of God taking sins into and upon Himself. At this crucial point of soteriology, Niebuhr has not been able to break from his liberal tradition.

VI

Antithesis: The Foolishness of the Cross

BECAUSE the revelation of the cross issues from the mind of God and thus is grounded in a perspective which transcends the limits of human wisdom, that revelation, to the extent of its transcendence, is foolishness to the natural man. The cross could not have been anticipated by human wisdom because it contains insights which outrun historical vindication. The cross will remain offensively related to the immanent ethos of human culture. "The truth which is revealed in the Cross is not a truth which could have been anticipated in human culture and it is not the culmination of human wisdom. The true Christ is not expected. All human wisdom seeks to complete itself from the basis of its partial perspective. The pride of nations and of national and imperial cultures is only a primitive form of the pride of man as man, who will seek to complete the meaning of life from the standpoint of some human virtue or achievement and who will confuse and corrupt life's meaning by that very attempt."[1]

I. The Nature of Foolishness

A. *The First Offense: There are No Righteous.*

It is characterististic of the natural man to interpret the moral program in such a way that its terms may easily be met. Sensing, quite properly, that degrees of truth and error must be respected within history, he concludes, quite improperly, that our moral relativities will remain undisturbed in the final judgment. In the *final* judgment "the distinction between the righteous and the unrighteous disappears."[2] This is foolishness to the natural man, both righteous and unrighteous. There are three basic elements in the last judgment.

1. *Human Destiny*, p. 62.
2. *Ibid.*, p. 46.

1. *The norm is Christ.* "It is Christ who will be the judge of history. Christ as judge means that when the historical confronts the eternal it is judged by its own ideal possibility, and not by the contrast between the finite and the eternal character of God."[3] Natural wisdom, failing to reach the absolute demands of eternity, is not able to understand how it is possible for men to be judged by a perfection of *agape* which can stand only at the edge of history. Such a perfection is either unfair or irrelevant. It is unfair because it involves the imposition upon history of a rule which history cannot accommodate; and it is irrelevant because the finite and the conditioned are quite able to yield their own order.

It is not the literal historical Jesus, but the abstract Christ, which is the rule by which men are finally judged. Jesus remains condemned by Christ. The mere fact that Jesus was *in* history, rather than remaining *tangent* to history, forever sullies His candidacy as the basis for final judgment. Although Niebuhr quotes Augustine's words with approbation that God "has given His judgment to His Son who shall show himself *as a man* to judge the world,"[4] he means no more than that Jesus the man remains a *symbol* of Christ the abstraction. Jesus lived that consistent life of *agape* which reminds free men of absolute *agape,* the Christ, their rule of absolute fulfillment. This is sort of a Christianized Platonism: the world of flux (Jesus) reminds men of the world of Ideas (Christ).

The following observations support this: *First,* neither a part nor the whole of the life of Jesus could be completely sinless. "Where there is history at all there is freedom; and where there is freedom there is sin."[5] Since history at every moment must be kept suspended under the tension of the dialectic, it follows that sin was present even at the very moment Jesus died on the cross. If history could bear its own ideal other than as a symbolism, the dialectic would be corrupted. It makes little difference who corrupts it. Jesus,

3. *Ibid.,* pp. 291-292.
4. *Ibid.,* n.
5. *Ibid.,* p. 80.

therefore, though He created the Christ in His life and doctrine, did not Himself become the Christ; *He created an ideal larger than His own possibilities. Jesus is judged by the Christ.* "Perhaps it is sufficient to say that the Jesus of history actually created the Christ of faith in the life of the early church, and that his historic life is related to the transcendent Christ as a final and ultimate symbol of a relation which prophetic religion sees between all life and history and the transcendent."[6] Nothing could be clearer: The "Jesus of history" and the "Christ of faith" must be two different entities or the dialectic is sullied.

Second, Jesus is not actually the Christ or we would have idolatry. "If some vitality of existence, or even some subordinate principle of coherence is used as the principle of meaning, man is involved in idolatry. He lifts some finite and contingent element of existence into the eminence of the divine."[7] If we may univocally identify Christ and Jesus at any point, the finite is then endowed with the prerogatives of divinity. But this would lead to idolatry.

Third, Jesus had only finite perspective. The Christ is absolute. "For there is no self in history or society, no matter how impartial its perspective upon the competitions of life, which can rise to the position of a disinterested participation in those rivalries and competitions. It can symbolize disinterested love only by a refusal to participate in the rivalries."[8] The historical Jesus was a participant in His own partial interests. Jesus "expected the historic interim between the first and second establishment of the Kingdom to be short. In this error he was followed both by St. Paul and the early church, with the consequent false and disappointed hope of the *parousia* in the lifetime of the early disciples. This error was due to an almost

6. *An Interpretation of Christian Ethics*, p. 120. Christ is the "true mythical symbol of both the possibilities and the limits of the human." *Ibid.*, p. 15.
7. *Human Nature*, p. 164. "The identification of Christ with the 'Sacred Host' on the altar is the perfect fruit of the Catholic error. The host on the altar is an historically conditioned symbol of the ultimate sanctity." *Human Destiny*, p. 224, n.
8. *Human Destiny*, p. 72.

inevitable illusion of thought which deals with the problem of the relation of time and eternity."[9]

Christian faith is quite aware of the sinfulness and errors of Jesus; it merely says that it is more interested in the symbol of perfection in Jesus than in the earthen vessel through which that symbolism came. "Christian faith believes that the ideal of love is real in the will and nature of God, *even though he knows of no place in history where the ideal has been realized in its pure form.*"[10]

The "Christ," therefore, which God uses as a rule by which to make the righteous feel sinful and the unrighteous surprised at how righteous they actually are, is but a pure abstraction designed to designate man's historical possibilities. These potentialities are exhibited in the life of Jesus in an imperfect, but remarkably consistent, way. Jesus reminds us of a Christ we already knew in a hidden way through general revelation.

This calls to our attention again the confusion of Niebuhr's mind in matters of Christology. "Does not Niebuhr here confuse general and special revelation? It is difficult to see in what sense Jesus, as a man in history, represents the *absolute* which is said to *invade* history . . . Is not Niebuhr talking about Jesus as a *general* revelation, and not as the Incarnation? Niebuhr only gives us intimations of his Christology. It is not worked out. His position is even rather dim, because it is evident that he wants to transcend liberal theology at this point also."[11] The only way that Niebuhr can break from liberal errors is to take his presuppositions from Scripture instead of the existentialism of Sören Kierkegaard.

The final judgment is foolish to men, therefore, because it is grounded in the Christ, a rule which man learns both in moments of prayerful transcendence and in reading the life of Jesus. Only the immanent can be meaningful to those whose perspective is confined to history. Christ is a transcendent principle.

---

9. *Ibid.,* pp. 49-50.
10. *An Interpretation of Christian Ethics,* p. 8. (Italics mine).
11. Hammar, *Christian Realism in Contemporary American Theology,* p. 231.

2. *Conjunction and disjunction.* In the final judgment God initially respects the relative distinctions in history between good and evil, while yet pronouncing a final judgment against such relativities because of their inherent ambiguities. "All historical realities are indeed ambiguous. Therefore no absolute distinction between good and evil in them is possible. But this does not obviate the necessity and possibility of a *final* judgment upon good and evil."[12]

When a man judges according to his own perspective from within history, he may be tempted to conclude either that good and evil remain inconsequential distinctions in eternity, for all will revert back to God in an absolute oneness; or that the distinctions are so absolute that they will be carried into eternity without alteration. The final judgment shatters both conclusions. Against the first, the final judgment commences with a provisional respect for the degrees of righteousness and unrighteousness among men. "The very rigour with which all judgments in history culminate in a final judgment is thus an expression of meaningfulness of all historic conflicts between good and evil."[13] Against the second, the final judgment exposes the deep-rooted partiality and ambiguity of these provisional distinctions. When seen with an eye to the full norm of Christ, the righteous clearly perceive why their own self-pride and personal interest have sullied their right to a *final* pretension to righteousness. The difference between good and evil in history is so important that God had to take historical sins into and upon Himself; but they are never sufficiently unmixed with relative and ambiguous elements that they can stand unaltered in the presence of Christ.

3. *History as judgment and fulfillment.* "The third facet in the symbol of the last judgment is to be found in its locus at the 'end' of history. There is no achievement or partial realization in history, no fulfillment of meaning or achievement of virtue by which man can escape the final judgment."[14] Christianity refutes all views which suppose that history either

12. *Human Destiny,* p. 292.
13. *Ibid.,* pp. 292-293.
14. *Ibid.,* p. 293.

has the potentialities within it to rid itself of its own guilt, on the one hand, or those which conclude that history does not need redeeming — either because history is inconsequential or because sinlessness has already been achieved within history. Modernity, blinded to "the historical being involved, on every level of achievement, in contradiction to the eternal,"[15] is prone to see "the end only as fulfillment"[16] and not judgment; while the self-righteous do "not see that all history and all historic achievements must remain under the judgment of God; that the 'Kingdom of God' which we achieve in history is never the same as the Kingdom for which we pray."[17]

The dialectic is foolish because man cannot understand either how one can be drawn by an ideal which history cannot contain, or how God can use that ideal as the basis for a just judgment. What is forgotten is that God's perspective of judgment proceeds from the direction of the eternal and reaches back into history. The partial is both recognized and judged. For this reason Niebuhr rejects both the "literalistic conceptions of the allegedly everlasting fires of hell"[18] and the "moral sentimentality in modern Christianity."[19] Neither does justice to the idea of history as ending in judgment, for each fails to understand the relation between time and eternity as a dialectic.

By remaining within the counsel that eternity both fulfills and negates history, Christ is the true prophet. "The mark of false prophecy is that it assures the sinner peace and security within terms of his sinful ambitions."[20] A false prophet counsels men to defy the laws of life in favor of a tenuous, self-established security. The true prophet seeks to open the eyes of men to the realistic terms of life, so that in confessing blindness they might see, and in confessing weakness they might be strong. "Christianity as judgment is precisely to bring man to despair, which is reality, to the acknowledgment

15. *Ibid.*, p. 167.
16. *Ibid.*, p. 166.
17. *Ibid.*, p. 180.
18. *Ibid.*, p. 294.
19. *Ibid.*
20. *Beyond Tragedy*, p. 94.

of his utter inability ever to fulfill the ideal. But in the realization of that very despair lies man's great hope; for in the realization of despair judgment becomes mercy. Despair becomes the avenue of a rebirth of the whole man. And this is the profundity of the relevance of Christian faith to every historical situation. It is to deprive man of his pride, which dooms civilization to perpetual frustration. Christianity as judgment is the point of a new leverage in historical frustration."[21] The final judgment seems foolish only when the dialectical relation between time and eternity seems foolish; but such a condition is sustained only when man understands neither the height of his freedom nor the depths of his involvement, on the one hand, nor the incomplete way in which what is ideally known in the self as transcendent is inconsistently applied in the self as empirical, on the other.

B. *The Second Offense: Suffering*

"The second reason for the 'offensive' character of Jesus' Messianism was in the answer which he gave to the problem emphasized by this reinterpretation of life and history. This answer is most succinctly stated in his own words, 'The Son of man must suffer.' The answer introduces the outrageous idea of a suffering Messiah into the Messianic thought, which had not entertained any other conception than that of a triumphant Messiah."[22] As general revelation the cross reveals that there is ultimately only one fate for *agape* action in a sinful society: *suffering*. Selfless love grows out of an appreciation of a law and rule behind history; it does not stem from the hope that final vindication may be expected within history. The Christian maxim is as follows: "Find your satisfaction not in the triumph over evil in existence, but rather in the conformity of your life to its ultimate essence."[23]

The cross establishes both the possibilities and the limits of history. Because the cross was preceded by the epical life of

21. D. R. Davies, *Reinhold Niebuhr: Prophet from America*, (London: James Clarke & Co., LTD), p. 80.

22. *Human Destiny*, p. 44.

23. *An Interpretation of Christian Ethics*, p. 47. Christian love "is oriented by only one vertical religious reference, to the will of God; and the will of God is defined in terms of all-inclusive love." *Ibid.*, p. 51.

Jesus, a life in which a remarkably consistent commitment to the will of God was exhibited, history is shown its possibilities; but because that life ended on the cross, history is shown its limits. History cannot assimilate the heights of selfless love because the best security within history seems to be gained when men love only those who love them. *Agape* love is misunderstood by the world to the degree that eternity transcends time. "From the standpoint of history mutual love is the highest good. Only in mutual love, in which the concern of one person for the interests of another prompts and elicits a reciprocal affection, are the social demands of historical existence satisfied. The highest good of history must conform to standards of coherence and consistency in the whole realm of historical vitality . . . The sacrifice of the self for others is therefore a violation of natural standards of morals, as limited by historical existence."[24] Giving oneself for another appears to run cross-grained to the law of self-preservation within the individual. This only increases the foolishness of suffering.

The selfless lover is often taken advantage of by the one who has not broken with mutuality. Because sin is inevitable, it is not possible for action grounded in reverence for the eternal either so to alter history that sin disappears, or to be finally understood when sin remains. The cross exhibits the fact that those who follow selfless moral commitments will themselves suffer. "The New Testament never guarantees the historical success of the 'strategy' of the Cross. Jesus warns his disciples against a too sanguine historical hope . . . Whatever the possibilities of success for *agape* in history . . . the final justification for the way of *agape* in the New Testament is never found in history. The motive to which Christ appeals is always the emulation of God or gratitude for *agape* of God."[25]

Because the temporal cannot ultimately defy its own norm, however, *agape* love may partially be justified in history.

24. *Human Destiny,* pp. 68-69.
25. *Ibid.,* pp. 87-88.

Men give provisional respect to the lover. But such respect cannot be final, since the understanding of selflessness presupposes a prior understanding of God's love.

II. The Wisdom of Foolishness

There is a wisdom in foolishness. But it can be appreciated only when the free individual is willing to examine the cross in relation to his own height and depth. "Precisely because it is such a foolishness, transcending human wisdom, it becomes, once accepted, the basis for a satisfactory total explanation of life. It becomes truly wisdom. Revelation does not remain in contradiction to human culture and human knowledge. By completing the incompleteness, clarifying the obscurities and correcting the falsifications of human knowledge it becomes true wisdom to 'them that are called.' "[26] The individual who comes to himself will know the truth of the doctrine.

A. *The Self is Explained*

The universal reaction of all who have made spiritual contact with the law which defines ideal selfhood, is what Niebuhr calls "the fall." The free self tends to engage the whole self with more obligations than can be made good within the sinful tensions of history. And in acknowledging this fall the foolishness of the cross converts to profound wisdom; for once the self understands the struggle that it has in making *agape* love good in history, it will immediately assent to the *a fortiori* that those who know not the Christ will succeed in selfless love even less. Love must suffer.

The Christian doctrine of the fall is a mythological description of a universal experience of the race. Knowing the good and performing it are two different experiences. Although man alacritously accepts the word and will of God, he immediately is "tempted by the serpent" to be equal with God "by eating of the fruit." The limits of man are set by the dialectic, and sin is the refusal of man to remain within

26. *Ibid.*, p. 67.

this tension. "Man is tempted, in other words, to break and transcend the limits which God has set for him. The temptation thus lies in his situation of finiteness and freedom."[27] The occasion of all temptation is the free spirit's seeking a security which will defy the precarious terms of its human situation; but finding none, it converts itself into a citadel of egoistic pretensions. The free spirit outruns the legitimate claims of the whole self by mistaking imagined grounds of security for those actually possessed. Anxiety over insecurity goads the self on to promote pretensions of security which are not justified. The temptation to pass beyond justifiable claims to self-sufficiency is as inevitable in our own experience as the love for self. Pretension is but self-love extending itself into self-sufficiency. It is simply a cover for a fear of actual insufficiency. The free self betrays the involved self by convincing it of its right to claim as a possession what really belongs to it only as an earnest. Riches are a partial security, but the individual is not satisfied here; the individual converts this partial security into a final security. Its trust, thus, completely outruns the evidence upon which it rests.

The individual who examines his own conduct in the light of *justitia originalis* will thus discover that, while he gives assent in his free self to the height of that rule, he never matches that perfection in his involved self with absolute conduct. In other words, he falls. The fall is localized in that moment in freedom where the free self, assenting to the law of *agape*, peers down into the empirical self and discovers selfishness. "Perfection before the Fall is, in other words, perfection before the act; but it is important not to give too narrow a connotation to the concept of 'act.' The self may act even when the action is not overt. It acts whenever, as anxious self, it thinks or moves for its own protection in the welter of perils and passions which constitutes its world."[28]

For this reason "every man is Adam." The fall is a mythological expression for what is psychologically true in

27. *Human Nature*, pp. 179-180.
28. *Ibid.*, p. 278.

each person. When we wake in the morning determined to live *agape* consistently, we find that even that very determination is compounded with egoistic impulses. Hence, we fall. Only a person in the adulthood of moral responsibility can understand and appreciate the fall, however. The fall is an inward "conflict between the *is* and the *ought* of life, between the ideal possibilities to which freedom encourages man and the drive of egoism, which reason sharpens rather than assuages."[29] The fall is a marching, moment-by-moment experience of the race. It is a contemporaneous truth, an existential truth. We fall whenever we understand both the law of the second Adam and our own personal failures as the first Adam. In our transcendent self we know the *ought* of love; in our empirical self we know the *failure* to love.

Corruptions of the fall take two different forms. Those, such as the Pelagians, who suppose that man enjoys plenary ability to fulfill all known law, dismiss the fall as an unnecessary theological pessimism. "The essential characteristic of Pelagianism is its insistence that actual sins cannot be regarded as sinful or as involving guilt if they do not proceed from a will which is essentially free. The bias toward evil, that is, that aspect of sin which is designated as 'original' in the classic doctrine is found not in man's will but in the inertia of nature. It is in other words not sin at all." Pelagians "find no real place for the myth of the Fall in their thought, though of course they seek to incorporate the Bibical story in their system."[30] Pelagianism follows the Renaissance motif. Man can work out his historical dignity without reference to the full terms defined in the second Adam. Pelagianism forgets that "the rational freedom with which man is endowed represents an ideal possibility of harmonizing the forces of nature upon a higher level than they achieve in nature. But this ideal possibility is not realized."[31]

The second corruption is on the side of those who take the fall literally as an historic, once-for-all event. "Christian

29. *Beyond Tragedy*, pp. 137-138.
30. *Human Nature*, p. 245.
31. *Beyond Tragedy*, p. 138.

theology has found it difficult to refute the rationalistic rejection of the myth of the Fall without falling into the literalistic error of insisting upon the Fall as an historical event."[32] The objections to a literal theory of the fall are precisely the same as those listed against a literal *justitia originalis* in history. They need not be repeated. Niebuhr simply feels that when interest is directed to an historical Adam away from the psychological experience of the race than each man is Adam, the result is the breaking of the dialectical relation between time and eternity. Unless each man is related to the source of his being the same as all other men, one cannot affirm that what is true at one point in the relation between time and eternity is likewise true for all others. If it is to be normative, the Christ must stand over history to challenge the first as well as the last man on earth. Whoever the first man might have been (a scientific question inconsequential for faith), he was as suspended within the tension of the dialectic as the last man will be. This is Niebuhr's way of expressing the symbol of the "sovereignty of God." Process is always related to its source with the same possibility/impossibility dialectic. The law was just as high for the first man as it is for us; and it was just as impossible for him perfectly to mediate its terms as it is for us. Degrees of achievement in history cannot modify the essential truth that none have performed the whole law. "The particular virtue of the myth of the Fall is that it does justice to the paradoxical relation of spirit and nature in human evil . . . According to the myth of the Fall, evil came into the world through human responsibility. It was neither ordained in the counsels of God nor the inevitable consequences of temporal existence."[33]

Niebuhr regards metaphysics as irrelevant for Christian faith — although it is almost unbelievable to think that the free spirit can be satisfied apart from a metaphysical ex-

32. *Human Nature,* pp. 267-268. "When the Fall is made an event in history rather than a symbol of an aspect of every historical moment in the life of man, the relation of evil to goodness in that moment is obscured." *Human Nature,* p. 269.

33. *An Interpretation of Christian Ethics,* p. 72.

pression of the relation between time and eternity. Thus the value of the doctrine of the fall is only existential and psychological. "'The metaphysical connotations of the myth of the Fall are, however, less important for our purposes than the psychological and moral ones. It is in its interpretations of the facts of human nature, rather than in its oblique insights into the relation of order and chaos as such, that the myth of the Fall makes its profoundest contribution to moral and religious theory. The most basic and fruitful conception flowing from this ancient myth is the idea that evil lies at the juncture of nature and spirit."[34]

Before leaving this matter, the evangelical would certainly wish that note be taken of the following observations:

First, Niebuhr not only adds confusion to use the term "fall" in describing this mythological insight; but he likewise exposes the limits of his own ability to coin exact words to express himself. The historic church has always defined the fall as historical. For Niebuhr to persist in using the term "fall" to express something altogether different, therefore, only subtracts from precision.

Second, the race's psychological experience of a fall does not exclude the possibility of an historic fall by Adam. No possible analysis of psychological experiences within the tension of obligation/failure yields the following proposition: There was no literal fall in history. Niebuhr is masterful in his understanding of our inward experiences; but he reasons *non sequitur* to conclude from this analysis that the non-existence of an historical fall is necessarily implied. The two may simultaneously be true.

Third, Niebuhr believes that orthodoxy's metaphysical statement of the fall results in the metaphysical embarrassment of making God the author of sin. "John Calvin is, in a sense, typical of the tendency in Christian orthodoxy, in his provisional denial of God's responsibility for sin and his final acceptance of the idea, 'Man falls, the providence of God so

34. *Ibid.*, p. 76.

ordaining.' "[35] In contrast to this the psychological explanation of the fall is supposed to localize the responsibility for evil solely in man. The existentialist says he is not obliged to pass beyond the experience of sin in the self. The question need not be related to God.

In reply to this, one can only remark that though Niebuhr may not personally care to talk about ultimate relations in metaphysical terms, those who come to the free height of their transcendent selves do. The self discovers that there *are* metaphysical relations which must be discussed. Does not existentialism even more so make God the author of evil by teaching that God sovereignly created a universe which would *necessarily* be sinful through the tension of the dialectic? Did not God deliberately create man with an evil tendency in his will? These questions may be legitimately asked of existential theology. They must be faced or the transcendent self may conclude that it has been cheated. And if the existentialist refuses to face these issues on the ground that he is not interested in such non-sanguine relations, he surely cannot blame people for rejecting Christianity. One should give himself to a *Weltanschauung* which stabilizes and satisfies the whole man — feeling, will, and intellect. "A religion based on mere feeling is the vaguest, most unreliable, most unstable of all things. A strong, stable, religious life can be built up on no other ground than that of intelligent conviction. Christianity, therefore, addresses itself to the intelligence as well as to the heart. It sounds plausible indeed to say, Let us avoid all doctrinal subtleties; let us keep to a few plain, easy, simple propositions, in regard to which there will be general agreement. But, unfortunately, men *will* think on those deep problems which lie at the root of religious belief — on the nature of God, His character, His relations to the world and men, sin, the means of deliverance from it, the end to which things are moving, — *and if Christianity does not give them an answer,*

35. *An Interpretation of Christian Ethics*, p. 74.

suited to their deeper and more reflective moods, they will simply put it aside as inadequate for their needs."[36]

Fourth, the deep-down reason why Niebuhr cannot accept the doctrine of a real Adam in history is not that the logic of existentialism compels him, but rather that he unconsciously assumes the truth of his liberal presupposition that science and higher criticism have destroyed our right intelligently to believe the Bibical documents as historically accurate. It never occurs to Niebuhr that this obsequious devotion to science may itself be part of an unwarranted liberal optimism which has trailed along in our bourgeois culture. Niebuhr understands quite well how all men judge from their own perspectives and from within their own presuppositions, but he does not seem to consider the possibility that he himself judges both the Bible and the orthodox doctrine of the fall on the ground of presuppositions imbedded into his thinking while a liberal studying at Yale. It is surely a mystery why Niebuhr bows so respectfully before science whenever Biblical history and metaphysics are in question, but then recoils with profound shock when science seeks to negate the validity of the existential myth.

Before leaving this topic, it is well to summarize the exact way in which the foolishness of the cross contains a wisdom to all who have faith. At first blush it appears foolish that Christ should reveal a wisdom which *ex hypothesi* cannot enjoy final concretion within history. But this foolishness becomes a profundity when one realizes the way in which he himself likewise gives assent to an ultimate which history cannot contain. While we pray to be selfless in our love, we find that even that request itself is vitiated by our pride over being willing to be selfless. If we ourselves cannot be converted by the doctrine of *agape,* can we realistically expect that a token living of *agape* will convert the world? We cannot deny the truth of our *duty* in love; but we cannot likewise deny the truth of our *fall* from love.

36. James Orr, *The Christian View of God and the World,* (Grand Rapids, Eerdmans, 1947), pp. 20-21. (Italics mine.)

The depth to which a man descends in grief is proportioned to the height to which he ascends in freedom. Both the righteous and the unrighteous pass through the experience of the fall; but whereas the righteous understand their declension *coram deo,* the unrighteous know only the loss of personal security in history. The "sorrow of the world" and "'godly sorrow" are not identical. The one is sorrow within immediacy and the other is guilt before God. Genuine repentance comes only when the individual first knows God. "All experiences of an uneasy conscience, of remorse and of repentance, are therefore religious experiences, though they are not always explicitly or consciously religious. Experiences of repentance, in distinction to remorse, presuppose some knowledge of God. They may not be consciously related to Biblical revelation but yet they do presuppose some, at least dim, awareness of God as redeemer as well as God as judge. For without the knowledge of divine love remorse cannot be transmuted into repentance. If man recognizes only judgment and knows only that his sin is discovered, he cannot rise above the despair of remorse to the hope of repentance."[37]

B. *History's Possibilities are Explained.*

Because the cross was preceded by a remarkably consistent life of selfless love, its foolishness suddenly converts into a realistic explanation of the relation between possibility and fulfillment in history.

First, "Sacrificial love (*agape*) completes the incompleteness of mutual love (*eros*), for the latter is always arrested by reason of the fact that it seeks to relate life to life from the standpoint of the self and for the sake of the self's own happiness."[38] When a man comes to himself he realizes the heights of his spiritual possibilities. Being capable of *agape,* he instinctively assents to *agape.* He knows that he is more faithful to himself when he passes from mutual to selfless love. Conscience tells him that only in and through selflessness can he

37. *Human Nature,* p. 257.
38. *Human Destiny,* p. 82.

find true security. The self can always discover a residue of pride and self-love in all its moral expressions. Therefore, it is always subject to improvement through *agape*. "There are no limits to be set in history for the achievement of more universal brotherhood, for the development of more perfect and more inclusive mutual relations."[39]

Second, "The Cross represents a transcendent perfection which clarifies obscurities of history and defines the limits of what is possible in historic development."[40] When a man sees only Jesus' life, forgetting that such a life had to suffer in history, he is always tempted to conclude that the fufillment of history's transcendent norm is a simple possibility. One need merely employ the proper strategy and the world will be saved. "This error runs through the thought of most sectarian versions of Christianity and through the secularized forms of Christianity in the Renaissance and the Enlightenment. It is an error to which American liberal Protestantism has been particularly prone because sectarian and secular perfectionism have been compounded in this form of the Christian faith. Marxist apocalypticism also shares in this error. Whether by sanctifying grace (as in sectarian interpretations) or by the cumulative force of universal education (as in secular liberalism) or by a catastrophic reorganization of society (as in Marxism), it is believed possible to lift historic life to the plane upon which all distinctions between mutual love and disinterested and sacrificing love vanish."[41] The optimist errs, not knowing the inevitability of sin in freedom. He does not perceive how some residue of anxiety goes before every act. He does not sense how greatly the element of personal interest threads through all his supposed selflessness.

There is wisdom in the defeat of love on the cross because it is symbolic of the defeat which the Christian can expect. He is already briefed on the tragic side of history, and thus is neither upset nor discouraged when history does not vindicate

39. *Ibid.*, p. 85.
40. *Ibid.*, p. 86.
41. *Ibid.*

his efforts. "The *agape,* the sacrificial love, which is for Christian faith revealed upon the Cross, has its primary justification in an 'essential reality' which transcends the realities of history, namely, the character of God. It does not expect an immediate or historical validation but looks towards some ultimate consummation of life and history."[42]

Third, "The Cross represents a perfection which contradicts the false pretensions of virtue in history and which reveals the contrast between man's sinful self-assertion and the divine *agape.*"[43] The assertiveness of egotism is exhibited in all forms of remedial justice in history, for it is not possible for one to stand in judgment over another without unconsciously relating the question to the issue of his own security. The powers which rally to preserve society from anarchy are always informed by egoistic assertiveness, the will to live, and partiality. The contrast between the perfection of divine *agape* and the mixed motives in human love will remain until the end of time. *Agape* as *telos* corrects and interprets history through to its *finis.* "As freedom develops, both good and evil develop with it. The innocent state of trust develops into the anxieties and fears of freedom; and these prompt the individual and the community to seek an unjust security at the expense of others. On the other hand it is possible that the same freedom may prompt larger and larger structures of brotherhood in human society."[44] History can justify the norm of love only as a norm; it cannot absorb it as a reality.

Niebuhr gives a succinct summary of the conversion of foolishness to wisdom as follows: "In the realm of ethics as in the realm of truth, the revelation of Christ is foolishness, in the sense that experience does not lead us to expect or anticipate the answer which it makes to the ethical problem. But it is 'wisdom to them that are called' in the sense that, once accepted, it becomes an adequate principle for interpreting the ethical problem in history. It is the only principle of interpretation

42. *Ibid.*, p. 96.
43. *Ibid.*, p. 89.
44. *Ibid.*, p. 95.

which does justice to the two factors in the human situation: Man's involvement in natural process, including the imperative character of his natural impulse of survival; and his transcendence over natural process, including his uneasy conscience over the fact that the survival impulse should play so dominant a role in all his ethical calculations."[45]

C. *The Triumph of the Eternal.*

Faith is able to perceive in the cross the grounds for accepting the validity of all those Christian symbols which express the eternal triumph of the *agape* ideal on the one hand, and the chronic defiance of that ideal in the historical process, on the other. Without the cross the symbols which express valid insights into the relation between time and eternity remain groundless.

1. *The second coming of Christ.* The temporal end of history is *finis*. The normative end is *telos*. *Telos* sums up all that we mean when we say that history has a purpose or goal. Christ, the wisdom of God, is the *telos* of history. Selfless love expresses the purposive end of history. It is the norm to which history is responsible, and it is the expression of the way that God himself will sovereignly solve the problems raised by history's defiance of that norm. "This double connotation of end as both *finis* and *telos* expresses, in a sense, the whole character of human history and reveals the fundamental problem of human existence. All things in history move towards both fulfillment and dissolution, towards the fuller embodiment of their essential character and towards death."[46]

In the collision between *telos* and *finis,* it seems at times from within the historical process that the purpose of history will be frustrated by the dissolution of history. The individual is cut off before he comes to the full flower of *agape*. Nations rise and fall.

45. *Human Destiny,* p. 97.
46. *Ibid.,* p. 287.

The sinful solution to this precariousness is to inject false eternals into history, making pretensions which are unwarranted by the facts. Christian faith solves the problem by the belief that Christ came to reveal both the meaning of history and the sovereign way that God will vindicate *agape* at the end of history by taking our sins into and upon himself.

The *parousia,* or second coming of Christ, is the symbolic way faith declares its assurance that Christ, who has already overcome the world, as *telos,* will assuredly achieve that triumph at the *finis* of history. *Telos* will never be overthrown by *finis*. The dialectical tension of history is, symbolically, an interim "between the disclosure and the fulfillment" of history. The first coming — Christ after the flesh — is the disclosure, and the second coming is the fulfillment. "To believe that the suffering Messiah will return at the end of history as a triumphant judge and redeemer is to express the faith that existence cannot ultimately defy its own norm. Love may have to live in history as suffering love because the power of sin makes a simple triumph of love impossible. But if this were the ultimate situation it would be necessary either to worship the power of sin as the final power in the world or to regard it as a kind of second God, not able to triumph, but also strong enough to avoid defeat."[47] Faith believes that God is sovereign to make good both the revelation and the triumph of love.

Niebuhr disagrees both with those who dismiss the idea of the second coming with the scorn that it is simply prescientific fancy, on the one hand, and the literalists who believe that a living Christ will personally appear in the clouds with power and great glory to redeem the historical process, on the other. *The second coming is simply a mythical symbol.* It is an expression of faith that those who are devoted to *agape* are on the right side in conflicts of life.

The locus of the second coming, therefore, is both in and out of history. It is in history whenever selfless love enjoys vindication, and it is out of history wherever history needs eternity for its fulfillment. This double significance provides

47. *Human Destiny,* p. 290.

Niebuhr with an opportunity to review a theme which is woven skillfully into every major book he has written: "Against utopianism the Christian faith insists that the final consummation of history lies beyond the conditions of the temporal process. Against other-worldliness it asserts that the consummation fulfills rather than negates, the historical process. There is no way of expressing this dialectical concept without running the danger of its dissolution."[48] If history did not give tokens of love's triumph, the ideal would be irrelevant; but if history absorbed the ideal, *agape* would not be an absolute.

In evaluating this — and all the other *eschatological* symbols espoused by Niebuhr — one cannot but repeat the charge that greater accuracy would have been achieved if historic Christian terms had not been used to express the symbols. The church universal has always believed that the Son of God as a Person would sovereignly come at the end of history. When Niebuhr uses this term, "the second coming," but means to express the thought that the abstract norm of history will finally triumph, he only increases misunderstanding and confusion.

2. *The resurrection of the body.* In his student days Niebuhr abandoned the doctrine of a physical resurrection of the body as scientifically stupid. He has had no occasion to recant that decision. But he has seriously rethought the validity of that doctrine as a *symbol* of Christian faith. Sensing that the tension of the dialectic would be severed the moment it made no difference in the judgment how men conducted themselves here on earth, he quickly reinstated the hope of the resurrection as a valid dialectical symbol. The hope of the resurrection "embodies the very genius of the Christian idea of the historical. On the one hand it implies that eternity will fulfill and not annul the richness and variety which the temporal process has elaborated. On the other it implies that the condition of finiteness and freedom, which lies at the basis of historical existence, is a problem for which there is no solution by human power. Only God can solve this problem."[49] One

48. *Ibid.*, p. 291.
49. *Ibid.*, p. 295.

can perceive by this that the symbols of the second coming, the resurrection, and the final judgment lie so close to one another that their difference is only one of perspective.

To believe that the graves will open and men will literally be raised (as the Bible teaches with unmistakable clarity) is, to Niebuhr, literalistic nonsense. Without the slightest effort to validate this rejection of a bodily resurrection, Niebuhr dismisses it almost with ridicule. One might be tempted to dismiss his own existential solution as nonsense, too, but that course of action would hardly support the *agape* rule that one do by others as he would that they do by him. "Why is it thought incredible by any of you that God raises the dead?" (Acts 26:8).

The body is the symbol "of the contribution which nature makes to human individuality and to all historical realizations."[50] Since "the eternal is the ground and source of the temporal,"[51] it follows that there is partial continuity between these spheres. The movement of the present process of history, therefore, is meaningfully related to its end as *telos*. What man does in history makes a difference in eternity. "The doctrine of the resurrection of the body implies that eternal significance belongs to the whole unity of an historical realization in so far as it has brought all particularities into the harmony of the whole. Consummation is thus conceived not as absorption into the divine but as loving fellowship with God."[52] Historical differences are not ultimate, however, for Christ shows all men in final judgment to be unrighteous. Niebuhr does not believe in the *final* separation of the righteous and the unrighteous on the grounds of the imputed righteousness of Christ. God is provisionally justified in making a relative distinction between the righteous and the unrighteous. But this distinction is ultimately done away with when we are "clothed upon" by God.

---

50. *Human Destiny*, p. 296.
51. *Ibid.*, p. 299
52. *Ibid.*, pp. 296-297

At this point the inconsistency of Niebuhr again shows itself. He is exemplary in his humility when he deals with the details of his own existential eschatology, for "it is not possible to give a fuller or more plausible account of what is implied in the Christian hope of the fulfillment of life; and it is well to remember that the conditions of finiteness make a more explicit definition of the consummation impossible."[53] But when he negates the details of other possible eschatologies — such as those of Jesus and Paul who thought that the body would literally be raised — he pontificates *ex cathedra.* Heaven is his witness that the body cannot possibly be raised from the dead. Science teaches that. When existentially discussing what the future *may* hold, Niebuhr whispers in a modest tone; but when discussing what the future positively *cannot* hold, he speaks mouth to mouth. A radical empiricist ought to leave all possibilities open.

3. *The antichrist.* With amazing skill Niebuhr converts even the doctrine of the antichrist into an existential symbol. Because eternity remains both continuously and discontinuously related to time at all points within history, it follows that moral growth and opposition to moral growth will likewise contend together to the end of time. Evil frustrates pure good at all times.

Some symbol is needed by faith as a rallying point for this insight. "The New Testament symbol for this aspect of historical reality, this new peril of evil on every new level of the good, is the figure of the Antichrist. The Antichrist belongs to the *eschata,* to the 'last things' which herald the end of history. The most explicit denial of the norm of history must be expected in the most ultimate development of history."[54]

The literalists, again, are guilty of corrupting the symbol by believing that the antichrist is localized in a person. "The inclination of contemporary millenarian literalism to identify some current embodiment of evil with Antichrist, corresponds

53. *Human Destiny,* p. 298.
54. *Ibid.,* p. 316.

to a recurrent tendency in all apocalypses."[55] The liberals corrupt the symbol by seeing no validity in it at all. They do not understand the way in which history will defy its own norm until the end.

The antichrist is present wherever the Christ is resisted. The *righteous* are antichrist when they pretend to be righteous — for the final judgment of Christ finds none righteous. The *unrighteous* are antichrist when they deny that there is a Christ — for eternity is the valid norm of history. Antichrist is as ubiquitous as sin and as variegated as sinfulness.

When once the antichrist is confessed by faith, it may be seen that history can move its own problems to new levels but it cannot solve them. The reason for this failure is that there can be no freedom to create without a freedom to destroy. Evil is serious. Evil is chronic in history.

It is well to notice the locus of the defeat of the antichrist, therefore. Man can only reduce the relative power of antichrist. Only the norm of history can finally destroy the antichrist. Thus, while the "Antichrist stands at the end of history to indicate that history culminates, rather than solves, the essential problems of human existence,"[56] the same "Antichrist who appears at the end of history can be defeated only by the Christ who ends history."[57] The *telos* destroys the defiances against itself which have marched through history within the terms of the dialectic.

In summary: the cross exhibits a judgment about the relation between time and eternity which on the surface appears to be foolishness; but the more sensitively a person meditates upon Christ's death, the more its foolishness is displaced by a satisfying wisdom. It is initially painful to learn that we are responsible for doing what we know we cannot do: but there is a comfort in learning that the rule we embrace in faith is part of the plan by which God himself will solve history's contradiction. Faith gains a confidence in God which in turn gives

55. *Ibid.*, p. 317.
56. *Ibid.*, p. 318.
57. *Ibid.*, p. 319.

it a confidence in history. "By its confidence in an eternal ground of existence which is, nevertheless, involved in man's historical striving to the very point of suffering with and for him, this faith can prompt men to accept their historical responsibilities gladly. From the standpoint of such a faith history is not meaningless because it cannot complete itself; though it cannot be denied that it is tragic because men always seek prematurely to complete it."[58]

---

58. *Ibid.*, p. 321.

VII

Synthesis: The Power of the Cross

IN 1938 Niebuhr released a series of essays under the title, *Beyond Tragedy*. The title is not only striking in its own rights, but it also points in a unique way to the synthesis of the cross. The same cross which reveals the tragedy of love in history likewise has a message which is *beyond* tragedy.

I. The Final Problem of the Cross

An analysis of the Christian world view reveals that man must remain tensionally suspended within the dialectical contrarieties of finity and infinity, history and eternity, sinful, inward impulses and the rule of *justicia originalis.* Neither side of the tension may be relaxed in favor of the other or the dialectic is broken.

But is this tension the final word? The thesis of the cross is the rule of life, and the antithesis the fact that history cannot bear the fulfillment of that rule; but is there no synthesis? Is man consigned to remain suspended within this tension, guilty when he performs and guilty when he fails to perform?

It now becomes clear that apart from the gift of God's grace, man, who remains but a creature of dust and not an angelic being having powers commensurate with a heavenly office, will simply collapse from despair. Initiative vanishes whenever the free spirit finds itself confronted with futility. Man cannot continue striving for what is known in advance must terminate in historical defeat.

This is the final problem of the cross. How can man sustain interest in a goal which is defined in advance as unattainable? Until the thesis and antithesis of the cross are sublimated in a synthesis, the dialectic will once again be destroyed. Since the task of fulfilling *agape* involves a goal which is beyond human possibility, man must have a power beyond himself to labor toward that goal.

The answer of the cross, however, is steady. Christ is the revelation of the *grace* as well as the truth of God. Truth stands for the "mind of God," the plan God has for both history and man. Grace "stands for powers and possibilities beyond all human possibilities."[1] The moment a person assumes the posture of repentance before God and confesses helplessness in the inward man, that instant God injects power into his heart. These resources are at once recognized as vitalities which have come from beyond man. By grace man is given powers which outrun his Renaissance possibilities.

Christian faith denies that the individual is deprived of the moral undergirding needed to remain content within the tensions of the dialectic. Positive graces are supplied to afford man contentment in his commitments. As by grace God takes sin into and upon Himself, so by grace He empowers man to be faithful to a rule which cannot vindicate itself within history. The Great Physician is no less engaged in providing the balm of healing for the sinful than in initially exposing the diseased tissue itself.

There are two types of grace. The first is the mercy of God whereby the individual, being forgiven of his sins, is given faith and hope for a new life in Christ. This is grace unto forgiveness, or justification. Until the individual is assured that his past sins and shortcomings do not irretrievably condemn him, he cannot even begin a serious walk with Christ. The other type of grace is power which God implants in the justified heart to insure a successful walk of faith subsequent to cleansing. It is not sufficient for one simply to have a clean start in life. Justification must always be fortified with power to prevent past defeat from leading to future defeat. This is grace unto sanctification. Justification is grace *unto* man, while sanctification is grace *in* man. "Grace represents

1. *Human Destiny*, p. 208.

on the one hand the mercy and forgiveness of God by which He completes what man cannot complete and overcomes the sinful elements in all of man's achievements. Grace is the power of God over man. Grace is on the other hand the power of God in man; it represents an accession of resources, which man does not have of himself, enabling him to become what he truly ought to be."[2] Justification clears a man with God's wrath, releasing and settling him to commence a life of serious holiness. Justification supplies man with a "new nature." Sanctification releases a flow of grace to empower one to complete heights of *agape* normally impossible on one's own strength.

The working of grace unto and in man is a dialectical counterpart in the individual to the generic way God is related to the process itself. God justifies history whenever history pledges to accept *agape* as the rule of life; while history waits for sanctification graces at every moment through its refusal fully to complete itself through such pledges. In like manner the individual is completed and fulfilled in the moment of justification, while he waits at every moment to be fulfilled as he grows in sanctification. "The idea of 'power' and 'grace' in Christian thought is ambiguous. On the one hand the believer is regarded as capable of fulfilling life as it has been disclosed to him. On the other hand he remains in both the finiteness of history and in the corruption of sin. The 'grace' of God is on the one hand a power of God in man which completes his incompleteness. It is on the other hand the merciful power of God over man, whereby sin is overcome by God's mercy, but not by human goodness. The fulfillment of history, according to Christian faith, has two facets. According to the one there is fulfillment in every moment in which man establishes relation to God in contrition and faith. According to the other, life waits for its fulfillment and 'we are saved by hope.' "[3]

---

2. *Human Destiny*, pp. 98-99.
3. *Ibid.*, pp. 61-62.

II. *Pro Nobis* and *In Nobis*

Through the device of an existential exegesis of Galatians 2:20, Niebuhr covers the entire sweep of the experience of grace as mercy towards, and power in, man.

A. *I am Crucified with Christ: Conversion.*

Grace is relevant only as one antecedently recognizes his own impotency. Justification enters only that heart which has been broken by seeing the impossibility of fulfilling what it acknowledges as the law of its life. When once man perceives the contradiction of being responsible for more than the self can make good, he is in a position to plead the grace of God. Conversion must precede justification. "The plight of the self is that it cannot do the good that it intends. The self in action seems impotent to conform its actions to the requirements of its essential being, as seen by the self in contemplation. The self is so created in freedom that it cannot realize itself within itself. It can only realize itself in loving relation to its fellows. Love is the law of its being. But in practice it is always betrayed into self-love."[4] The self can find a release from this moral dilemma only when there is a "crucifixion" of the self through conversion. One must confess that there is no salvation apart from the intrusion of God into the life with new power. The self "cannot be saved merely by being enlightened. It is a unity and therefore cannot be drawn out of itself merely by extending its perspective upon interests beyond itself. If it remains self-centred, it merely uses its wider perspective to bring more lives and interests under the dominion of its will-to-power."[5]

Conversion is an unknown experience in Renaissance optimism, for a crucifixion of the ego is always postponed under the pretense that the ego has yet limitless possibilities of self-development. The Renaissance mind always fondly imagines that the deficiency in man is but a want of resolution and determination, never of resident power. A more consistent application of our own native resources will solve our problems.

4. *Human Destiny,* p. 108.
5. *Ibid.,* p. 109.

"One school holds that men would be good if only political institutions would not corrupt them; another believes that they would be good if the prior evil of a faulty economic organization could be eliminated. Or another school thinks of this evil as no more than ignorance, and therefore waits for a more perfect educational process to redeem man from his partial and particular loyalties. But no school asks how it is that an essentially good man could have produced corrupting and tyrannical political organizations or exploiting economic organizations, or fanatical and superstitious religious organizations."[6] Modern scientific advances have served to augment the pretensions of Renaissance optimism. A triumph of the law of life in history is confidently expected. But this optimism is supported only through an oversight of the fact that "every heightened potency of human existence may also represent a possibility of evil."[7]

Man must come to himself and understand that it is no easy thing to fulfill the law of existence. The self must be shattered by the Christ at the very root of its pretensions. "The self is shattered whenever it is confronted by the power and holiness of God and becomes genuinely conscious of the real source and centre of all life."[8]

One must guard against concluding that Niebuhr has reference to that type of conversion experience where, in a once-for-all religious crisis, one "hits the sawdust trail." On the contrary, "existential conversion" is theoretically as repetitious in the individual as the experience of the "fall" itself. Man can be shattered as often as he renews contact with the power and holiness of God over against him. If the individual were to have once-for-all conversion experience, he would be, in the words of Karl Barth, a "blessed possessor." The dialectic is broken if the conversion experience is not kept as much a marching truth within history as the experience of falling. "The shattering of the self is a perennial process and occurs in every

6. *The Children of Light and the Children of Darkness*, p. 17.
7. *Human Destiny*, p. 166.
8. *Ibid.*, p. 109.

spiritual experience in which the self is confronted with the claims of God, and becomes conscious of its sinful, self-centred state."[9] The departure of Niebuhr from historic Christianity is evident. The classic Reformers taught with singleness of mind that conversion was a unique experience in man and was not repeated.

Niebuhr likewise departs from the Biblical doctrine that there is a necessary relation between Jesus of history and conversion. The Bible gives no encouragement that men may have hope apart from the historical Christ. "If you confess with your lips that Jesus is Lord and believe in your heart that God raised him from the dead, you will be saved." (Romans 10:9) The antecedent here is clearly Jesus of history. Niebuhr, however, faithful to his controlling presupposition that eternity and time are dialectically related, contends that only the abstract "Christ," and not "Jesus after the flesh," is needed for conversion. "While Christians rightly believe that all truth necessary for such a spiritual experience is mediated only through the revelation in Christ, they must guard against the assumption that only those who know Christ 'after the flesh,' that is, in the actual historical revelation, are capable of such a conversion. A 'hidden Christ' operates in history. And there is always the possibility that those who do not know the historical revelation may achieve a more genuine repentance and humility than those who do. If this is not kept in mind the Christian faith easily becomes a new vehicle of pride."[10]

The "hidden Christ" is another existential symbol for the complex way God has informed history with the rule of *justicia originalis*. Men are converted by the Christ in whatever way they may come to understand Christ. The mechanics of conversion are irrelevant.

B. *Nevertheless I Live*: *Justification.*

Justification, the "assurance of divine forgiveness,"[11] follows immediately upon the experience of conversion. It is a feeling

9. *Human Destiny*, p. 109, footnote 5.
10. *Ibid.*, pp. 109-110, footnote 6.
11. *Ibid.*, p. 103.

in the heart that the ego which has been shattered is now cleansed and forgiven.

One of the barriers to understanding Niebuhr at this point is his repeated employment of Biblical terminology, when what he means is an existential experience and not a literal transferal to the individual of a righteousness purchased by the blood of Jesus Christ. The language used both by orthodoxy and by Niebuhr to express justification is remarkably similar. Orthodoxy expresses itself as follows: "Justification is an act of God's free grace, wherein he pardons all our sins, and accepts us as righteous in his sight, only for the righteousness of Christ imputed to us, and received by faith alone."[12] Niebuhr expresses himself thus: "The final peace of the soul is gained on the one hand by the assurance of divine forgiveness; and on the other by 'faith.' The Christ who is apprehended by faith, *i.e.* to whom the soul is obedient in principle, 'imputes' his righteousness to it."[13] But the most remarkable feature of this similarity of language is that diametrically different conceptions are being conveyed. Orthodoxy follows a realistic Biblical pattern, concluding that justification is a forensic, judicial act upon the part of God the Father whereby the righteousness of Christ, earned in the Messianic office, is applied to the account of all who put their trust in His substitutionary atonement as a full payment for sins. When God the Father imputes the righteousness of His Son unto believers, therefore, an actual corpus of righteousness is put to the sinner's account. The perfection was earned step by step through the obedience of Jesus Christ, the Messiah. Niebuhr, however, means that after the heart morally contacts the law of life, it feels a consequent release. The ego is at peace. This peace is a proof that God has accepted man's intention to live righteously as the *act* itself. No literal body of righteousness is imputed to the sinner, for Jesus Christ, being a sinner Himself, stood in need of righteousness.

---

12. *Westminster Shorter Catechism,* Answer 33.
13. *Human Destiny,* p. 103.

Existential justification is not a forensic, judicial relationship of God to man, therefore. Justification is a feeling in the heart of a forgiveness which could not have come as a result of one's own merit. "The Christian experience of the new life is an experience of a new selfhood. The new self is more truly a real self because the vicious circle of self-centeredness has been broken. The self lives in and for others, in the general orientation of loyalty to, and love of, God; who alone can do justice to the freedom of the self over all partial interests and values. This new self is the real self; for the self is infinitely self-transcendent; and any premature centering of itself around its own interests, individually or collectively, destroys and corrupts its freedom."[14]

The power which displaces self-love in this "new birth" is the "Holy Spirit." "The Holy Spirit is the spirit of God indwelling in man."[15] One knows that it is the spirit of God, and not an extension of his own powers which overtakes him, because this spiritual power is greater than the self in its empirical reality and yet comprehensive enough to satisfy the transcendent self in its ultimate freedom. The Holy Spirit is *essentially* related to *agape*. All other forms of power are "demons." Whoever permits himself to be overtaken by a spirit less than the definition of *agape's* full height is "demon possessed." All expressions of egotism are manifestations of demon possession. But "the most striking, contemporary form of it is a religious nationalism in which race and nation assume the eminence of God and demand unconditioned devotion. This absolute claim for something which is not absolute identifies the possessing spirit as 'demonic'; for it is the nature of demons to make pretensions of divinity . . . The invasion and possession of the self by spirit, which is not the Holy Spirit, produces a spurious sense of transfiguration."[16] The demons are not ontological entities. They are simply existential symbols for the fact that, since "human life is actually subject to

14. *Human Destiny,* p. 110.
15. *Ibid.,* p. 99.
16. *Ibid.,* p. 111.

power and not merely to mind,"[17] the human spirit may be devoted to a power which claims more absoluteness than it has a right to. When once one makes the mistake of reifying the demons (as did Jesus Christ), he then converts a profound experiential truth into poor science.

The symbol of imputed righteousness takes its place beside all other Christian symbols. It must be dialectically understood. It is corrupted, therefore, both by a simple moral philosophy which is unable to comprehend how one may have a moral credit imputed to him which he has failed to earn, and by the literalists who formulate the doctrine "in juridicial and legalistic terms in such a way that it never conveys the religious truth which strikes man in the very centre of his spiritual being."[18] Justification is a feeling in the free self of a spiritual relief following upon the occasion of conversion and repentance. This relief cannot be accounted for on the ground that one has merited release himself, for he remains a sinner; therefore, it must be the imputed righteousness of Christ. God accepts the intention to live according to the rule of Christ as the very act itself. The possession is always a righteousness *by faith.* "It is not an actual possession except 'by faith.' "[19] Man is free from guilt "in principle" only, never "in fact." Our sinful nature remains, although we feel that we are sinless. If man were constituted perfect through infused righteousness, then the dialectic would be spoiled by history's containing its own ideal. "It is not easy to express these two aspects of the life of grace, to which all history attests without seeming to offend the canons of logic. That is one reason why moralists have always found it rather easy to discount the doctrine of 'justification by faith.' But here, as in many cases, a seeming defiance of logic is merely the consequence of an effort to express complex facts of experience. It happens to be true to the fact of experience that in one sense the converted man is righteous and that in another sense he is not."[20]

17. *Ibid.*
18. *Ibid.*, p. 104.
19. *Ibid.*. p. 103.
20. *Ibid.*, pp. 124-125.

Justification is to be understood solely from the perspective of the existing, experiencing individual, not from the vantage point of an *a priori* theological system. Logically, justification may be a "foolishness"; while experientially, it is a "wisdom." It is foolishness "in prospect and wisdom only in retrospect."[21]

Some charge that justification by faith cuts the nerve of moral striving. Niebuhr skillfully engages such an objection by showing that *without* this doctrine, striving is enervated; for either one despairs of attaining, or he prematurely claims to have attained. In either case the real nerve of moral enthusiasm has been cut. "To understand that Christ in us is not a possession but a hope, that perfection is not a reality but an intention; that such peace as we know in this life is never purely the peace of achievement but the serenity of being 'completely known and all forgiven'; all this does not destroy moral ardour or responsibility. On the contrary it is the only way of preventing premature completions of life, or arresting the new and more terrible pride which may find its roots in the soil of humility, and of saving the Christian life from the intolerable pretension of saints who have forgotten that they are sinners."[22] Possessing righteousness by faith, man is preserved from despairing; while at the same time realizing that this righteousness is no more than a possession by intention, man is saved from pride.

Justification does not injure the unity of the self. In contrast to mystical absorptions of the individual into the Absolute, justification completes, but does not destroy, the person. It is the *I* which nevertheless lives. The self which is justified is the same self which is shattered in conversion.

Before examining the doctrine of grace unto sanctification, it is in order to indicate some essential reasons why evangelical Christians remain unpersuaded by Niebuhr's construction. Evangelical thought admits that, for the most part, Niebuhr is *formally* right in his description of the experience of jus-

21. *Ibid.*, p. 121.
22. *Ibid.*, pp. 125-126.

tification from the perspective of the existing individual. It simply happens to be true in Christian experience that one feels an inward release through justification. And this feeling supports the seemingly incompatible experiences of being freed from the law on the one hand, while yet being obliged to fulfill the law on the other. It would be difficult to improve formally on Niebuhr's description of justification from this perspective. Justification does not *constitute* a person righteous.

What the evangelical seriously questions, however, is whether feeling apart from metaphysics can completely satisfy the transcendent self. Niebuhr has no metaphysical grounding for his feeling theology. The scriptures, while fully detailing the exhilaration of the release which attends forensic justification, nevertheless move on to anchor this feeling in an objective structure of divine-human relations. The Biblical doctrine of justification is set squarely within the framework of the covenant of grace. The Father, accepting the Messianic work of the Son as fulfilling all righteousness, imputes to the account of the penitent believer a release from the penalty of law. The act of justifying sinners is Biblically explained as a forensic, judicial act upon the part of God, not simply the inward feeling of a release accompanying the confession of an abstract rule of *agape* as the law of one's life. Niebuhr is unable to pass beyond a feeling theology, however, because he has no adequate understanding of the Messianic office of the ontological Son of God in history. According to the dialectic structure, Jesus Himself needs the righteousness of Christ as does any other man. How could Jesus' Messianic office be the basis of a genuine imputation of righteousness therefore?

But is not feeling an extremely precarious epistemology? How is it possible for the existing individual to test feeling for error? How does one know for certain that he is not being deluded when he thinks he is justified? Why may not the actual cause of his feeling be Descartes' omnipotent demon? Perhaps this demon delights in fooling him. How can one even be certain that what he feels is actually the *Holy Spirit* overtaking him and not simply an expression of his own powers which has escaped his notice up to date? Has science come to comprehensive knowledge on the question of what constitutes the full expression of man's resoures? In a feeling theology the ubiquitous specter of the problem of error hovers near. If ignorant people can persuade themselves that they are very well informed, and if ill-dressed people can convince themselves that they are socially decorous, what is to prevent man from self-deception that he is justified? Are our feelings suddenly exempt from error when they turn to the pious work of *agape?*

The reply of existentialism is that "the experience of the race" presents a uniform pattern which is not subject to the problems of individual experience. Drugs may soothe the race for a while, but here is a phenomenon which outruns time. The race has found justification true.

One can only inquire, however, what is this mythical "race?" When did it live? Where did it live? Texts on anthropology list no race of people whose distinguishing characteristic is that they, over against others, have had an experience of justification. The simple fact is that there is no race of this kind.

If Niebuhr has reference to the Christian church, is it accurate to call so variegated and widely distributed a body of people "a race?" Futhermore, far from presenting a solid front on the question of justification by faith, the Christian church itself is divided on this issue. Niebuhr charges that Roman Catholic concepts of justification break the dialectic. Luther was overbalanced. Calvin did not fully understand the doctrine of *agape*. The sectarian movements corrupt justification by their perfectionism. Who, then, is left to form this mythical "race?" Where is this solid testimony of mankind that justification by faith is true? The specter of the problem of error remains.

Once more the unsatisfying side of Niebuhrian existentialism protrudes. All that the existing individual has to rest his everlasting salvation on are the following: (a) The simple phrase, "God takes our sins into and upon himself"; (b) A feeling of release the moment one acknowledges *agape* as the rule of life; (c) The "experience of the race." Exactly how, however, and in precisely what way, is the death of Christ on the cross a proof that God takes our sins into and upon Himself? The symbol of the cross is not that unambiguous. Why may it not just as plausibly be a symbol for the somber fact that each man must suffer for his own sins, even as Christ Himself hung on the tree? Why is it not a symbol of hell to come? Why is the symbol of vicarious suffering so compelling?

Another point: Since the "hidden Christ" will serve quite as well as the basis of the dialectic — for the historical Jesus is not always needed to bring men to salvation — why is it necessary that the dialectical framework be *Christian?* Will not a "hidden Christ" in Socrates do? Socrates reveals Christ whenever he performs works of *agape*. The "latent church" or "race" is the totality of Socratic witnesses in all generations — including those not knowing Socrates "after the flesh" who yet follow the Christ. "The cross" is the hemlock. The "wisdom of the cross" is the insight that *agape* is the true Christ — *agape* exhausts our free heights. The "foolishness of the cross" is the warning of the hemlock that love cannot be vindicated in history, but waits for its completeness in eternity. The "synthesis of the cross" is the feeling of release and satisfaction which attends submission to the Socratic insight into *agape* (conversion and justification).

Niebuhr has so emasculated the Biblical witness in his penchant for the dialectic, that Christianity is robbed of its uniqueness. The only difference between Jesus and a Gandhi is quantitative consistency. But faith need be concerned only with the symbol of *agape* in either Jesus or Gandhi. The dialectic is so accommodating a frame of reference that it serves to justify not only the *agape* life of Jesus but also all others in which the least deed of selflessness is performed.

If God has actually deposited a trustworthy revelation of Himself in Holy Scripture, then one is forced to the conclusion that existentialism may be encouraging a feeling of complacency which men have yet no right to claim. The Bible nowhere teaches that God will automatically take sins into and upon Himself as a blanket, gratuitous act of mercy for all men, thus completing history. The picture in Scripture is more complex and more awful. There is a very definite condition which the heart must meet before it may claim justification. That condition is personal faith in the atoning work of the sinless Messiah, Jesus Christ. Jesus Christ as the ontological God-man on the cross poured out His blood as a vicarious payment for the sins of all who put their personal trust in Him. Biblical faith terminates upon the person of Jesus Christ, not upon an abstract "Christ" which is the rule of our life. Salvation comes only when one trusts Jesus Christ for what He personally did on the cross for men. His blood was a literal payment for sins to satisfy the wrath of God against sinners. Existentialism, however, seeks to persuade men that they have a right to claim the fruits of justification on the ground that they have announced their sincere intentions to abide by the abstract rule of life, Christ. If the Bible is right in its structure, then Niebuhr clearly is wrong. In a rational universe both cannot simultaneously be true.

Niebuhr, however, being a moralist pragmatically concerned with ends, is little interested in the exact mechanics by which one finds salvation. Since the "hidden Christ" *works* as well as Jesus "after the flesh," it follows logically that it is quite accidental to the dialectical experience whether one is saved through Jesus or through another. It is inconsequential under what circumstances one is shattered by *agape,* for it is the shattering which has the existential value.

But would it not be an unspeakable tragedy for the followers of existentialism if at the final judgment Jesus of Nazareth were right, and Niebuhr wrong, that the basis of judgment is one's having had his sins atoned for by the blood of Christ and not devotion to an abstract, bloodless "Christ" as the *agape* rule of men's lives? Whereas Jesus warned of that fearful sight in judgment when the wicked will hear their fate of being consigned to everlasting separation from God's sight, Niebuhr counsels us to believe that God will forgive all men.

One must decide between these authorities. "Do not fear those who kill the body but cannot kill the soul; rather fear him who can destroy both soul and body in hell" (Matthew 10:28). The Father whom Jesus Christ worshiped was a Father, wrathful against sin, determined that all who crucify His son afresh shall suffer eternal separation from His fellowship. It may be existentially distressing to think that God will deal harshly with sinners, but a question of authority is at stake here. Shall we trust our own feelings or the counsel of Jesus Christ? "Again, the kingdom of heaven is like a net which was thrown into the sea and gathered fish of every kind; when it was full, men drew it ashore and sat down and sorted the good into vessels but threw away the bad. *So it will be at the close of the age. The angels will come out and separate the evil from the righteous, and throw them into the furnace of fire; there men will weep and gnash their teeth*" (Matthew 13:47-50). These are frightful words, they cannot be dismissed lightly.

A very curious, yet pathetic, epistemological inconsistency of Niebuhr's method is the way he is a Biblical literalist wherever the Bible supports his antecedently conceived dialectic, but a Biblical critic at most other points. The parable of the last judgment, for example, is worked over with precision. Every word is exegeted carefully, for the structure of an existential judgment is made to rest upon it. If literalism were ever employed, it surely is here. But when Christ prophesies that men will perish in hell for trampling under foot the Son of God and counting the blood of his covenant an unworthy thing, the critical side emerges. "Hell" is not even a symbol, let alone a fact. But how can Christ be the Son of God at some points and a deluded Rabbi at others?

Niebuhr claims a great advancement over evangelicalism. Armed with "the mind of Christ" he can come to the Jesus of history and sort out what is worthless from what he feels is true. The evangelical, on the other hand, persuaded that Jesus is genuinely an objective authority, must submit humbly to His words at every point, constructing a theology out of that counsel. It is surely true that there are *difficulties* in the evangelical approach. They are freely admitted.[23] But are there not *absurdities* in the existential alternative? Suppose a trusted king issued a decree to his subjects. Would it be in order to examine that decree armed with "the mind of the king" to sift out of that message what matches the existential witness of the self and discard what does not? This would be clearly an arrogant act of insubordination, for an *obedient* subject follows the king as the words are spoken. Is it not contradictory, therefore, to imagine one standing with Jesus Christ on the steps of the temple, confessing, on the one hand, that "Christ is the Lord of his life," but then telling Jesus that he is using "the mind of Christ" to determine what he shall accept of His own teachings, on the other? Jesus Christ divided men into the obedient and the wicked. The obedient were those who, having submitted themselves to the authority of His person, followed Him at the cost of leaving father, mother, husband, wife, sister, and children. The wicked were those who ate bread with Him but refused to eat the bread of His broken body and drink the cup of His blood. They were "critical" of what they would accept of Christ's words.

One is forced to conclude that Niebuhr remains a liberal in soteriology. While he rejects the conventional liberal optimism that God will solve our problems through an immanent movement of the Kingdom within history, he retains the optimism that God will solve our problems through a transcendent movement in eternity. Niebuhr simply exchanges an historical optimism for an eternal optimism. He relocates the locus of optimism. He forgets that the Bible is pessimistic about *both* history and eternity for all who remain unjustified by the blood of Jesus Christ. *Niebuhr is a transcendental optimist with a fiat theory of forgiveness.* The pleasant consolation of all men at the end of history is that, regardless how good or bad they were, their provisional historical differences will be overcome by a final forgiveness.

---

23. See, *e. g.*, my *An Introduction to Christian Apologetics*, pp. 111, 206ff.

Niebuhr, therefore, does not really take sin seriously at all. Man is only in an existential predicament. He does not stand under the wrath of a severe God into whose hands it is a fearful thing to fall. The transition from sinfulness to eternal salvation is rather painless. Sin will easily be forgiven, for God will take all our sins into and upon Himself. Niebuhr speaks very often of judgment, but his descriptions are always informed with a half-hearted liberalism. God is pictured in a way man *hopes* that He is, and not according to the way Jesus Christ warned in advance that He actually *is*. Christ pictures the final separation of men at the end of judgment as an awful scene: heaven and hell mark the difference between the redeemed and the lost. Niebuhr claims that the separation is only provisional, for in the end a great reunion results. God is love; He will not cast men away forever. In the end the wicked are shown their partial righteousness and the righteous their partial unrighteousness. No *ultimate* separation of men into the camps of sheep and goats is made, however. Conduct on earth does not make a heaven-or-hell difference in eternity. God quietly finishes off the dialectic by saving everybody — since nobody deserved it anyway. How could anybody deserve salvation when the criterion of judgment is good works performed according to the rule of *agape* and not the imputed righteousness of the historical Jesus?

It is not surprising to see Niebuhr's liberalism finally triumphing, but it is surprising to observe that this doctrine of universalism is itself a new corruption of the dialectic. Niebuhr is realistic in his analysis of human nature at one point, but he is idealistic and inaccurate at another. He realizes that love will not succeed in history because men seek their own security. A legitimate system of rewards and punishments must inform history to urge men on to moral duty. But what he does not see is that there must likewise be a system of rewards and punishments in eternity if man is to respond selflessly to God's law. Why should an individual sacrifice himself for others under the rule of *agape* when both he and the one who does not love will be saved anyway? What motive is there for striving selflessly? Why struggle? It makes no final difference whether one struggles or not, for God will oblige by overcoming all our sins and ills, taking them into and upon Himself. Why be crucified if one will gain nothing ultimately by it?

It would be difficult to find a more convincing way to corrupt the dialectic than that which Niebuhr himself has introduced by his "transcendental optimism." By shifting the locus of optimism from history to eternity one does not give man a challenging basis for selfless struggle. Since nothing is lost ultimately not to struggle, why struggle?

It is true that one probably will not become a Hitler when the glad gospel news is given him that he will be saved in eternity regardless what he does in history, but surely one who does decide to be such a culprit cannot effectively be answered. In the judgment Hitler and Gandhi will stand together. Hitler will be amazed to learn all the ways he fed the hungry and clothed the naked, while Gandhi will be humiliated to understand that every *agape* deed he performed was corrupted by pride and personal interest. And in the end both will enter into felicity because of the mercy of God.

Niebuhr's dialectical theology is another image of Daniel. The head of the image is pure gold. Niebuhr has given a final, formal account of *agape* as the absolute expression of law. There is no thinkable perfection beyond *agape;* one leaves Christianity if he leaves *agape*. The thigh of the image is of silver, however. The ramifications which Niebuhr draws out of this *agape* insight are of mixed value. One must read them selectively. The feet and toes, finally, are of clay. At the end of a matchless insight into a formal statement of both the law of life and personal justification in Christ, the case for salvation rests upon the crumbling props of a personal feeling in the heart, the experience of the race, and the formal pronouncement, "God takes our sins into and upon himself." These are the only consolations the transcendent self has. The image is top-heavy; it is bound to collapse.

C. *Yet not I; but Christ Lives in Me: Sanctification*

The transition to sanctification is accomplished by observing that "justification by faith is a release of the soul into action."[24] Justification is not an end in itself. One is now to engage in the labor of working out his salvation, for it is God which works within him both to will and to do. Sanctification offers grace to man for performance of *agape* after conversion. It is the power by which man continues to strive for what he knows he will never attain. One must abide in holiness. The proof of justification is the stepping up of sensitivity and personal responsibility in matters of holiness.

Sanctification is grace *in nobis*. Man feels a continuing flow of power in his heart as he remains within the tension of the dialectic. It is the individual himself which strives; yet it is not. I live — yet not I; but Christ lives in me. The life that one lives subsequent to seeing the rule of his life is a devotion empowered by the Christ which dwells within him. If we believe that we can sanctify ourselves without Christ, we retreat to the moralism of immanence where grace is not respected and over which the delusions of Renaissance ideology hover; and if we believe that God alone does the sanctifying, we cut the nerve of striving. Man works; but God works within him. That is what experience finds. Without this balance the dialectic is destroyed. "Both affirmations — that only God in Christ can break and reconstruct the sinful self, and that the self must 'open the door' and is capable of doing so — are equally true; and they are both unqualifiedly true, each on its own level. Yet either affirmation becomes false if it is made without reference to the other."[25]

Sanctification constitutes a person righteous only by degrees. An individual may always make progress in sanctification, but he may never claim perfect attainment. Whenever man comes to self-conciousness in freedom (as Kiekegaard showed in *The Concept of Dread*) anxiety and, finally, sin emerge. Sin posits itself. One could not sin if he were not

24. *Human Destiny*, p. 188.
25. *Ibid.*, p. 118.

already a sinner. These dialectical affirmations must always be borne in mind when evaluating both justification and sanctification. "The possibilities of new evil cannot be avoided by grace; for so long as the self, individual or collective, remains within the tensions of history and is subject to the twofold condition of involvement in process and transcendence over it, it will be subject to the sin of overestimating its transcendence and of compounding its interests with those which are more inclusive."[26] A necessary conflict abides in the heart, therefore, a conflict which will accompany the existing individual to the grave. Man is holy, but he is full of sin. He is completed, but he waits for completion. Niebuhr calls this tension between grace *pro nobis* and grace *in nobis* "the paradox of grace."[27] It is a feeling in the heart of "having and not having."[28] The morally conditioned man is justified "in principle" at every point in history, but justified "in fact" at no point. Man, therefore, is enjoined to be holy because he is already holy. Here the dialectic reaches its climax. "These injunctions declare in effect: you are now sinless. Therefore you must not sin any more. The exhortation implies that the original statements have a slightly different meaning than their obvious connotation. They really mean: self-love has been destroyed in principle in your life. See to it now that the new principle of devotion to God in Christ is actualized in your life."[29]

III. Corruptions of the Paradox of Grace

One may appreciate the delicacy of "the paradox of grace" after being briefed cursorily on the easy ways in which the paradox is broken even by those making profession of *agape*.

A. Grace as forgiveness.

Roman Catholic theology vitiates the dialectic by confusing justification and sanctification. At an early date in Catholic

26. *Human Destiny*, p. 123.
27. *Ibid.*, p. 213.
28. *Ibid.*, p. 226.
29. *Ibid.*, p. 102.

history "forgiveness becomes a single remission *of sins that are past*."[30] Here the wedge was set for the pretension that man is able to complete the law of his life at one point in history. The baptized Catholic is completely released from the stains of original sin. Self-love is broken in fact. If he dies before committing sin, he goes to heaven on the ground of his constituted and infused righteousness. In the final judgment he is given full clearance on the basis of what he is in himself. The breaking of self-love in the Catholic is all of grace, to be sure, but that fact is irrelevant. The issue is that a baptized Catholic enjoys an exemption from the judgment of Christ. The justified Catholic can storm heaven with a legal claim to eternal life.

Niebuhr is stern at this point, for he (correctly) detects in this error the fountainhead of all Catholic prides and pretensions. "The point at issue may seem academic to the casual student. It may even appear to the critical as a case of that futile theological hairsplitting, which seems to make theological debate so fatuous. But all important issues, whether in philosophy or theology, are finally defined in very precise distinctions, which may easily hide from the unwary, even as they reveal to the initiated, the importance of the issue which is at stake. The issue at stake here is whether man's historical existence is such that he can ever, by any discipline of reason or by any merit of grace, confront a divine judgment upon his life with an easy conscience. If he can it means that it is possible for a will centred in an individual ego to be brought into essential conformity with the will and power which governs all things. On this question the Catholic answer is a consistently affirmative one."[31]

The easy distinction in Catholicism between "mortal" and "venial" sins stems out of this initial error of believing that man is judged by sacramental performances rather than by the full heights of *agape* rule. The infinitely complex shades of selfishness cannot be processed by the machinery of the

30. *Human Destiny*, pp. 130-131.
31. *Ibid.*, pp. 140-141.

church. There is no way to correlate sacramental forgiveness, days of indulgence, and the delicate hues of pride which neither exhibit social manifestations nor which fall directly under any of the Ten Commandments. "Here the complexities of the moral life are obscured by too simple a statement of them. The actual situation is that man may be redeemed from self-love in the sense that he acknowledges the evil of it and recognizes the love of God as the only adequate motive of conduct; and may yet be selfish in more than an incidental sense. The pride of a bishop, the pretensions of a theologian, the will-to-power of a pious business man, and the spiritual arrogance of the church itself are not mere incidental defects, not merely 'venial' sins. They represent the basic drive of self-love, operating upon whatever new level grace has pitched the new life."[32]

Paul Blanshard, in his classic volume *American Freedom and Catholic Power,* has fully documented the charge that the church sins as a collective ego. Whenever either an individual or a church believes that it reigns with, rather than stands under, Christ, it supposes itself free from the judgment which is meted out to all men by Christ. Catholicism has usurped the majesty of God. "It pretended that the church could mediate the divine mercy and judgment without itself standing under that judgment or requiring that mercy. It was, in short, involved in an intolerable pretension."[33] Pretending to be an "extension of the incarnation of Christ," the Catholic Church moves in an aura of sanctimoniousness which makes herself infallible and her head the vicar of Christ on earth. A new will-to-power results in the name of a Christian finality. "When an institution which mediates the judgment of God upon all the ambiguities of historic existence claims that it has escaped those ambiguities by this mission, it commits the same sin which the prophets recognized so clearly as the sin

---

32. *Ibid.,* p. 137.

33. Niebuhr, "The Pope's Domesticated God," *The Christian Century,* January 18, 1950, p. 74.

of Israel. This sin becomes particularly apparent — and intolerable — when it expresses itself in political will-to-power."[34]

Niebuhr turned an unsympathetic ear toward Rome when the Pope in his 1949 Christmas message, asked all of the dissidents and schismatics to return to the true fold; for he detected neither modesty nor logic in the pope's words. "We would be more secure if the Roman Catholic Church were anxious with us under the divine judgment and not so anxious about us. We would be willing to dispense with the assurance of its fatherly forgiveness towards us if we were certain that it sought divine forgiveness with us for the evils in which we have been jointly involved."[35] One does not solve the problem of sin by fleeing to an institution which itself commits the sin of claiming exemption from the judgment of Christ against it. Rome cannot solve our problems because it does not yet see its own sin. "The Roman church has a favorite explanation of all the ills of modern life. They are due to mankind's departure from 'God's plan' as incorporated in the church. We have an equally plausible explanation, not for all the ills of modern world but for a serious aggravation of all our difficulties. The animosities of modern men are exacerbated on the one hand by priest-kings of a secular religion who make ridiculous pretensions of omniscience and omnipotence from the Kremlin; and on the other by priests of a true religion who give the final glory to God but meanwhile are too certain that they are privy to his counsels and the sole dispensers of his grace."[36] Niebuhr's courage and forthright honesty call for highest praise.

It was inevitable that the Catholic synthesis would be challenged, for the free self cannot honestly continue in the delusion that it enjoys a righteousness "in fact" at any point, individually or institutionally. "Here lies the signifiance of the Reformation. It is the historical locus where that side of the gospel, which negates and contradicts historical achieve-

34. *Human Destiny,* p. 145.
35. "The Pope's Domesticated God," *op. cit.,* p. 75.
36. *Ibid.*

ments, became more fully known."[37] The Reformers understood that every historical achievement is sullied and corrupted by insinuations of human pride and pretense. Freedom is always an instrument of chaos as well as of order. "The Reformation understands that therefore we are 'justified by faith' and 'saved in hope'; that we must look forward to a completion of life which is not in our power and even beyond our comprehension. It realizes that the unity of human existence, despite its involvement in, and freedom from, natural process, is such that it cannot be 'saved' either by disavowing its freedom in order to return to nature, or by sloughing off its creaturely character so that it may rise to the 'eternal.' This is the final enigma of human existence for which there is no answer except by faith and hope; for all answers transcend the categories of human reason. Yet without these answers human life is threatened with scepticism and nihilism on the one hand; and with fanaticism and pride on the other. For either it is overwhelmed by the relativity and partiality of all human perspectives and comes to the conclusion that there is no truth, since no man can expound the truth without corrupting it; or it pretends to have absolute truth despite the finite nature of human perspective."[38]

B. Grace as Power.

The delicacy of grace unto sanctification was broken from the other side. The cults did not understand the limits of personal sanctification and the Reformers did not understand the cultural potentialities of grace.

The sects do not contest the Catholic pretension to complete personal sanctification. "Their primary quarrel with Catholicism is that they suspect sacramentalism of achieving a pseudo-perfection and of 'piping' and infusing grace too painlessly into the soul of the sinner and thus failing to induce a genuine change towards a new life."[39] The "Pietistic sects" claim individualistic perfection on the ground of an "inner light" or

37. *Human Destiny,* p. 148.
38. *Ibid.,* p. 149.
39. *Ibid.,* p. 169.

"hidden seed" which is too pure and uncorrupted a vein of spiritual possession to be subject to an indictment of judgment. The "eschatological sects," while sharing this same individual pretension, claimed in addition that history itself may finally be exempt from judgment. The anabaptists *suffered* for the coming of the kingdom of God on earth, and the Cromwellian sects *fought* for it; but each expected it. "The sectarians sought for an ideal society in which every contradiction to the law of love would be eliminated. But such a society is no more possible in history than are sanctified individuals who have no law in their members warring against the law that is in their mind."[40] Neither the individual nor the collective ego can finally claim exemption from sinfulness.

Of no less a serious nature was the cultural pessimism of the Reformers. While recognizing the prophetic truth that judgment and mercy are relevant at every point in history, thus reaching a high-water mark in Christian thought which has yet to be surpassed; they yet did not always appreciate the fine balance between *Christus in nobis* and *Christus pro nobis* in cultural realms.

Luther illustrates both the heights and the depths of Reformation insight. He saw the need for grace everywhere. The prides of both the individual and the church destroy any claim to righteousness "in fact." Luther saw the height of *agape,* "particularly its transcendent freedom over all the prudential considerations of natural ethical attitudes."[41] Completely disinterested motives characterize Christian perfection. But Luther then failed to relate these insights to the realm of culture and to individual, Christian action. "Despite these great merits of the Lutheran position there are quietistic tendencies in it, even when Luther is analysing the intricacies of personal religion, where he is on the whole most faithful to the Biblical paradox. Sometimes he lapses into mystic doctrines of passivity or combines quietism with a legalistic con-

40. *Ibid.,* p. 180.
41. *Ibid.,* p. 186.

ception of the imputation of righteousness."[42] Realizing the futility of taking pure *agape* into the collective ego, Luther overlooked the power of grace *in nobis* and the responsibility of a justified Christian to struggle for the increase of justice in society. Luther did not appreciate that a justified man must carry the rule of Christ into society and strive for justice. "By the inspiration of grace the law is extended as well as overcome. Repentance and faith prompt a sense of obligation towards wider and wider circles of life. The need of this neighbour, the demands of that social situation, the claims of this life upon me, unrecognized today may be recognized and stir the conscience to uneasiness tomorrow. There is a constantly increasing sense of social obligation which is an integral part of the life of grace. To deny this is to be oblivious to one aspect of historic existence which the Renaissance understood so well: that life represents an indeterminate series of possibilities, and therefore of obligation to fulfill them."[43] The Reformation tended to be socially defeatist.

Calvin never understood the fullness of *agape* in the first place. While he rejected the idea that man or history has any merit to which to claim pretension before God in judgment, he nevertheless subsumed love under faith in the catalogue of Christian virtues. A new casuistry resulted. "The history of Puritan self-righteousness reveals the weakness of Calvinism on this point. Calvin does not fully understand the law of lové as the final law."[44] Calvin's pitiless attitude toward the heretics, together with his stern rule over Geneva, illustrate perfectly the absence of self-judgment. Calvin forgot that the mercy which God had showed toward him must likewise be showed toward heretics. Vengeance belongs to God, not to man. "The final proof of the genuine spirit of humility in the 'elect,' of their 'brokenness of spirit,' is their capacity for mercy and forgiveness. Without conciousness of

---

42. *Ibid.*, p. 187.
43. *Ibid.*, pp. 189-190.
44. *Ibid.*, p. 201.

their own need of forgiveness, 'good' people never show mercy towards 'bad' people."[45]

Niebuhr summarizes the strengths and weaknesses of both Reformation and Renaissance insights in the following rather lucid way: "The Reformation understands that every possible extension of knowledge and wisdom falls short of the wisdom which knows God. It realizes that the 'world by its wisdom knew not God' and it rejoices in the grace, apprehended by faith, which overcomes the sinful egocentricity of all human knowledge. But it has no interest in the infinite shades and varieties of the amalgam of truth and falsehood which constitutes the stuff of science and philosophy, and of all human striving after the truth. The Renaissance was undoubtedly wrong in imagining that the final truth could be found by the cumulative process of the history of culture. It did not recognize the peril of new errors on each new level of wisdom; most particularly the error of assuming that an age which had a point of vantage over all preceding ages would thereby arrive at the final truth. But was it not right, in comparison with the Reformation, to take the obligation towards the truth seriously? And was not the Reformation delivered into the sin of cultural obscurantism by its indifference towards the relative distinctions of truth and falsehood which are so important in the history of culture?"[46] These words need only assent, not comment.

IV. The Final Synthesis

If Reformation insights were overbalanced by both a defeatism and a cultural obscurantism, and if Renaissance insights were overbalanced by an unwarranted optimism in both truth and culture, the final truth must lie in a synthesis between these extremes. The Reformation thesis and the Renaissance antithesis must pass into a synthesis of a dialectical Christianity. The Reformation has discovered the final truth that all of history stands under both judgment and mercy, while the

45. *Ibid.*
46. *Human Nature*, p. 191.

Renaissance has discovered the final truth that history contains more possibilities for the increase of justice than are tapped at any point within the process. History waits to be fulfilled at every point, but history is likewise fulfilled at every point. If this balance is upset, the dialectical relation between time and eternity is destroyed; and either an unwarranted pessimism or an unwarranted optimism results. Each, however, is sin.

"A new synthesis is therefore called for. It must be a synthesis which incorporates the twofold aspects of grace of Biblical religion, and adds the light which modern history, and the Renaissance and Reformation interpretations of history, have thrown upon the paradox of grace. Briefly this means that on the one hand life in history must be recognized as filled with indeterminate possibilities. There is no individual or interior spiritual situation, no cultural or scientific task, and no social or political problem in which men do not face new possibilities of the good and the obligation to realize them. It means on the other hand that every effort and pretension to complete life, whether in collective or individual terms, that every desire to stand beyond the contradictions of history, or to eliminate the final corruptions of history must be disavowed."[47]

47. *Human Destiny*, p. 207.

Part IV

CONCLUDING IMPLICATIONS

CHAPTER VIII

AGAPE and the Realm of Culture

NIEBUHR correctly perceives, while many others apparently do not, that there is no simple statement of the relation between individual and group ethics. It goes without saying that the gospel program *is* the basis of both individual and collective morals, but how, exactly, is it? This is one further difficult question Niebuhr courageously faces.

I. The Inevitability of Dualistic Ethics

In partly solving this problem Niebuhr resorts to a formula of "dualistic ethics." The moral sensitivity which characterizes the individual ego cannot be absorbed by the collective. The development of this thought is as follows:

Man cannot consistently live unto himself. Neither saint nor sinner may altogether dispense with the aid and cooperation of the other. The righteous require the ships, cranes, and distribution centers held by the unrighteous before they can distribute food effectively to the poor. The unrighteous need the purchasing power of the righteous to sustain their economic privileges. The complexity which results from this competitive mingling together of contesting ideologies is staggering, and all hope of finding a simple moral program to cover both the individual and collective mind vanishes. The group lacks the organs of sensitivity of the individual. Furthermore, neither saint nor sinner can remain satisfied with a common denominator between them; for either the saint interprets such a standard as too diluted or the sinner as too demanding.

In the competition of group life both the children of darkness (the unrighteous) and the children of light (the righteous) enjoy provisional advantages over the other. The children of darkness, realistically perceiving the inevitability ot power in society, are alert to the value of force to achieve their ends; while the children of light, not deluded by an unfounded historical optimism, are not disheartened when history does not vindicate their efforts to establish social justice.

A. The Children of Darkness.

Because they have never been overtaken by the law of life, the children of darkness are devoted with whole absorption to the task of carving out security in history without the aid of divine grace. They are Renaissance, as opposed to Reformation, in their perspective. While completely blinded to the judgment of God against history, they yet compensate for this sightlessness by developing a sensitivity to a realistic use of power. "The children of darkness are evil because they know no law beyond the self. They are wise, though evil, because they understand the power of self-interest."[1] Man's freedom to create is misunderstood because human nature is never fully related to the law of Christ; but man's freedom to destroy is well known. "For man, unlike other creatures, is gifted and cursed with an imagination which extends his appetites beyond the requirements of subsistence. Human society will never escape the problem of the equitable distribution of the physical and cultural goods which provide for the preservation and fulfillment of human life."[2] The unrighteous know enough about the strategy of their own selfish tactics in life to generalize that all men enter social relations armed with a determination to increase their own security. The ambitious individual always craves far more than physical and social necessity calls for. Freedom overtakes every possession by lusting for more. "Man, being more than a natural creature, is not interested merely in physical survival but in prestige and social approval. Having the intelligence to anticipate the perils in which he stands in nature and history, he invariably seeks to gain security against these perils by enhancing

1. *The Children of Light and the Children of Darkness,* p. 10.
2. *Moral Man and Immoral Society,* p. 1.

his power, individually and collectively. Possessing a darkly unconscious sense of his insignificance in the total scheme of things, he seeks to compensate for his insignificance by pretensions of pride."[3]

Niebuhr, having directly observed the unjust fruits of a capitalistic ideology while serving a Detroit pastorate, inevitably moved farther to the left in his social theory. The realism of the children of darkness contained a wisdom which was absent in liberal Christian ethics. The lofty optimism of a middle class, capitalistic ideology was being strangulated by realistic socialistic forces. It was only natural that liberal-educated Niebuhr was deeply affected by the Marxian philosophy of social conflict. Marx, though evil, yet is wise in understanding that men always demand more than either security requires or justice permits, and so must be restrained by force or power. "Rejecting a mild political reformism based on the assumptions of a middle-class outlook which did not challenge the deeper roots of social injustice, he was finally driven to embrace a Marxist ideology which apparently offered the key to the problem of building a new world. Marxism to him was the clue because it saw the realities of inevitable class conflict, the root of injustice in the disproportions of power and privilege inherent in the very structure of bourgeois society, the coming doom of capitalism by its own inner chaos and disintegration, the impossibility of avoiding force, even destructive violence, in a social order torn by irreconcilable economic interests, the locus of political power in the possession of property, and an organized militant proletariat as the only means for effectuating a genuine transfer of power essential for basic justice."[4] The disillusionment of a liberal Christian optimism lashed Niebuhr on to a provisional acceptance of the Marxist social theory. In time, to be sure, he tempered his Marxism with *agape* insights.

---

3. *The Children of Light and the Children of Darkness*, p. 20.
4. J. Neal Hughley, *Trends in Protestant Social Idealism*, (Morningside Heights, King's Crown Press, 1948), pp. 121-122.

The early publications of Niebuhr are therefore sprinkled with propositions of extreme pessimism about the possibility of social reconstruction through capitalism. An unmistakable Marxian influence can be traced. "Since it is impossible to count on enough moral goodwill among those who possess irresponsible power to sacrifice it for the good of the whole, it must be destroyed by coercive methods and these will always run the peril of introducing new forms of injustice in place of those abolished . . . The future peace and justice of society therefore depend upon, not one but many, social strategies, in all of which moral and coercive factors are compounded in varying degrees."[5] Even after the postwar triumph of Russian communism as a world power — with its godless, vicious presuppositions — Niebuhr yet clung to the unbelievable optimism that the program of Marx is but quantitatively removed from the program of Jesus Christ. "The judgment of the late Archbishop Temple is still correct: Communism is a Christian heresy and Nazism is an anti-Christian paganism. Communism is not morally cynical as Nazism is. It does not glorify race or nation. It does not worship power for its own sake. It believes in a universal rule of justice. It may be provisionally cynical but not in the ultimate sense. It still belongs to civilization."[6] One wonders if the six erstwhile communists who wrote the now famous confessional document, *The God That Failed*, would agree with this unusually optimistic view of communism.

Because their plan in defeating injustice rests on moral commitments that never fully enjoy validation in time, the children of light stand at a disadvantage in history. "Since the political defeat of the mighty is more verifiable in historic terms, and probably more significant socially, than their moral defeat, the religio-political dreams of the Marxians have an

---

5. *Moral Man and Immoral Society*, p. 21.

6. Niebuhr, "Our Relations to Russia," in *Christianity Takes a Stand*, William Scarlett ed., (N. Y., Penguin Books, Inc., 1946), p. 41. Marx is "not cynical but only realistic, in maintaining that disproportion of power in society is the real root of social injustice." *Moral Man and Immoral Society*, p. 163.

immediate significance, which the religio-ethical dreams of the Christians lack."[7] The children of light must learn a lesson of history from the children of darkness: To establish social justice effectively reason and love must be complemented by threats of force. As long as the righteous continue unmindful of the perils of history, that long will they be less wise than the unrighteous. Their wisdom toward eternity does not justify a blindness toward history. "The children of light are virtuous because they have some conception of a higher law than their own will. They are usually foolish because they do not know the power of self-will."[8]

B. The Children of Light.

As Niebuhr was drawn deeper and deeper into the vortex of transcendental ethics, he perceived more and more clearly that Marx's insights were at best but provisional; and that ultimately force without the tempering vitality of love is demonic. In Niebuhr's final dialectic liberal and Marxist elements cross-fertilize each other. The shift to the left politically was complemented by an ethical shift to the right. The Marxian insight justifies an historical pessimism and the liberal insight a transcendental optimism. "Marxism is a perversion of a profound truth. It understands, as the purely progressive view of history does not, that civilizations and cultures do not merely grow but that they must die and be reborn if they are to have a new life. Its program of the socialization of property is a proximate answer to the immediate problem of achieving justice in a technical age . . . But Marxism falsely made it into a final fact of history which was supposed to bear within itself the possibility of an ultimate redemption of history. The illusions of Marxism are thus the end-products of a Christian civilization which either failed to realize the highest possibilities of life in history or which claimed the realization of a perfection which can never be achieved in history."[9]

7. *Ibid.*, p. 156.
8. *The Children of Light and the Children of Darkness*, pp. 10-11.
9. *Faith and History*, p. 212.

The profundity of the children of light lies in the fact that their faith rests on insights which judge as well as fulfill history. One may realistically resort to force and power to mitigate one obtrusive injustice; but one is blinded if he believes that out of that effort a stable justice will result. Every new effort to achieve justice is compounded with the sullying forces of self-love and pretension. Since the children of light realize this, they enjoy a perspective lacking among the children of darkness. They remain wiser than those who expect to achieve final justice. The Marxian juxtaposing of violent revolution besides a peaceful, classless society perfectly illustrates the pathos of sinful optimism. "The Marxist dialectic challenged the confidence of Hegelian rationalism in the power of reason. It saw that reason may be an instrument of interest and passion. But unfortunately it transmuted this discovery into a mere weapon of social and political conflict by attributing an ideological taint to the moral and social ideals of every group except the proletariat. The pretension that one group in human society is free of sin, naturally became the source of new and terrible fanaticisms."[10]

Men who substitute pure force for force plus morals obscure the fact that the law of our nature, which alone can define perfect social equality, *excludes* the use of power as a means of uniting spirit with spirit. The continued employment of force to dislodge inequalities inevitably leads to further inequalities; and the less tangent to the law of love such forces are, the more terrible are the resulting inequalities. The children of light realize this. Therefore, they are wise.

All resort to force would be excluded *ex hypothesi* if men accepted love as the law of their own nature. *Agape* love levels off inequalities wherever they exist. Christ, not Marx, therefore, has a right to define the terms of the classless society, for only Christ based final justice on the exhaustiveness of *agape*. Marxian communism is actually a contradiction in terms. Sordid means are employed to reach an end which only love can gain. Christian communism, while it may never

10. *Ibid.*, p. 160.

be realized in history, is at least consistent in its elements. "Such perfect love as he demands would obviate the necessity of coercion on the one hand because men would refrain from transgressing upon their neighbor's rights, and on the other hand because such transgression would be accepted and forgiven if it did occur. That is anarchism in other words. It would mean communism because the privileges of each would be potentially the privileges of all. Where love is perfect the distinctions between mine and thine disappear."[11]

When history fails the children of darkness, pessimism results; but when history fails the children of light, faith is verified. The Christian refuses to allow token successes of power in history to encourage the faith that an ultimate completion of history's norm may be expected. For this reason a motive to continue for the right is sustained even in times of defeat — even though it may be very difficult to remain consistently within that motive. "We are to forgive because God forgives; we are to love our enemies because God is impartial in his love. The points of reference are vertical and not horizontal. Neither natural impulses nor social consequences are taken into consideration."[12]

C. *Ethical Dualism.*

Agape, which remains a law for the individual as a vertical reference, must suffer in purity when taken into social relations. *Agape* is at best a regulative social norm. It sets the outside definition of ideal justice as well as tempering whatever realistic means must be employed to dynamite recalcitrant centers of pride and injustice. Love remains a leaven in society, permeating the whole and giving texture and consistency to life. Love is the salt which preserves social relations from corruption. The balanced Christian, therefore, must be both loving and realistic. As an individual who in moments of prayerful self-transcendence has been justified by faith, he gives

---

11. Niebuhr, "The Ethic of Jesus and the Social Problem," in *Contemporary Thinking about Jesus,* Thomas S. Kepler ed., p. 287.
12. *An Interpretation of Christian Ethics,* p. 46.

final allegiance to Christ; but as an individual in complex social relations he must realistically meet mind with mind, power with power. Since sanctification is always by degrees, love is carried into social relations only at a risk. Two perspectives always vie for primacy. "One focus is in the inner life of the individual, and the other in the necessities of man's social life. From the perspective of society the highest moral ideal is justice. From the perspective of the individual the highest ideal is unselfishness. Society must strive for justice even if it is forced to use means, such as self-assertion, resistance, coercion and perhaps resentment, which cannot gain the moral sanction of the most sensitive moral spirit. The individual must strive to realize his life by losing and finding himself in something greater than himself."[13] The Christian, being in though not of the world, is never fully free from the complexities of acting as a vicar of Christ in his intentional life and a social and political agent in his actual life. Such a conflict is most acute in the instance of the politician who represents both his country and own responsible self before God. It is least acute in either a monkish withdrawal into the desert or an inarticulate sectarian isolationism. The more aggressively one relates the gospel to life, the more sensitively he realizes that the social unit can accomodate only justice, not *agape*.

Agape is always a possibility/impossibility. It remains perennially relevant in society as the regulative principle of morals, but it is realized in society only through infinite degrees of justice. "A rational analysis reveals both the ideal possibility and the actual situation from which one must begin. In that sense there are really two natural laws — that which reason commands ultimately and the compromise which reason makes with the contingent and arbitrary forces of human existence. The ideal possibility is really an impossibility, a fact to which both Stoic and Christian doctrine do justice by the myth of the Golden Age in Stoic doctrine and the age of perfection before the Fall in Christian doctrine. The ideal is an im-

13. *Moral Man and Immoral Society*. p. 257.

possibility because both the contingencies of nature and the sin in the human heart prevent men from ever living in that perfect freedom and equality which the whole logic of the moral life demands. The ideal equality will be relativized, as has been previously observed, not only by the fortuitous circumstances of nature and history, but by the necessities of social cohesion and organic social life, which will give some men privileges and powers which other men lack; and finally by human sin, for it is inevitable that men should take advantage of privileges with which nature or necessity has endowed them and should enhance them beyond the limits of the one and the requirements of the other. Yet this impossibility is not one which can be relegated simply to the world of transcendence. It offers immediate possibilities of a higher good in every given situation. We may never realize equality, but we cannot accept the inequalities of capitalism or any other unjust social system complacently."[14]

Niebuhr freely admits that justice is morally inferior to equality in love, but (and this is what makes him unmistakably brilliant as a moralist) one will err in rejecting a "second best" — to use a Platonic formula — simply because he despairs of achieving perfection. Individuals are justified by faith and saved by hope, but the end of justification is the active engagement of evil and injustice wherever, and under whatever guises, they may be found. One must realistically adjust himself to the fact that the ethic which controls the individual cannot inform the group. The individual ethic "is oriented by only one vertical religious reference, to the will of God; and the will of God is defined in terms of all-inclusive love."[15] Consequently, the group, which is the focal point of individuals increasing their own security either at the expense of, or indifference to, others, lacks the organs of self-transcendence

---

14. *An Interpretation of Christian Ethics*, pp. 147 148. "The Christian religion is thus an ethical religion in which the optimism, necessary for the ethical enterprise, and the pessimism, consequent upon profound religious insights, never achieve a perfect equilibrium or harmony." *Reflection on the End of an Era*, p. 213.

15. *An Interpretation of Christian Ethics*, p. 51.

to understand *agape*. And "the larger the group the more difficult it is to achieve a common mind and purpose and the more inevitably will it be unified by momentary impulses and immediate and unreflective purposes."[16] Justice is a this-worldly value; all understand and strive for it. While *agape* is an eternal value; only the initiated understand and strive for it.

Justice is never discontinuously related to love, however. Justice is a negative application of love. Whereas love seeks out the needs of others, justice limits freedom to prevent its infringement upon the rights and privileges of others. Justice does not establish the security of a neighbor; it simply restricts the self-interest of others from encroaching upon the rights and interests of that neighbor. Justice is a check (by force, if necessary) upon ambitions of individuals seeking to overcome their own insecurity at the expense of others. It is a mistake for the religious mind to disregard degrees of justice in society, even though society cannot accommodate the purity and perfection of the law of love. Justice *is* love's message for the collective mind. "In a struggle between those who enjoy inordinate privileges and those who lack the basic essentials of the good life it is fairly clear that a religion which holds love to be the final law of life stultifies itself if it does not support equal justice as a political and economic approximation of the ideal of love... The relativity of all moral ideals cannot absolve us of the necessity and duty of choosing between relative values; and that the choice is sometimes so clear as to become an imperative one."[17]

Neither liberal nor orthodox Christianity has fully understood the relation between love, justice, and a dualistic theory of ethics. Orthodoxy, while properly sensing the inevitability of sin in the world and the consequent defeat of pure love as a moral force, inclines to be pessimistic about the cultural possibilities of love. It tends to withdraw from the world in preference to interacting in it. Reformation pessimism

16. *Moral Man and Immoral Society*, p. 48.
17. *An Interpretation of Christian Ethics*, p. 131.

has its modern disciples, in other words. Christian orthodoxy "failed to derive any significant politico-moral principles from the law of love... It therefore destroyed a dynamic relationship between the ideal of love and the principles of justice."[18] Orthodoxy has not yet found the exact relation of justice to love. It periodically capitulates to lower standards of social justice because of this deficiency. Individual perfection is too often made an end in itself. "The failure of Christian orthodoxy to relate the principles of equality to the law of love on the one hand and to the problems of relative justice on the other, resulted in a constant temptation to a complacent acceptance of historic forms of relative justice which ought to have been regarded, and by later ages were regarded, as injustice. A perfectionist ethic thus had the tragic consequence of increasing complacency toward remediable imperfections in justice."[19] Niebuhr (properly) senses that when those who hold the true answer are inarticulate about remedying injustices in society they only encourage the pretensions of those — such as Marx — who, while blinded to eternal love, are alert to the realistic use of force and power in society for securing justice.

The liberal ethic is a religious expression of the Renaissance fallacy. It illustrates the blindness of the children of light from another side. Enlightened on the law of love, but insensitive to the inevitability of sin in history, liberalism vainly seeks to overcome justice through purely moral and rational suasions. "The unvarying refrain of the liberal Church in its treatment of politics is that love and cooperation are superior to conflict and coercion, and that therefore they must be and will be established."[20] Liberalism confuses the ideal itself with the realistic means which must be employed to coerce society into an approximation of that ideal. Perfect

18. *Ibid.*, p. 144.
19. *An Interpretation of Christian Ethics*, p. 150. "Ideally the Christian religion therefore is rooted in a mythology which does justice both to the necessity for moral tension in life and the need for the relaxation of this tension." *Reflections on the End of an Era*, p. 292.
20. *An Interpretation of Christian Ethics*, p. 176.

justice will not come by a simple statement of the moral superiority of brotherhood in the world, for men are controlled by power, not mind alone. There is a recalcitrant power in the will which refuses to submit to ideal law. "If the liberal Church had had less moral idealism and more religious realism its approach to the political problem would have been less inept and fatuous. Liberal solutions of the social problem never take the permanent difference between man's collective behavior and the moral ideals of an individual life into consideration. Very few seem to recognize that even in the individual there is a law in his members which wars against the law that is in his mind." [21]

II. The Inevitability of Government

Even as the Christian must become realistic in ethics, so he must become realistic in his attitude toward the power which employs force to coerce justice.

A. *The Ambiguity of Government.*

Since forceful suasions are irrelevant wherever a love for God is perfected, government, ideally, is unnecessary. The man who loves will naturally prefer the needs and securities of his neighbor. Actually, however, government is very necessary, for men inevitably corrupt their potentialities of love through a lust for self-security which outruns natural needs. Men must be restrained by force. Otherwise they will swallow up their neighbors in a desperate effort to make themselves secure. Government is approved of God. "Government is divinely ordained and morally justified because a sinful world would, without the restraints of the state, be reduced to anarchy by its evil lusts." [22] The force of sinfulness is so stubborn a characteristic of human nature that neither moral nor rational suasion will restrain men from exploiting each other. Anti-social vitalities can be restrained only when the social unit is armed with both moral and physical might.

---

21. *An Interpretation of Christian Ethics,* pp. 178-179.
22. *Reflections on the End of an Era,* p. 220.

Without the protection of government the children of light would stand at a grave disadvantage in history. Freed from all restraint, the children of darkness would eventually swallow up the righteous. Love is forgiving and kind, patient and long-suffering. The lover is easily preyed on by a mind which respects only coercion of force. A penchant for power in the individual must be matched by power in the collective mind. Government wields this power.

Government is holy as an instrument for restraining the sinful, but it is sinful because the sin of rebellion from God has provoked its necessity. "According to the absolute ideal, man was intended to live in perfect love and complete equality with his fellow men. But his fall into sin made this impossible and created a situation in which the evil lusts of men needed to be checked by the governments, the restrictions of property and even the inequalities of slavery."[23] The Christian may assume no easy attitude toward the collective ego, therefore. His reverence for government extends only as far as the purpose for which that unit was created. When the government pretends to be divine, the Christian serves God rather than man. "According to the one, the government is an ordinance of God and its authority reflects the Divine Majesty. According to the other, the 'rulers' and 'judges' of the nations are particularly subject to divine judgment and wrath because they oppress the poor and defy the divine majesty." [24]

Because of the easy pretensions of the collective ego to both power and dignity of commission, the sinful perils of government are legion. Rulers are ordained for the praise of the good and the condemnation of the evil. Therefore megalomania — the pride of being exempt from the judgment of God — is an easy sin to commit. Because the state enjoys a *prima facie* claim to immortality unknown in precarious individual life, it is extremely easy for it to identify its own mission with that of the divine. Government must learn to respect its limits.

---

23. *Ibid.*, p. 215.
24. *Human Destiny*, p. 269.

When it forgets its role of establishing justice, the judgment of Christ stands over it.

The Christian must constantly maintain a "dialectical" attitude toward government. He must remain obedient to government while the collective ego remains within its bounds, while being critical whenever these bounds are overpassed.

Because the Scriptures teach both obedience and the right of disobedience, conservatives and radicals have found equal Biblical support for their extremes. "Unfortunately a single text from St. Paul has done much to destroy the force of the Biblical paradox. St. Paul's very 'undialectical' appreciation of government in Romans 13 has had a fateful influence in Christian thought, particularly in the Reformation. But its influence was fortunately never able to extinguish the power of prophetic criticism upon the evils of government in Christian history." [25]

The dialectic has perennially been corrupted by both classical and Christian thinkers. Classical polity, optimistically concluding that the will of man is on the side of the good, defined government fundamentally in moral and rational terms. The fear of anarchy is only mildly accented in classical political theories. "The approach is, in the parlance of modern philosophy, 'non-existential.'" [26] The rougher vitalities of life are easily brought into moral and rational harmony through the cohesion of the *logos*. Because the philosopher king is the most consistent participant in *logos*, he is most qualified to arbitrate the prejudices and evils of others. Thus, an unmistakable optimism informs classical political theory. The contest between classes can be mediated through simple, moral and rational efforts (together with force when necessary).

Augustine, enlightened by the Pauline insight of the sinfulness of man, corrected the Stoic-Ciceronian optimism by denying that the rational order of government is simply a compact of justice. "He regarded the peace of the world as an uneasy

25. *Human Destiny*, pp. 270-271.
26. *Ibid.*, p. 271.

armistice between contending social forces."[27] Society is constantly threatened by anarchy within and tyranny above. Peace, paradoxically, is based on strife. "Such a morally neutral definition of political cohesion allows Augustine to compare the harmony of the state with the harmony which thieves maintain among themselves and to suggest that there may be little difference except size, between a state and a robber band." [28]

Medieval Catholicism, by-passing much of Augustine's insights, partly returned to classical optimism. The medieval synthesis never finally excludes criticism against unjust rulers. Yet, since the state becomes an instrument for the extension of papal pride and authority, such criticism was always provisional. Moral and rational optimism informed much medieval, social and political theory. It "failed to comprehend the political order as a vast realm of mutually dependent and conflicting powers and interests, and to appreciate the contingent and relative character of any 'justice' which might be achieved at a given moment by the power of government and by the specific equilibria of forces existing at that moment. This failure was one cause of its inability to deal realistically with the new forces, and the consequent disbalances introduced into the medieval political economy by rising commerce." [29] The Biblical insight that government is a necessary evil tended to encourage the optimism that government is also just.

The Reformation presents a perfect potpourri of attitudes toward the collective ego. Luther was uncritical, appealing to Paul as an authority for justifying a faith that the status quo is "ordained of God." Barth, a modern disciple, has so tempered his Lutheranism as a result of an emotional reaction to Nazi domination, that his Lutheran quietism is complemented by a Calvinistic activism. The state, while remaining within divine providence, is yet subject to the judgment of God. This new feeling toward government, however, is not yet integrally related to crisis theology.

27. *Ibid.*, p. 273.
28. *Ibid.*, p. 273.
29. *Ibid.*, pp. 275-276.

The extreme sects, while appreciating the inevitability of injustice in government, nevertheless broke the dialectic from the other side. "The perils of government are appreciated, but not its necessity. The contradiction between the majesty of government and the majesty of God is emphasized; but the legitimate majesty of government is not apprehended."[30] The radical sects remained inarticulate in formulating a careful statement of the relation between *agape* and justice. But their extreme reactionary individualism inevitably enriched modern democratic theories.

The evolution of Calvinism contains a surprisingly satisfying dialectical approach to government. In its earliest inception Calvinism was uncritical toward government, prohibiting, along with Lutheranism, the right of the individual to resist injustice. One may *disobey* the ruler who conflicts with God's law, but he may not *resist*. Later Calvinists wisely distinguished between the necessity of government *per se* and the relativity of any particular form of rule. Through this device both reverence and the right to criticize were mingled together in a balanced political theory. Calvinism did not lead to democracy as an inevitable consequence of this balance, for the leaven of many secular and religious forces was yet needed for the development of a purely democratic ideology.

The dialectic is the best way to express that tension which alone can avoid the twin evils of anarchy and tyranny. "An intelligent society will constantly strive toward the goal of a more equal justice by initiating a more rigorous policy just as soon as a previous and more tentative one has been accepted and absorbed into the social standards of the community. If this is not done by gradual process, with the unrealized goal of essential equality beckoning each generation to surpass the approximations of justice achieved in the past, the inequalities of the social order, always increasing through natural process, are bound to grow until an outraged sense of justice (probably spurred by actual physical want on the part of the least privileged members of a community) will

30. *Human Destiny*, p. 279.

produce a violent revolt."[31] The higher possibilities of justice, together with an appreciation of the relative forms of justice already achieved, must always be balanced. The perils of society are expressed in strife and conflict. Marx was right. But Marx was wrong when he sought to solve the problem of strife through mediums which themselves were not subject to the criticism of eternity. "Every society needs working principles of justice, as criteria for its positive law and system of restraints . . . But every historical statement of them is subject to amendment. If it becomes fixed it will destroy some of the potentialities of a higher justice, which the mind of one generation is unable to anticipate in the life of subsequent eras."[32]

Niebuhr is far from optimistic about the final prevention of either war or tyranny. In ruling and ordering an unwieldy social mind one may unconsciously destroy the very forms needed to preserve order. Society often stumbles into total war. But Niebuhr is optimistic in his belief that the same Christian symbols which sustain the individual in personal faith can likewise guide him in the realm of culture. "To understand this is to labor for higher justice in terms of the experience of justification by faith. Justification by faith in the realm of justice means that we will not regard the pressures and counter pressures, the tensions, the overt and the covert conflicts by which justice is achieved and maintained, as normative in the absolute sense; but neither will we ease our conscience by seeking to escape from involvement in them. We will know that we cannot purge ourselves of the sin and guilt in which we are involved by the moral ambiguities of politics without also disavowing responsibility for the creative possibilities of justice."[33]

31. Niebuhr, "The Ethic of Jesus and the Social Problem," in Kepler ed., *op. cit.*, p. 289.

32. *The Children of Light and the Children of Darkness*, p. 71. "There is no difficulty in understanding Niebuhr's practical interest in attaching guilt to every action, for Niebuhr is convinced in all his writings that the tension of inevitable sin is necessary to keep men up to a higher mark than they would otherwise attain." Mary Thelen, *Man as Sinner*, p. 79.

33. *Human Destiny*, p. 284.

B. Democracy and the Dialectic.

While the ambiguity of government is deeply embedded in every conceivable political form, it would be undialectical to deny that perceptible shades of virtue and vice are expressed in alternative political types. The pragmatic rule reveals that some political cohesions expose a greater surface of self-criticism than others. No easy sliding scale of expressions of government can be formed. But critical insight quickly perceives that the most desirable cohesion is democracy, even as the least desirable is totalitarianism. Democracy stands highest, while tyrannical overlord ranks lowest, because the checks and balances which are cultivated in the one are missing altogether in the other. "For certainly one perennial justification for democracy is that it arms the individual with political and constitutional power to resist the inordinate ambition of rulers, and to check the tendency of the community to achieve order at the price of liberty."[34] Ideal democracy is Renaissance in its faith that there are always limitless possibilities of growth in history. Ideally it remains true to the Reformation that no particular expression of democratic rule is ever finally free from the sins and guilt of injustice, pride, and personal interest.

Actual democratic expressons are always informed by far too much optimism, to be sure. A bourgeois, *laissez faire* optimism, inherited from Renaissance sanguinity, dominates much modern democratic rule. The foundation of a democratic society is faith in the dignity and worth of the individual. For this reason democracy always stands perilously close to the false expectancy that man will follow the path of righteousness by simple suasions of moral and rational appeal.

Democracy is not adequately equipped to detect anarchical elements within its own boundaries. It may always erroneously conclude that isolated instances of unrest and upheaval are but normal expressions of man's privilege to criticize his government. Both constitutional monarchies and oligarchic and dictatorial forms of political power always have the ad-

34. *The Children of Light and the Children of Darkness*, pp. 46-47.

vantage over democracy of interpreting social unrest as a potential movement of anarchy. "While democratic theorists failed to measure the full dimensions and the dynamic quality of human vitalities, the undemocratic constitutionalists saw the destructive but not the creative possibilities of individual vitality and ambition and appreciated the necessity, but not the peril, of strong government."[35] The democratic preference for the "least government possible" betrays its optimism about human sinfulness; while the undemocratic preference in dictatorship for the strongest possible government betrays its optimism about the sinfulness of the collective ego.

Pragmatically, therefore, though not absolutely, democracy is the most satisfactory form of collective rule. Its adequacy lies in the measure in which it realistically lends itself to the dialectical relation between time and eternity. "An adequate approach to the social and moral problem must include a political policy which will bring the most effective social check upon conflicting egoistic impulses in society."[36] Democracy anticipates in its normal operation the right of the individual to criticize the ruler. Impeachment is the final expression of this right. The power to rebel against a ruler goes beyond anything understood in the Reformation; yet it is achieved in the name of norms perceived by reformers. Since the state is not God, it is subject to prophetic indictment whenever it arrogates to itself a hegemony reserved for God alone. "It is the highest achievement of democratic societies that they embody the principle of resistance to government within the principle of government itself. The citizen is thus armed with 'constitutional' power to resist the unjust exaction of government. He can do this without creating anarchy within the community, if government has been so conceived that criticism of the ruler becomes an instrument of better government and not a threat to government itself."[37] There is risk in arming men with the power of resistance, but the alternative risk is worse. If society

---

35. *The Children of Light and the Children of Darkness*, p. 47.
36. *Reflections on the End of an Era*, p. 229.
37. *Human Destiny*, p. 268.

is not empowered with rights to free expression, it will, as Marx predicted, explode from internal combustion.

A perfect democracy is just as impossible to reach as either a perfect society or a perfect individual. Sanctification in cultural and political realms is achieved by the same tortuous effort as sanctification in the individual. Unless every expression of democratic order is kept suspended under the judgment of Christ (perfect justice and love), the corruption of pledging final obedience to but a provisional form of justice will result. This in turn will exacerbate new and wider corruptions.

The evils of democracy are patent. The most self-evident is that democracy is founded on an initial deception. "The ballot never determines which class is to govern a community. It may determine which faction of a class is to govern, whether Whig or Tory, Democratic or Republican."[38] Democracy promises the purely moral arrangement that people may choose whomever they wish to rule. This is not true. The issues of government are determined by proud, powerful parties months before the individual has the privilege of selecting the lesser evil to a worse. "The factor of consent does not create governments because the general public is never able to conceive political programs or fashion political strategies. It can only say yes or no to various alternatives presented to it. The public as such is without organs of conscious direction."[39] Democracy is a perfect shelter for the prides of a bourgeois, capitalistic class. The moral elevation of the state cloaks the pride and greed of individual minds within it. Democracy is a cover for the prides and pretenses of will-to-power. In this mid-century, *e.g.*, Washington, D. C. is a seething mass of power conflicts. At the present hour there are three times as many registered lobbyists in Washington as there are congressmen. And the congressmen, in addition to pressing home their own interests and securities, are swayed from organized pressure groups on the field, constituents at home, and a tangle of opportunist

38. *Reflection on the End of an Era*, p. 152.
39. *Ibid.*, p. 154.

government bureaus and agencies grasping to retain, or increase, their own security.

The salvation of both democracy and capitalism is the continual reshuffling of its centers of power until a perceptible increase of justice and equity is evidenced. If the political unit becomes a veiled support for class interests, not only does it champion the very sins of injustice and partiality in opposition to which it initially took its rise, but the prophecies of doom pronounced by Marx are clearly written on the wall against it.

C. The Balance of Power.

Not the least of Niebuhr's brilliant strokes is his positive defense of the balance of power as an admission that perfect justice is impossible, on the one hand, but that degrees of justice must yet be respected by the Christian mind, on the other. Niebuhr's dialectic makes him unqualifiedly pessimistic about the future of things. "As long as the character and nature of man is not changed into something now quite unknown in human history, neither a new and more perfect social pedagogy nor a more perfect social organization will be able to eliminate all possibilities of injustice and conflict in human society."[40] But he is likewise unqualifiedly optimistic about our responsibility to maintain the best possible order as a "second best." This realistic compromise is the balance of power. Morally inferior to either a moral and rational form of collective cohesions or the community of love, it nevertheless is our only realistic expedient to promote justice. "The very essence of politics is the achievement of justice through equilibria of power. A balance of power is not conflict; but a tension between opposing forces underlies it. Where there is tension there is potential conflict, and where there is conflict there is potential violence."[41]

The balance-of-power strategy turns on the inevitability of strife through a sinful assertion in both individual and collective minds. "The selfishness of human communities must be regarded as an inevitability. Where it is inordinate it can be

40. *Reflections on the End of an Era*, p. 243.
41. *An Interpretation of Christian Ethics*, p. 189.

checked only by competing assertions of interest."[42] Through the expedient of balancing power against power the pretensions of a collective ego are checked. One power is brought to bay through an equally ambitious power over against it. Balance of power "is in fact a kind of managed anarchy."[43]

Because power balance is at best a war of attrition, however, it is always subject to the simple criticism of an easy idealism. What could be more facile than to conclude from the precariousness and delicateness of the balance that it is not the best solution ideally? But despite "its defects the policy of the balance of power is not as iniquitous as idealists would have us believe. For even the most perfectly organized society must seek for a decent equilibrium of the vitalities and forces under its organization. If this is not done, strong disproportions of power develop; and wherever power is inordinate, injustice results."[44]

With brilliant foresight Niebuhr prophesied the drastic consequences of breaking the balance of power through World War II. Our contemporary political impasse flows directly out of the appeasement policies followed by those in command of our war effort. Russia, unfettered by the checks of a European balance of power, is now pretentiously reaching out for absolute world domination. The normal checks of fear and uncertainty are missing. The present armaments race between the east and the west exposes the determination of each collective mind to tip the balance of power in its own favor. Niebuhr, therefore, is pessimistic (though not cynical) about the present world situation. "It would be easier to maintain the peace of the world if there were either only one center of power in it, or if there were ten. Actually there are only two. If the world had only one center of power, the world community might be managed in a fashion analogous to the Pax Romana in the ancient world. The Pax Romana did not achieve an ideal justice but it did maintain a tolerable order . . . If on the other hand there were seven or ten fairly equal cen-

42. *Moral Man and Immoral Society*, p. 272.
43. *The Children of Light and the Children of Darkness*, p. 174.
44. *Ibid.*

ters of power in the world they could be federated into a world organization, with a greater hope of stability than is now the case. There is, in other words, an inherent peril in the division of the world into two primary centers of power."[45] The expedience of the Atlantic Charter is but another frantic effort upon the part of the democracies to retain the hegemony in this final world balance of power.

Since "no participant in a balance is ever quite satisfied with its own position,"[46] the balance is always precarious. Niebuhr has no fond illusions either of the moral worth of this solution or of its resulting problems. The best he can proffer is a realistic approach to a wretchedly complex situation, believing only that within the terms of a dialectic balance of righteous and unrighteous insights can the probability of either anarchy or tyranny be lessened.

In the following remarkably concise way Hughley has charted Niebuhr's solution:[47]

> 1. That the struggle for social justice is always involved in a contest of power. It is never a question of mere morality versus power.
>
> (a) Because all contending groups lay claim to 'right,' to morality, giving moral justification to their position or demands.
>
> (b) Because men are always power-seekers, even the most moral of them. Even their 'ideals' express themselves in a quest for power.
>
> (c) Because groups are even more concerned for power (less for morality) than individuals, and thus justice becomes a question of continual adjustment of group claims.
>
> 2. That the essence of social justice is a full consideration of the claims of all parties, with every system of justice resulting from compromise. No contending group can have all it wants or contends for, and hence must be restrained by force in its selfish aspirations.
>
> 3. That achievement of justice is dependent upon a relative equality of power (or balance of power), for

45. Niebuhr, "Our Relations to Russia," in Scarlett ed., *op. cit.*, p. 34.
46. *The Children of Light and the Children of Darkness*, p. 175.
47. *Trends in Protestant Social Idealism*, p. 127.

(a) Where vast disproportions of power exist, justice is a mockery — it becomes the will of the mighty. The system of order resulting is merely the law of the ruling power which never fully considers the claims of the weaker.

(b) Where equality of power exists all contenders get a hearing because the power of an opponent always tends to check one's pretensions and claims.

4. A structure of justice based on a balance of power is morally inferior to a community of love. But corrupt human nature will require a rough balance to the end of time. To imagine otherwise is to be victimized by illusions concerning man and social processes.

III. The World Brotherhood

Since the ideal always lasts longer than the real (for history as *finis* will be both triumphed over and completed by history as *telos*), Niebuhr does not hesitate to complement his pessimistic observations with a strikingly optimistic reaffirmation of *agape*. Culturally, man is always responsible for, and capable of making measurable gains toward, world brotherhood. Love and justice are perfect tangents in a world brotherhood.

Because Niebuhr appeals to our *lack* of final truth as a ground for maintaining tolerance in brotherly relations, however, it is necessary to examine the background of world brotherhood somewhat critically.

A. The Basis of a Forgiving Spirit.

Niebuhr is unambiguous in his announcement that it is impossible for men to have final truth. "However we twist or turn, whatever instruments or pretensions we use, it is not possible to establish the claim that we have the truth. The truth remains subject to the paradox of grace. We may have it; and yet we do not have it. And we will have it the more purely in fact if we know that we have it only in principle. Our toleration of truths opposed to those which we confess is an expression of the spirit of forgiveness in the realm of culture. Like all forgiveness, it is possible only if we are not too sure of our own virtue."[48] The point is that when men have no final truth themselves, they are hardly in a position to be censorious or bitter against those who do not agree with them. Man has truth "in principle," perhaps, but never "in fact." And the reason for this is that every knowledge situation is corrupted by personal interest and finite perspective.

Niebuhr traces through the bitter controversies of both Catholic and Protestant history to support what he believes is the logical conclusion to one's claiming a final truth to which others must submit. Pride and intolerance result when justification and sanctification are confused in the realm of culture. Because history is asked to bear the very ideal which ultimately explains history, all final truth destroys the dialectic.

The objection to the claim that we have no final truth is perfectly obvious. If *no* truth is final, then it is not final either that the relation between time and eternity is dialectical or that *agape* defines the rule of our free responsibilities. In this case it is no longer a final truth that grace is paradoxical, and the case for final tolerance in the realm of culture collapses. Since personal interest and finite perspective corrupt and sully *all* truth, they likewise corrupt and sully the truths of both Christ and the dialectic. *Any principle which explains the corruption of all knowledge explains the corruption of no knowledge, for it has already corrupted itself.*

Niebuhr is determined not to be caught off guard on this question. He dips deeply into Tillich's *The Interpretation of History* for a philosophical statement to extricate himself from the above objection. "The doctrine of the character of knowledge as a decision, like everything that makes truth relative, elicits the objection that this doctrine makes itself relative and thus refutes itself . . . What is true, however, of all knowledge cannot be true of the knowledge of knowledge, otherwise it would cease to have universal significance. On the other hand, if an exception is admitted, then for one bit of reality the equivocal character of being is broken . . . Is that possible? It would be impossible if the removal of the ambiguity of exis-

48. *Human Destiny*, p. 243.

tence were to occur at any place in existence. Whatever stands in the context of knowledge is subject to the ambiguity of knowledge. Therefore such a proposition must be removed from the context of knowledge . . . It must be the expression of the relation of knowledge to the Unconditioned . . . The judgment that is removed from ambiguity . . . can be only the fundamental judgment of the relationship of the Unconditioned and Conditioned . . . The content of this judgment is just this — that our subjective thinking never can reach the unconditioned Truth . . . This judgment is plainly the absolute judgment which is independent of all its forms of expression, even of the one by which it is expressed here. It is the judgment which constitutes truth as truth."[49]

The remarkable feature of this appeal to Tillich is the argument's complete irrelevance to Niebuhr's defense of the paradox of grace as a final truth. The argument (if true) establishes only the formal proposition that all truth is relative. It does not establish the final truth of the inference that *agape* is the law of our life and that the relation between time and eternity is adequately expressed only through the paradox of grace. There is an immense difference between the formal proposition, "All knowledge is relative," and the material inference, "Christ is the rule of our life and the relation between time and eternity is dialectical." The first proposition (if true) expresses only the relation of all finite knowledge to the unconditioned; while the inference expresses a genuine claim to knowledge. One is a formal statement and the other is an inference drawn from it. The inference, lying within the context of knowledge, cannot enjoy the security of the formal statement itself, for the only possible finality is the absence of all finality. One must regrettably conclude that Niebuhr's dialectic provides him with no absolute ground to defend the preference of tolerance to intolerance, justice to injustice, truth to error, goodness to evil, and beauty to ugliness. There is no final truth except the formal statement of the relation

49. *Human Destiny*, pp. 217-218 n. (Quoted from *The Interpretation of History*, pp. 169-170).

of all finite knowledge to the unconditioned. The existing self recoils from this implication of dialectical thinking, for it senses with a perfect intuition that justice, truth, goodness, and beauty are absolute values which rest on final claims to knowledge.

Niebuhr, indeed, cannot be consistent in his skepticism, for his dialectical theology fairly bristles with finality claims. The Christ is final, love is final, tolerance is final, Reformation insights are final, Renaissance truths are final, Kierkegaardian psychology is final, grace is final, justification and sanctification are final — in short, *the entire Christian view of man and history is final.* But by what right does Niebuhr introduce these as finalities when he has already admitted that the only final knowledge we can have is the formal statement that nothing is final? Tillich at best can put only a roof over Niebuhr's skepticism. He cannot justify the Christian edifice itself. *Agape* as the rule of life is a positive claim to knowledge. Yet, Niebuhr is unhesitant to claim that *agape* is a finality. On what ground can he support this pretension, however? If *all* knowledge is corrupted through personal interest and finite perspective, then the knowledge of *agape* suffers the same fate as all other judgment claims. If Niebuhr were consistent, thus, he would be forced to admit that it is neither final that *agape* is the rule of life nor that tolerance is preferable to intolerance.

An absolute impasse must be admitted. If one claims that the dialectical relation between time and eternity *is* a final piece of knowledge, he destroys the dialectic by admitting that finite creatures have overcome the ambiguity of existence at one point in history; and if one claims that the dialectical relation between time and eternity is *not* a final piece of knowledge, then he destroys the dialectic by leaving open the possibility that a non-dialectical view of life may serve us. In either decision a *final* Christian dialectic is destroyed.

Niebuhr may preface his discussion of world brotherhood with the plea that finitude should lead to humility and toleration, but he cannot significantly show with finality that one *ought* to be either humble or tolerant. All inferences are pieces of knowledge which are relative.

The evangelical believes that it is a far more satisfying alternative to base humility and toleration upon the *presence,* not the *absence,* of final knowledge. Because it is finally true that Christ has atoned for our sins and that out of love for Him men are to love one another, tolerance has a genuinely secure basis in life. "If," as I have expressed it elsewhere, "all truth is relative, then the truth that we should be tolerant is also relative; this leaves the horrors of the inquisition open as a possibility for tomorrow. Is it not evident that without final truth, it cannot be shown that one must love his neighbor today, and tomorrow?"[50]

If the price one has to pay for reconstructing his theology along dialectical lines is the loss of final truth, the sacrifice is too great. Shall one dismiss the significant that he may enjoy the insignificant? The free self knows only too clearly that the preference of justice to injustice, love to hatred, goodness to evil, truth to error are final truths. If they cannot be accommodated in a dialectical system, so much worse for the dialectic.

B. The New World.

World brotherhood has the regulative value of defining the outside goal of our free, creative possibilities. Through moments of prayerful self-transcendence we confront the rule of life. We know our responsibilities. But running through this insight are the vitiating vitalities of self-assertiveness and pride. These make the literal realization of the law of our life in society an impossibility. "Confronted with this situation humanity always faces a double task. The one is to reduce the anarchy of the world to some kind of immediately sufferable order and unity; and the other is to set these tentative and insecure unities and achievements under the criticism of the ultimate goal."[51] Freedom must tack within the tensions of necessity and possibility, possession and hope. Final justice

50. *An Introduction to Christian Apologetics,* p. 221.
51. *An Interpretation of Christian Ethics,* pp. 60-61.

within a world community is a possibility/impossibility. "The world community, toward which all historical forces seem to be driving us, is mankind's final possibility and impossibility. The task of achieving it must be interpreted from the standpoint of a faith which understands the fragmentary and broken character of all historic achievements and yet has confidence in their meaning because it knows their completion to be in the hands of a Divine Power, whose resources are greater than those of men, and whose suffering love can overcome the corruptions of man's achievements, without negating the significance of our striving."[52]

The mid-century predicament of man is frightfully apparent. Whether our culture will survive this final test or not is unknown at the present hour. In facing this plight, however, we can either delude ourselves by concluding that our situation is hopeless, on the one hand, or that all will naturally work out for the good, on the other; or we can admit the possibility of both defeat and victory, determining with resolute faith that we shall perform the full height of our responsibilities to make the outcome a victory. Niebuhr elects the latter, and more noble, alternative. "The new world must be built by resolute men who 'when hope is dead will hope by faith'; who will neither seek premature escape from the guilt of history, nor yet call the evil, which taints all their achievements, good. There is no escape from the paradoxical relation of history to the Kingdom of God. History moves toward the realization of the Kingdom but yet the judgment of God is upon every new realization."[53]

"History is today, as it has always been, filled with hours of decision in which we can relate ourselves to its promises or contribute to its disasters. It is therefore more important to seek to do our duty in watchfulness and soberness than to speculate overmuch about the perils which lie before us."[54]

Finis

---

52. *The Children of Light and the Children of Darkness,* pp. 189-190.
53. *Human Destiny,* pp. 285-286.
54. Niebuhr, "Can We Avoid Catastrophe?" *The Christian Century,* May 26, 1948, p. 506.

INDEX

www.ingramcontent.com/pod-product-compliance
Lightning Source LLC
LaVergne TN
LVHW050618100826
845148LV00011B/1638